Cambridge Opera Handbooks

Giuseppe Verdi
*Falstaff*

D0077987

Costume design for Falstaff by Adolph Hohenstein, 1892
(Archivio Storico Ricordi, Milan)

# Giuseppe Verdi
## *Falstaff*

JAMES A. HEPOKOSKI
*Associate Professor of Music History*
*Oberlin College Conservatory*

CAMBRIDGE UNIVERSITY PRESS

*Cambridge*
*London   New York   New Rochelle*
*Melbourne   Sydney*

Published by the Press Syndicate of the University of Cambridge
The Pitt Building, Trumpington Street, Cambridge CB2 1RP
32 East 57th Street, New York, NY 10022, USA
296 Beaconsfield Parade, Middle Park, Melbourne 3206, Australia

First published 1983

Printed in Great Britain
at the University Press, Cambridge

Library of Congress catalogue card number: 82-23493

*British Library Cataloguing in Publication Data*

Hepokoski, James A.
Giuseppe Verdi: Falstaff. – (Cambridge opera handbooks)
I. Verdi, Giuseppe. Falstaff
I. Title    II. Series
782.1'092'4    ML410.V4

ISBN 0 521 23534 0 hard covers
ISBN 0 521 28016 8 paperback

ME

# CAMBRIDGE OPERA HANDBOOKS

# *General preface*

This is a series of studies of individual operas, written for the serious opera-goer or record-collector as well as the student or scholar. Each volume has three main concerns. The first is historical: to describe the genesis of the work, its sources or its relation to literary prototypes, the collaboration between librettist and composer, and the first performance and subsequent stage history. This history is itself a record of changing attitudes towards the work, and an index of general changes of taste. The second is analytical and is grounded in a very full synopsis which considers the opera as a structure of musical and dramatic effects. In most volumes there is also a musical analysis of a section of the score, showing how the music serves or makes the drama. The analysis, like the history, naturally raises questions of interpretation, and the third concern of each volume is to show how critical writing about an opera, like production and performance, can direct or distort appreciation of its structural elements. Some conflict of interpretation is an inevitable part of this account; editors of the handbooks reflect this − by citing classic statements, by commissioning new essays, by taking up their own critical position. A final section gives a select bibliography, a discography and guides to other sources.

**Books published**

Richard Wagner: *Parsifal* by Lucy Beckett
C. W. von Gluck: *Orfeo* by Patricia Howard
W. A. Mozart: *Don Giovanni* by Julian Rushton
Igor Stravinsky: *The Rake's Progress* by Paul Griffiths
Leoš Janáček: *Kát'a Kabanová* by John Tyrrell
Benjamin Britten: *Peter Grimes* by Philip Brett

*other volumes in preparation*

To my wife, Barbara

# Contents

# *Illustrations*

# Acknowledgments

I should like to thank G. Ricordi & C., S.P.A., for permission to reproduce some of the original sets and costumes (Figs. 3-12) and portions of the January 1893 vocal score (Figs. 1-2), for permission to translate from both the unpublished correspondence in their extensive collection and the letters published in Franco Abbiati's *Giuseppe Verdi*, and for permission to quote musical passages from the autograph score and the published Ricordi scores. In particular, I should like to acknowledge the kind assistance of Mimma Guastoni, Luciana Pestalozza, Carlo Clausetti, and Francesco Degrada during my year of research in Milan. I should also like to thank the Library of the Conservatorio di Musica 'Giuseppe Verdi' in Milan and its director, Agostina Zecca Laterza, for permission to use material from the 1892 *Falstaff* proofs; Alberto and Gabriella Carrara Verdi for so generously making Boito's manuscript libretto available to me some years ago and for permission to quote from it in subsequent publications; The Fogg Art Museum, Harvard University, for photographing and supplying the relevant score pages for Figs. 1 and 2; Larry Mowers of the Harvard Music Library for assistance in obtaining these pages; the Istituto di Studi Verdiani in Parma and its director, Pierluigi Petrobelli, for permission to translate from the recent *Carteggio Verdi–Boito*; William Ashbrook for sharing his insights into *Falstaff*'s performance history (some of those insights, undoubtedly, have crept into the book); Ursula Günther, Philip Gossett, and Joseph Kerman for their advice and support during an early stage of this book; the American Institute of Verdi Studies in New York and its director, Martin Chusid, for making available many documents crucial to the final text of portions of this book; Warren Darcy and Paul Mast for their astute suggestions concerning an early draft of the chapter on musical style; Sylvan Suskin and Steven Plank for advice on various portions of the book; Graham Bradshaw for his splendid epilogue on Verdi, Boito, and

Shakespeare; Malcolm Walker for the discography; and, above all, the staff of Cambridge University Press, and particularly Rosemary Dooley, Michael Black, and Judith Nagley, for their help and support.

James A. Hepokoski

*Oberlin College Conservatory*
*November 1982*

# 1 Synopsis

Few operas begin with such a rush of activity as that which launches Verdi's last opera, *Falstaff*. Gone are even the traces of the familiar overtures, preludes, *introduzioni*, and introductory choral tableaux of his previous works; all have been relinquished in favour of a sudden plunge into headlong activity. In *Falstaff* we have a mere seven bars of boisterous *fortissimo* music before we are swept up in rapid dialogue.

The action of the opera unfolds during a single day in early fifteenth-century Windsor. The first part of Act I takes place inside the Garter Inn, where we immediately encounter one of its standard fixtures, the witty Sir John Falstaff. Aging and corpulent, this knight is now concerned only with supporting the self-indulgence that produced his enormous girth in the first place. At curtain-rise Falstaff has just sealed two letters at his writing-desk – the beginning of another intrigue – and has settled down to drink his beloved sack, when an enraged Dr Cajus ('the renowned French physician' of Shakespeare's *The Merry Wives of Windsor*, although his occupation is never made explicit in the opera) bursts into the room to howl accusations at him.

The opening seven bars, jaggedly mirroring Cajus' fulminations, are justly famous for the momentum that they impart to both the scene and the whole opera. The very first sound – an explosive C major chord for full orchestra – trips the *commedia lirica* into immediate motion, largely because Verdi places it on the 'weak' second beat of the bar, after an initial beat of silence; the remainder of the three-bar phrase can be heard as an effort to regain one's balance, whereupon the *fortissimo* detonation (now on G) recurs to mix things up once again. The effect of all of this is to initiate an ongoing movement that comes to rest only at the conclusion of Act III.

Cajus proceeds to denounce the fat knight: Falstaff has beaten his servants, worn out his horses and broken into his house, and now the doctor demands an explanation. Throughout this thunderstorm of imputation Falstaff stretches out, unperturbed, in a large chair, surrounded by his thieving henchmen, the red-nosed Bardolfo and the inflammatory Pistola, and calmly orders more sherry from the Host. His response to Cajus is an unruffled acknowledgment of guilt:

> Ecco la mia risposta:
> Ho fatto ciò che hai detto . . . L'ho fatto apposta.
>
> Here is my answer:
> I've done what you said . . . On purpose.

The amazed Cajus, clearly a man with connections, threatens to bring the matter to the royal council, but Falstaff closes the issue by assuring the doctor that this would only provoke their laughter.

Defeated on his first charge, Cajus turns to Bardolfo to hurl a second, as the full orchestra again sounds the *fortissimo* wrath figure with which the opera began. Bardolfo and Pistola, he claims, got him drunk yesterday and used the opportunity to pick his pocket. When Bardolfo, feigning offence, denies the charge, all eyes turn to Pistola, who not only pleads innocence but also challenges his accuser as a liar: this provokes a round of name-calling. Finally, Bardolfo manages to come up with an explanation for Cajus: the doctor merely drank himself senseless and dreamed that he had been robbed. 'I fatti son negati,' concludes Falstaff, 'Vattene in pace' ('The facts are denied; Go in peace'). Cajus storms out, proclaiming:

> Giuro
> Che se mai mi ubbriaco ancora all'osteria
> Sarà fra gente onesta, sobria, civile e pia.
>
> I swear
> That if I ever get drunk again at the inn
> It will be with people who are honest, sober, civil, and pious.

Pistola and Bardolfo mock the doctor's exit with a canonic 'Amen' in academic counterpoint (a nearly strict canon at the second – the joke, of course, lies in the thieves' exaggerated following of the rules), until Sir John turns on them with hostility for their inept cozenage. The two attendants receive his short lecture by beginning another 'Amen'. Falstaff cuts them short and proceeds to examine his weekly bill at the inn. As he reads '6 polli: 6 scellini' ('6 chickens: 6 shillings'), we hear the first instance of the widely spaced, unusual orchestral effects that appear throughout the score: here, French horns play a sustained open fifth, E–B, with an enormous gap of two and a half octaves between the notes. After Falstaff asks Bardolfo to search his pocketbook for money, the orchestral texture changes to arpeggiated figurations in the low violas, and high, resonant intervals in the flute and piccolo help to suggest Falstaff's unnatural relish for the thirst-provoking 'acciuga' ('anchovy') that he finds listed on the bill.

When Falstaff learns that he possesses only two marks and a penny, he flies into a rage and blames his spendthrift lackeys, especially the hapless Bardolfo, whom he disparages in a sudden *arioso*:

> So che se andiam, la notte, di taverna in taverna
> Quel tuo naso ardentissimo mi serve da lanterna;
> Ma quel risparmio d'olio me lo consumi in vino.

> I know that if we go from tavern to tavern at night
> Your blazing nose serves me as a lantern;
> But what I save in oil you consume for me in wine.

Bardolfo and Pistola are becoming too expensive, he insists, shouting yet another order for wine. Too expensive indeed — for he dares not slacken his own gluttony, as he explains in a passage that begins with an extraordinary piccolo—cello doubling:

> Se Falstaff s'assottiglia
> Non è più lui, nessun più l'ama; in quest'addome
> C'è un migliaio di lingue che annunciano il mio nome.
>
> . . .                    Quest'è il mio regno.
> Lo ingrandirò.

> Were Falstaff to slim down
> He wouldn't be himself any longer; nobody would love him;
> In this abdomen there are a thousand tongues that announce
>    my name.
>
> . . .                    This is my kingdom.
> I shall enlarge it.

Everything to this point has been introductory. Falstaff now turns to the true plot of the comedy — his attempt to line his pocketbook by seducing the beautiful wives of the rich townsmen Ford and Page. The knight foolishly believes that Alice Ford even has a romantic interest in him, so much so that her sparkling desire seemed once to confide to him 'Io son di Sir John Falstaff' ('I am yours, Sir John Falstaff'). Meg Page also holds the key to her husband's wealth, he explains, and he hands his recently completed love-letters to his associates for a speedy delivery.

At that point the inconceivable occurs. Pistola refuses to be a pander; Bardolfo likewise declines to deliver the letter on the principle of honour. The outraged Falstaff calls for his page, gives him the letters, and, in one of the major solo pieces of the opera, wheels around to lecture his men about this so-called 'honour'. The main portion of this very free monologue is in the form of a catechism:

> Può l'onore riempirvi la pancia?
> No. Può l'onor rimettervi uno stinco? Non può.
> Né un piede? No. Né un dito? No. Né un capello? No.

> Can this honour fill your belly?
> No. Can this honour give you back a leg? No.
> Nor a foot? No. Nor a finger? No. Nor a hair? No.

Honour is a mere word, mere air, he asserts, and he concludes by emphatically rejecting the very concept of it: 'e per me non ne voglio, no, no, no!' ('as for me, I don't want it, no, no, no!'). The scene closes rapidly as the knight discharges his men and drives them from the inn with a broom, as *fortissimo* woodwind and brass recall the catechistic section of the Honour Monologue at whirlwind tempo.

The scene changes to a garden outside Ford's cottage. A brief, bustling introduction ushers in the four women of the comedy: Alice Ford, her very marriageable daughter Nannetta, Meg Page, and Mistress Quickly — for the purposes of this opera merely a friend, no reference being made to her role in *The Merry Wives* as Dr Cajus' housekeeper and general go-between. Alice and Meg soon discover that they have both received love-letters from Sir John. They exchange the letters and read aloud: 'Fulgida Alice! amor t'offro, amor bramo' ('Radiant Alice! I offer you love, I long for love'). They discover at once that, except for the names, the letters are identical. In this early portion of the letter the recurrent pseudo-melancholy English-horn phrase evokes Sir John in wooing mood: a triplet sigh leads to a gentle descent and thence to a concluding note awkwardly beyond the lower limit of the instrument — the final tonic has to be supplied by a clarinet, which thus without warning alters the mood established by the English-horn timbre. Falstaff's message, however, becomes increasingly ardent. Verdi provides the concluding lines of the knight's doggerel with a particularly lustrous setting:

> Facciamo il paio in un amor ridente
> Di donna bella e d'uom appariscente,
> E il viso tuo su me risplenderà
> Come una stella sull'immensità.

> In laughing love let's form a couple,
> Beautiful lady and striking man,
> And your face shall shine on me
> As a star upon immensity.

Breaking into laughter that quickly changes to mischief, the wives determine to be revenged on their plump suitor. In an unaccompanied quartet, 'Quell'otre! quel tino!' ('That wineskin! That barrel!'), the four women each discharge sixteen lines of insults at Falstaff — even the delicate Nannetta uncharacteristically insists that she would like to see 'quell'orco sudar' ('that ogre sweat'). Their quartet is succeeded by a quintet of men, likewise singing dissimilar texts simultaneously: the cashiered Bardolfo and Pistola are trying to inform Ford of Falstaff's plan to seduce his wife, while Dr Cajus, whom Ford intends to be Nannetta's future husband, and young Fenton, truly in love with Nannetta, are also present. As the confusion dies away, Pistola relishes the opportunity to tell Ford precisely what Falstaff is concocting. Bardolfo, for his part, delights in suggesting to Ford that he is already beginning to resemble a cuckold: 'Le corna!' ('Horns!'). 'Brutta parola!', shouts Ford ('Horrible word!'); he instantly resolves to keep a close watch on his wife and Falstaff.

Here occurs the first of the many mercurial shifts of mood — musical flicks of the wrist — that are among the most astonishing features of the opera. In the present instance the two plotting groups, men and women, catch sight of one another, each group believing itself to be unseen. Young Fenton now spots Nannetta Ford and lingers on stage as each group exits *sotto voce*. Within twelve rapid bars virtually everyone is whisked offstage, leaving only Fenton and Nannetta, whose love-meetings appear here and there throughout the work, precisely as Boito had suggested to Verdi in the early stages of their planning: 'from the beginning to the end of the comedy they will steal kisses from each other, hidden in corners, carefully, ardently, without being discovered, with short, fresh lines and brief, rapid, and clever dialogues' (*Carteggio Verdi–Boito* 1978: I, 145).

In this miniature duet, 'Labbra di foco' ('Lips of fire'), the young lovers have only a few moments in which to display the purity and innocence of their love, so much in contrast with the jaded propositioning of Falstaff and the growing jealousy of Ford. Very shortly after the *duettino* begins, it is interrupted by the sound of someone approaching. There is time only for an affectionate parting, a lingering on two lines (of Boccaccian origin: see Chapter 2) that suggest a mutual pledge of the perpetual self-renewal of their love:

> Bocca baciata non perde ventura.
> Anzi rinnova come fa la luna.
>
> A mouth once kissed loses not its future.
> Rather, it renews itself like the moon.

All at once the women are back to elaborate the details of their revenge; Alice designates Mistress Quickly as an ambassador to invite Falstaff to a liaison. Once the plot is laid and relished, the wives exit after a vocal fanfare to the words 'Che gioia!' ('What joy!'). Alone briefly again, Fenton and Nannetta sing a playfully varied repetition of their earlier love-music.

The men re-enter. Ford now explains that he has decided upon a visit to Falstaff under a false name – we later learn that this will be 'Signor Fontana' ('Master Brook') – to keep abreast of the knight's intentions. Bardolfo and Pistola, still smarting from their abrupt dismissal, agree to help him.

The remainder of the scene is reprise: a repetition of the polytextual men's quintet and women's quartet – now performed simultaneously, in different metres (2/2 and 6/8), leading to a new, lyrical melody for Fenton, sung against the remaining eight voices. After the men depart, the women excitedly bid each other farewell and affirm their intention of making Falstaff's belly swell to the point of bursting. Both the anticipated inflation and explosion receive graphic orchestral depiction: the former ('si gonfia') by brief, sequentially ascending lines in the woodwind, and the latter ('e poi crepa') by a raucous, rushing chromatic plunge in the bassoons and trombones. The act concludes with the wives' memory of the final two lines of their love-letters, with the words now modified to suggest that *they* have taken control of the situation ('But *my* face shall shine on *him*').

Act II Part i brings us back to the Garter Inn, where Falstaff is stretched out in his usual chair. Affecting contrition, Bardolfo and Pistola apologize to their master. Presumed amends having thus been made, Bardolfo introduces Mistress Quickly. Quickly curtsies in feigned respect, addresses Falstaff as 'Reverenza' ('Your Reverence'), and waits for him to order his two men out to insure privacy.

After another curtsy ('Reverenza') Quickly haltingly delivers her message: Alice Ford ('Ahimè! Povera donna!' – 'Alas! Poor woman!'), she claims, loves the knight and has bidden her to tell him that her husband is absent every day 'dalle due alle tre' ('from two until three o'clock'). Sir John is delighted, of course, and even more astonished when Quickly informs him that Meg Page (likewise a 'povera donna') has also sent her, but that her husband, unfortunately, rarely leaves the house. Falstaff gives Quickly a coin for her welcome information. She leaves after an even deeper curtsy, 'M'inchino' ('I bow'), to her 'Reverenza' music.

'Alice è mia!' ('Alice is mine!'), roars Falstaff, and the orchestra breaks into hearty, *fortissimo* laughter. In one of the many tiny solo pieces of the opera Falstaff now swaggeringly congratulates himself on his virile seductive powers: 'Va, vecchio John, va, va per la tua via' ('Go, old John, go, go your way'). No sooner do we hear again the exuberant orchestral laughter than Bardolfo returns to announce the arrival of a 'Mastro Fontana' — Ford in disguise. As 'Fontana' is being escorted inside the inn, Falstaff, riding high on his supposed invincibility, sings a fleeting memory of 'Va, vecchio John'. Ford enters — the string accompaniment with its hint of an ass's bray may well disclose his anxieties at the moment — bows, and, after the customary pleasantries, begins his story: 'In me vedete un uom' ch'ha un'abbondanza grande' ('In me you see a man of great abundance'). Learning of his visitor's wealth and generosity, Falstaff welcomes him with open arms: 'Caro signor Fontana!' ('Dear Master Brook!').

Realizing that Bardolfo and Pistola are overhearing all of this, Falstaff orders them out of the room. Ford then proceeds to display a sack of money (the jingle of the silver is suggested in the orchestra: triangle, arco and pizzicato strings, constant quaver motion with grace notes on virtually every half-beat) and offers to give it to Falstaff, providing that the latter can assist him in his unhappy pursuit of the married woman who has so far rejected all of his advances:

> C'è a Windsor una dama, bella e leggiadra molto,
> Si chiama Alice; è moglie d'un certo Ford.
>
> In Windsor there is a woman, very beautiful and graceful;
> Her name is Alice; she's the wife of a certain Ford.

Falstaff, amazed, begs this 'Master Brook' to continue. Ford relates his sorrowful tale with great passion, and expands particularly in a beautiful sequential phrase, 'Per lei sprecai tesori' ('For her I have squandered treasures'). All was in vain, he says; he has remained unnoticed, nervous, on her steps, singing a madrigal, 'L'amor, l'amor che non ci dà mai tregue' ('Love, love, that never gives us respite') — a melody that builds once again to the expansive sequential phrase, this time with even more powerfully directed harmonies.

Ford then comes to the point: Sir John is a gentleman, a warrior, and a man of the world, and he can spend all of 'Brook's' money ('Spendetele!') provided that he seduce Alice Ford — for it is only after she has succumbed to Falstaff's irresistible powers, he asserts, that he himself will have a chance to conquer her. All of this is expressed in a few smooth phrases of roguish insinuation, with Ford's lines sensuously doubled by cello and bassoon:

> Ma se voi l'espugnate, poi, posso anch'io sperar;
> Da fallo nasce fallo e allor . . . Che ve ne par?

> But if you besiege and win, then I too can hope;
> One sin leads to another . . . What do you think?

Falstaff jumps at the bargain, accepts the money, and assures 'Fontana' that he will indeed possess Ford's wife. And then, to Ford's surprise and mounting fury, he recounts his invitation to meet her 'dalle due alle tre' and brazenly mocks the husband whom he believes he has not yet met. As Ford listens in wide-eyed humiliation, Falstaff's ridicule climaxes in the repeated phrase 'Te lo cornifico, netto! netto!' ('I'll put horns on his head, neatly! neatly!').

After Sir John leaves to groom himself for his rendezvous, Ford begins a powerful soliloquy — one of the strongest solo pieces in the opera:

> È sogno? o realtà . . . Due rami enormi
> Crescon sulla mia testa.

> Is this a dream? Or reality? Two enormous branches
> Are growing out of my head.

The psychological accompaniment exposes Ford's deepest fears: as we hear the sound of 'horns' (the pun 'corni — corna' works equally well in Italian) and the bass-line triplets of 'dalle due alle tre', the anticipated hour of his cuckolding, Ford begins to complain:

> L'ora è fissata, tramato l'inganno;
> Sei gabbato e truffato!
> E poi diranno
> Che un marito geloso è un insensato!

> The hour is fixed, the deception planned;
> You are tricked and duped!
> And then they will say
> That a jealous husband is a madman!

Ford expresses his fears of ridicule, sneers, and whistles (represented by the humiliating 'Te lo cornifico' idea in the accompaniment) and declares with scorn that his wife cannot be trusted. In a rage his thoughts turn to Falstaff. He raises himself to fever pitch with thoughts of how he will first couple the knight with his wife and then catch him. The soliloquy ends with steel-fisted resolution:

> Vendicherò l'affronto!
> Laudata sempre sia
> Nel fondo del mio cor la gelosia.

I will avenge this affront!
From the bottom of my heart
May my jealousy be praised.

But, as is so common in *Falstaff*, the mood now shifts rapidly. The unsuspecting Sir John re-enters in new clothes − courting clothes − to invite Ford to accompany him for a short walk to Alice's house. As they leave, each pauses to permit the other to exit first − a mild bit of farce after Ford's intense monologue. Ultimately, they decide to go through the door at the same time ('Passiamo insieme'). The orchestra brings down the curtain by playing the exuberant laughter motive that had earlier framed Falstaff's 'Va, vecchio John'.

Meanwhile, in a room in Ford's house − Act II Part ii − Alice and Meg are gleefully setting the trap for Falstaff. The scene opens with a busy, staccato string introduction. Within a few moments Quickly enters, bursting with news about her visit to the Garter Inn. She requires little prodding to tell what happened:

> Giunta all'Albergo della Giarrettiera
> Chiedo d'esser ammessa alla presenza
> Del Cavalier, segreta messaggera.

> Once I had arrived at the Garter Inn,
> I asked to be admitted into the presence
> Of the knight − as a secret messenger.

Quickly's solo piece bears many of the qualities of Verdi's earlier operatic *racconti*, or narrative solos: she relates a story of past events in music flexible enough to capture the spirit of her tale but not to lapse into mere recitative. In fact, she holds the principal melodic flowering of her solo in reserve for the end of her story, when she assures the others that Falstaff actually believed her: 'Infin, per farla spiccia' ('Finally, to be brief').

Now realizing that Falstaff will arrive at any moment, the wives hurry to complete their preparations. Alice bids the servants to carry in the basket of laundry − an essential element of the plot. She notices, however, that Nannetta is not sharing in the mischievous mood; the latter explains that she is weeping because her father insists that she marry Dr Cajus. This is apparently the first that Alice has heard of this ridiculous complication, and she promises her daughter that she need fear no such marriage. Thus fortified in spirit, Nannetta joins the other three women in setting the traps to snare Falstaff: a chair here, a lute there, and an open folding screen placed between the laundry basket and the hearth.

In eager anticipation Alice sings a tiny solo piece:

> Gaie comari di Windsor! è l'ora!
> L'ora d'alzar la risata sonora!

> Merry wives of Windsor! It's time!
> Time to raise our hearty laughter!

The lightness and brilliance of this miniature can scarcely be overstressed: it is actually the principal 'aria' of the *prima donna*. Such an important piece would have demanded much more time in any of the earlier Verdi operas; here, one finds a wide range of soloistic gestures telescoped into a few moments. The central image of the text — and the music — is the 'favilla incendiaria' ('incendiary spark') of laughter: its electrical potency gains strength throughout the piece and at the end joyously discharges into the air ('Di gioia nell'aria') on a split-second high C.

After a brief three-voice reprise of 'Gaie comari di Windsor' Meg, Quickly, and Nannetta move to their assigned posts offstage. Expecting the knight momentarily, Alice sits at the table and dreamily strums a lute — the sound is actually provided by an offstage guitar. Falstaff enters singing to her accompaniment. He soon begins his strong wooing by stressing his ability to improve her middle-class social status. Alice responds with lines of alluring, flirtatious modesty, 'Ogni più bel gioiel mi nuoce' ('Each beautiful jewel only harms me'), and proceeds to allude to his enormous stomach — his 'vulnerabil polpa' ('vulnerable flesh'), so susceptible in its mass to worldly desires. He was not always so fat, he replies, in a brief solo:

> Quand'ero paggio
> Del Duca di Norfolk ero sottile.

> When I was page
> To the Duke of Norfolk I was slender.

The supposed seduction continues until Quickly runs in ('Signora Alice!') to 'warn' the couple that a highly upset Meg Page is about to enter the house. At this point the music leaps into an *allegro agitato*, and Falstaff hides himself behind the screen. Meg's entrance is even more frantic than Quickly's. In order to increase the concealed Don Juan's terror, she breathlessly reports that Ford is on his way home; that he suspects that his wife is hiding a lover; and that, surrounded by a group of neighbours, he is swearing deadly revenge.

Before long, Ford and his band of sympathizers (Cajus, Fenton, Bardolfo, and Pistola) invade the house. Spotting the laundry basket, Ford believes that he has discovered his quarry. He pounces upon the basket and tosses out the dirty clothes in all directions. 'Che uragano!' ('What a hurricane!'), exclaim the onlooking wives. After Ford and his men rush out of the room to search the rest of the house, the terrified Falstaff emerges from behind the screen. Desperate, he agrees to squeeze himself into the laundry basket and be covered with the washing.

Throughout all of this the orchestral accompaniment has been moving in a rapid *moto perpetuo*. Now Verdi again breaks the incessant motion and suddenly shifts the musical spotlight to the young lovers (clearly to permit the wives time to load the linen onto Falstaff). Fenton and Nannetta enter cautiously to begin another brief love-duet: a gently rocking triple-time exchange that is motivically related to their duets in the preceding act. Totally absorbed in their own world, they slip behind the screen recently vacated by Sir John — and just in time, as Ford and his troops return.

With Dr Cajus' shout 'Al ladro!' ('Get the thief!'), the perpetual motion is resumed. The men rabidly search the room for evidence of the lover. They ignore, of course, the previously investigated laundry basket that now holds the fat knight. Suddenly the sound of a kiss ('un bacio sonoro' — 'a resonant kiss' — according to the stage directions) is heard from behind the screen. 'C'è!', exclaims Ford, echoed by Cajus ('There he is!').

The passage from this moment to the end of the act is the pivot on which the whole opera hinges. Dramatically, Falstaff's lechery is about to be punished, Ford's jealousy exposed. Musically, we are treated to a *tour de force* of ensemble writing: six men, three women (i.e., Nannetta, Meg, and Quickly — Alice must remain offstage because Ford believes her to be behind the screen), and a chorus of neighbours, all venting individual emotions in a solidly grounded C major, the key in which the opera begins and ends.

The music moves at a relatively slow *andante* pace. Onstage, the action virtually freezes (an ensemble convention well over a century old by the time of *Falstaff*), as the men turn their attention to the screen and murmur quietly to each other, lest the presumed victim hear them. As all audiences have experienced, the hilarity of the situation is underscored when the real Sir John pokes his nose out of the basket to wail 'Affogo!' ('I'm suffocating!'), only to have the wives push him back down into the laundry basket — a comedic luxury not found in Shakespeare. And on top of the confused mutterings of the avengers and their wives, the groaning of the overheated Falstaff, and the nonplussed commentary of the neighbours float the *espressivo* vocal lines of Fenton and Nannetta, 'alone' with each other behind the screen.

Finally, Ford resolves to pull away the screen at the count of three ('Uno . . . Due . . . *Tre*') – only to discover not Falstaff and Alice, but Fenton and Nannetta. A *fortissimo* eruption in the voices and orchestra reflects everyone's surprise. Ford, whose choice for his daughter's hand is Dr Cajus, rebukes Fenton: 'L'ho detto mille volte: Costei non fa per voi' ('I've told you a thousand times: she is not to be yours'). Quite inexplicably, Bardolfo and Pistola suddenly believe that they see Falstaff on the steps outside. Once again to the *moto perpetuo*, all the men recommence the chase. This gives Alice (who had returned onstage near the end of the ensemble) the opportunity to order the servants to dump the laundry basket out of the large window and into the river below – and to send out Falstaff's little page to retrieve her husband to participate in the jest.

The servants struggle to lift the basket. After much strain (vividly depicted in the accompaniment) they manage to raise it and throw it out of the window, precisely as the men return to share in the wives' exclamation, 'Patatrac!' ('Crash!'). The act concludes with a short codetta of fanfare-like triumph.

The first part of Act III takes place at sunset (Sir John's?) just outside the Garter Inn. It opens with the longest purely orchestral passage in the opera: a fifty-two-bar prelude based on one of the perpetual-motion ideas from the previous scene. By means of such an unprecedented orchestral interpolation, Verdi prepares us for the third act, which will be more expansive and less dramatically concise than its predecessors. This newly found 'leisure' is appropriate, for the main plot is over, resolved in the last act. The third act serves as a kind of dramatic coda, in which additional tricks are devised to punish Falstaff further. The only real plot considerations that remain to be dealt with are relatively simple: the ultimate pairing of Fenton and Nannetta, and the consequent foiling of Ford's plans to give Nannetta to Dr Cajus. Thus, in the third act the rapid, fluid stream of the first two acts broadens into a delta of increasingly stylized pieces – Verdi's farewell to opera.

After the introduction dies down to a few *pianissimo* grumbles, we hear a sudden bright descending scalar passage in the first violins. The recently drenched Falstaff, now seated on a bench outside the inn, rouses himself in disgust. As he calls out to the Host, we hear the first appearance of a growling descending tetrachord in the low wind that clearly informs us of his bitter dejection: 'Mondo ladro. Mondo rubaldo. Reo mondo' ('Thieving world. Knavish world. Wicked world').

Falstaff's monologue here is freely constructed from a wide variety of motivic material. According to the textual demands of the opening, for example, one hears reiterations of the low growling motive; a brief, ironic reprise of 'Va, vecchio John' from Act II; another brief statement of the perpetual-motion idea as his mind turns to the events of the 'giornataccia nera' ('black, foul day'); and so forth. We hear the *fortissimo* string descent again as the Host enters with an order of warm wine. As Falstaff drinks it, his damp spirits rekindle, and he gradually becomes himself again. In the climactic conclusion of the monologue Falstaff compares the effect of the wine to that of a trill ('trillo') that grows in strength — the orchestra illustrates this — until its force escapes the confines of the mere individual:

> Trilla ogni fibra in cor, l'allegro etere al trillo
> Guizza e il giocondo globo squilibra una demenza
> Trillante! E il trillo invade il mondo!!!

> Every fibre in the heart trills; the merry sky itself quivers
> With the trill, and a trilling madness unbalances
> The joyous globe! And the trill invades the world!!!

Falstaff's recovery is short-lived. Mistress Quickly, again Alice's messenger, enters and interrupts with her obsequious 'Reverenza'. At first, Falstaff tries to dismiss her with enraged bluster, but Quickly pours out Alice's regrets and delivers another letter. The knight reads the message on a single pitch, as Alice, Ford, Nannetta, Meg, Dr Cajus, and Fenton (all on the far stage left) watch him unobserved:

> T'aspetterò nel parco Real, a mezzanotte.
> Tu verrai travestito da Cacciatore nero
> Alla quercia di Herne.

> I'll wait for you in the Royal Park, at midnight.
> Come disguised as the Black Hunter
> To Herne's Oak.

Quickly explains the strange terms of the assignation to Falstaff. According to popular legend the Black Hunter hanged himself on an oak tree (Herne's Oak); his ghost, adorned with horns, still prowls about the park at night. At death-march tempo Quickly begins to evoke the eerie scene: 'Quando il rintocco della mezzanotte' ('When the sullen knell of midnight'). As Falstaff and Quickly disappear to discuss matters inside the inn, Alice tells the same tale to her fellow conspirators. So vividly does she recount the legend that Nannetta feels a shiver of fear. Her mother, however, brushes it aside with the brief explanation that these are idle tales that nurses tell to sleepy children ('Fandonie che ai bamboli').

With Nannetta's fright quelled, Alice resumes the death-march story, now accompanied by four French horns: since Alice is telling the legend about the two horns sprouting on the Black Hunter's head, we encounter once again the *corni–corna* pun heard earlier in Ford's monologue. Ford delights at the prospect of seeing Falstaff horned. His glee is only mildly restrained by his wife's reminder that his own jealousy is almost as much at fault as Sir John's combination of greed and lust.

The remainder of the scene consists of instructions for the midnight masquerade. Nannetta will be dressed as the Queen of the Fairies, all in white; Meg is to be a forest nymph in green; Quickly a witch ('una befana', sung to a sour dissonance). As for herself, Alice sings:

| | |
|---|---|
| Avrò con me dei putti | I'll have some children with me |
| Che fingeran folletti, | Who will pretend to be goblins, |
| E spiritelli, | And little spirits, |
| E diavoletti, | And devils, |
| E pipistrelli, | And bats, |
| E farfarelli. | And butterflies. |

After Alice, Meg, Nannetta, and Fenton have left, Ford and Cajus remain on stage for a brief exchange that is overheard by Mistress Quickly, who at that moment is coming out of the inn. Ford hopes to capitalize on the midnight confusion in Windsor Forest by marrying his daughter to Dr Cajus. According to this plan Cajus is to put on monk's clothes and present himself and Nannetta to Ford immediately after Falstaff has been punished. As the two men leave, Quickly vows to thwart their plans. Her exit is accompanied by delicate music in the orchestra (beginning *pianissimo* with a descending sequence of parallel-seventh chords — hardly standard harmonic practice). The scene ends quietly, with the offstage voices of Quickly, Nannetta, and Alice refining their plans for the evening's revenge on Falstaff.

The final part of Act III, in Windsor Forest at midnight, comprises mainly a loose sequence of nearly self-sufficient pieces. Mystery and ritual now come to the fore (see Chapter 8 below): as the stage action unfolds more in archetypal gestures than in the free flow of 'normal' behaviour, so too the music becomes less fluid and more stylized.

And so the opening few minutes of this forest scene are given over to the sheer creation of atmosphere. The scene opens with mellow calls from a distant horn — Verdi specifies that it should be a natural horn in A♭ — answered by woodwind fragments from Fenton and Nannetta's duet in I.ii. Fenton enters alone and begins his principal solo of the opera, a formal, Petrarchan sonnet in ripe *endecasillabi*:

Dal labbro il canto estasïato vola
Pe' silenzi notturni e va lontano
E alfin ritrova un altro labbro umano
Che gli risponde colla sua parola.

From my lips the ecstasied song flies
Through nocturnal silences and into the distance,
And at last it finds another pair of lips
That answer it in their own words.

This is a wondrous, generalized evocation of love, to be perceived more as a deepening of Fenton's character than an advancement of the plot. But aspects of plot are nevertheless latent. The dramatic burden of III.ii is to discredit the plans of the adults and to allow the marriage of Fenton and Nannetta to effect a reconciliation and renewal among all parties. The highlighting of Fenton here and Nannetta later (in her parallel song) singles the young people out for elevation and endows them with an unquestioned purity of intent.

Fenton's sonnet initiates this process admirably: the disarmingly casual lyricism could not contrast more sharply with what we have been hearing during the past two acts. Moreover, as a kind of anticipatory symbol of the union that will conclude the opera, Nannetta sings the penultimate line of his sonnet offstage and enters to double his final line in vocal unison. This last tercet — pure magic — finally puts the young lovers' Boccaccian couplet from Act I into the context of an entire poem:

Bocca baciata non perde ventura.
Anzi rinnova come fa la luna.
Ma il canto muor nel bacio che lo tocca.

A mouth once kissed loses not its future.
Rather, it renews itself like the moon.
But the song dies in the kiss that touches it.

Such moments of perfection never last. Alice bursts in with Fenton's disguise: a monk's cloak. Having learned of her husband's plan to marry Nannetta to the disguised Dr Cajus, Alice intends to substitute Fenton in churchly garb for the doctor. All plans are now set. Everyone takes cover. We are even told that the children dressed as fairies have arrived to await the entrance of the victim.

The 'Black Hunter' Falstaff does indeed soon appear, wrapped in an immense cloak and sporting deer's antlers tied to his head. It is exactly midnight: Sir John counts the tolls of the bell and reflects on his bestial appearance. Recalling Ovid's story that Jupiter himself courted Europa in the guise of an ox, he declares that 'L'amore metamorfosa un uomo in una bestia' ('Love transforms a man into a beast').

Alice now begins the pretended flirtation. She tells the horned knight that Meg has come with her. Falstaff delightedly prepares to enjoy them both, when all at once Meg's distant voice is heard: 'Aiuto!!!' ('Help!!!'). Soon Meg darts onstage to warn the 'lovers' that she has sighted evil spirits. Alice flees, leaving Sir John alone to hear the noises of the apparent approach of fairies — Nannetta, offstage, marshalling her troops of costumed children. Falstaff throws himself on the ground: 'Sono le Fate. Chi le guarda è morto' ('These are the fairies. Who looks upon them will die'). Nannetta, Alice, and the children enter to twelve bars of gentle music, and Nannetta sings an evocative fairy song to her charges: 'Sul fil d'un soffio etesio' ('On the thread of a summer breeze'). Her song, like Fenton's, impresses through its delicate beauty (beginning, for example, with muted, staccato accompaniment in the high strings, coloured here and there with violin and harp harmonics) and its explicitly formalized construction: two strophes (Boito had originally written three), each containing eight lines of solo and a four-line choral response.

With a sudden shift to *prestissimo*, the remaining characters (all disguised except for Ford and some village neighbours) enter to accuse Falstaff. They surround the prostrate knight to hurl insults, Bardolfo and Pistola taking special pleasure in thus assailing their master. The physical portion of the onslaught begins with a virtually untranslatable song to accompany a thorough pinching:

| | |
|---|---|
| Pizzica, pizzica, | Pinch, pinch, |
| Pizzica, stuzzica | Pinch, poke, |
| Spizzica, spizzica, | Pick, pick, |
| Pungi, spilluzzica | Prick, nip, |
| Finch'egli abbài! | Until he barks! |

The tormentors swirl Falstaff around, raise him to his knees, shout further insults at him, and begin to beat him with a cudgel. 'Ahi! Ahi! mi pento', he cries repeatedly ('Oh! Oh! I repent!'), whereupon the wives begin a pseudo-litany in which they sing the first part of each of four lines to an 'ecclesiastical' melody (similar to that found in the 'Hostias' of Verdi's Requiem) and Falstaff gives the invariable response:

Domine fallo casto! Ma salvagli l'addomine.
Domine fallo guasto! Ma salvagli l'addomine.
Fallo punito Domine! Ma salvagli l'addomine.
Fallo pentito Domine! Ma salvagli l'addomine.

Lord, make him chaste! But save his abdomen.
Lord, make him ruined! But save his abdomen.
Make him punished, Lord! But save his abdomen.
Make him repent, Lord! But save his abdomen.

The verbal and physical abuse continues unabated, but Pistola and Bardolfo are letting things get out of hand: ultimately, Bardolfo shouts with such enthusiasm that the hood of his disguise falls back, allowing Falstaff to discover that at least one of these demons is very human indeed: 'Riconosco Bardolfo!' ('I recognize Bardolfo!'). Now the former victim rains insults on Bardolfo until his breath fails him. As Quickly sends Bardolfo offstage with brief instructions, Falstaff slowly realizes that his tormentors are people that he knows. 'Signor Fontana' turns out to be Ford; even Quickly introduces herself by singing 'Cavaliero' ('Knight') to her 'Reverenza' motive. The game is up. In music incorporating a twofold bray, Falstaff admits:

> Incomincio ad accorgermi
> D'esser stato un somaro.
>
> I do begin to perceive
> That I have been an ass.

After everyone laughs in agreement, Falstaff moralizes that, even as victim, his joviality provides the very spice of life: 'L'arguzia mia crea l'arguzia degli altri' ('My wit creates everyone else's wit'). All assent, and Ford now proposes what he believes will surprise everyone: a wedding for the Queen of the Fairies.

A graceful minuet serves as wedding processional for Cajus and the supposed Nannetta in disguise. Little does Cajus suspect that he is escorting Bardolfo, who, having agreed with the wives to upset Ford's plans, has just changed into the costume of the Queen. So sure is Ford that his plan is foolproof that he readily agrees to his wife's request to marry a similarly disguised couple — Fenton and the real Nannetta, of course — who suddenly enter into the festivities. The denouement is pure farce. Cajus discovers that he has married Bardolfo; Ford, that he has blessed the marriage of Fenton to Nannetta. To shouts of 'Vittoria!' and 'Evviva!' Ford is forced to admit that he has been duped as effectively as has Falstaff. As echoes of the nuptial minuet are heard in the orchestra, Nannetta asks for and receives her father's pardon.

Another grand 'Evviva!' leads Ford to ask everybody — even Falstaff — to join in a general chorus, to be followed by dinner. Sir John himself leads the ensemble, the celebrated concluding fugue:

> Tutto nel mondo è burla.
> L'uom è nato burlone.
>
> Everything in the world is a jest.
> Man is born a jokester.

What could be more fitting than this stylized final fugue? No other form could suggest as well the ultimate reconciliation of the characters, the restoration of order in Windsor society. But, in a larger sense, the fugue is far more than this. Is it not also a final display of technique, vitality, and sheer exuberance from a much-loved composer who refused to grow old?

> Ma ride ben chi ride
> La risata final.

> But he laughs well who laughs
> The last laugh.

# 2 *The forging of the libretto*

Italy learned the secret from Milan's *Corriere della sera* on 27 November 1890. Under the headline 'A New Opera by Giuseppe Verdi', the story revealed that the *gran maestro*, now seventy-seven years old, had already written more than half of a comic opera: 'It is entitled *Falstaff* and is drawn from Shakespeare'. The revelation took Italy by storm, and newspapers throughout the peninsula amplified the story at once. The delighted musical critic of the Milanese *La perseveranza*, for instance, was able to report the following day that

[Verdi] said that Boito's libretto is beautiful: so comic that even while composing it he has to break off work from time to time to burst into laughter. This reminds us of what he wrote to our late [critic] Filippi many years ago, that he would only compose a comic opera after finding a libretto that made him laugh first.

This was astonishing news. Public, critics, and musicians alike linked the composer's name with a brilliant succession of tragic operas from *Nabucco* (1842) to *Otello* (1887), for he had written no comic opera since the early, unsuccessful *Un giorno di regno* (1840). Doubtless many thought him incapable of it. As early as 1847 Rossini had maintained that Verdi's serious temperament was unsuited to comedy: 'He will never write a semi-serious opera like *Linda* [*di Chamounix*], much less a comic opera like *L'elisir d'amore*' – words that still hurt Verdi deeply in 1879, when Giulio Ricordi casually allowed them to be reprinted in the house journal of his publishing firm, the *Gazzetta musicale di Milano* (Abbiati 1959: IV, 88-90).

From time to time in his career Verdi had considered writing a second comic opera. When Marie Escudier had suggested in March 1850 that he write an opera for Covent Garden based on *The Tempest*, he showed some interest in the project but ultimately rejected it. Some eighteen years later, on 24 February 1868, after the Parisian performances of *Don Carlos*, his wife, Giuseppina, wrote to Léon Escudier that a comic opera was not out of the question, providing a suitable subject could be found, one without buffoonery and in which sentiment is present 'as a delicate, sympathetic nuance that serves to temper the gaiety and the laughter' (Ibid. IV, 380-1). In the summer of 1868 a Milanese journal reported that Verdi was writing a comic opera, *Falstaff* — the first pairing of his name with the title — with the librettist Antonio Ghislanzoni. Verdi denied the story privately in a letter to Opprandino Arrivabene; Ghislanzoni denied it publicly in the *Gazzetta musicale di Milano*.

It seems likely that he was indeed planning a comic opera to follow *Don Carlos*. His copy of a French scenario for such an opera, *Tartufo*, based on Molière, still exists at Sant'Agata. According to Alessandro Luzio (1935-47: II, 358-61), he prepared this copy some time between 1868 and 1870 but abandoned the subject in favour of *Aida*. One hears nothing more about an *opera buffa* until a decade later, when the composer, replying indignantly to Ricordi's publication of Rossini's words mentioned above, made the surprising assertion in August 1879: 'I have looked for a comic opera libretto for twenty years, and now that I have, so to speak, found it, you instil in the public a ready-made desire to hiss my opera before it is even written' (Abbiati 1959: IV, 88-9). Once again, despite Ricordi's interest in this opera, whatever it might have been, Verdi soon turned to the composition of another tragic opera, *Otello*, in collaboration with Arrigo Boito.

Had it not been for the latter's insistence, *Otello* might have remained Verdi's last opera. Boito, privately insisting to his friend Camille Bellaigue that he was 'eager to make that bronze colossus resound one more time' (Boito 1932: 315), began to hint at another collaboration soon after the success of that work. 'I would like that time to return', he wrote to the composer on 9 October 1888, 'when each of our letters was about the study of a great work of art' (*Carteggio Verdi–Boito* 1978: I, 132-3). But Verdi was not to be easily persuaded, although he had by no means abandoned composition: in March 1889 he wrote a brief *Ave Maria* that was later to be published as one of the four *Pezzi sacri*; and shortly thereafter — although this story cannot at present be confirmed — he may have been planning an atmospheric 'symphonic poem', *La notte dell'Innominato*, based on a portion of Manzoni's *I promessi sposi*, Chapter 21 (Osthoff 1977: 176-81).

Finally, during a trip to Milan in the summer of 1889, according to the usually well-informed Giulio Ricordi's report in the *Gazzetta musicale* on 30 November 1890, Verdi spoke with Boito about a comic opera, and Boito actually proposed a subject to him. Although Ricordi does not mention the precise date, this could well have occurred at the end of June, when Verdi passed through Milan before going to the spa at Montecatini (see Conati's discussion in *Carteggio Verdi–Boito* 1978: II, 383.) Whatever the circumstances of their preliminary arrangements might have been, it is clear that Boito sent Verdi a proposed *Falstaff* scenario based on *The Merry Wives* and the two parts of *Henry IV* some time before 6 July 1889. This is the date that Verdi first responded to the scenario:

Dear Boito,

Excellent! Excellent!

Before reading your sketch I wanted to re-read the *Merry Wives*, the two parts of *Henry IV* and *Henry V*, and I can only repeat: Excellent, for one could not do better than you have done . . .

I am talking for the sake of talking – take no notice. We have now very different matters to discuss, so that this *Falstaff*, or *Merry Wives*, which two days ago was in the world of dreams, now takes shape and becomes reality! When? How? . . . Who knows? I'll write to you tomorrow or the next day. (Walker 1962: 495)

The seven days from 6 to 12 July 1889 were critical for the *Falstaff* project. During this period Verdi wrote Boito four letters agreeing to compose the opera, suggesting slight alterations in the plot, and dealing with a few contractual matters; and Boito responded with four, eloquently alleviating Verdi's fears about his age and agreeing to the modifications that the composer was suggesting. From Verdi's letter to Boito of 7 July 1889:

In outlining *Falstaff* did you never think of the enormous number of my years? . . .

Supposing I couldn't stand the strain? And failed to finish it? You would then have uselessly wasted your time and trouble! . . .

How are we to overcome these obstacles? Have you a sound argument to oppose to mine? I hope so, but I don't believe it. Still, let's think it over (and be careful to do nothing that could be harmful to your career) and if you can find one for me, and I some way of throwing off ten years or so, then . . . what joy, to be able to say to the public:

*Here we are again!! Come and see us!* (Ibid. pp. 495-6)

And from 10 July:

Amen. So be it!

We'll write this *Falstaff* then! We won't think for the moment of obstacles, of age, of illness!

I too wish to conserve the profoundest *secrecy* – a word that I too underline three times, to tell you that no one must know anything about it! (Ibid. p. 496)

The correspondence of 6–12 July 1889 set in motion the process that would lead to a completed *Falstaff* and a La Scala première on 9 February 1893. Although the scenario that Boito sent Verdi is lost, these early letters, recently printed in their entirety (*Carteggio Verdi–Boito* 1978), permit one to determine many things about the first plans for the *Falstaff* story. Boito, for example, conceived it from the beginning in three acts and six parts. The general outline of the plot was much like that of the final version: Falstaff was to undergo two trials, not three, as in *The Merry Wives*; Fenton and Nannetta were to have loveduets scattered throughout the opera; the third act was to be more loosely constructed than the first two, and was to contain, as Verdi wrote in his letter of 6 July, 'little pieces, songs, ariettas, etc.' (Walker 1962: 495); Falstaff was to appear in horns and be interrogated in the third act; the final act was to contain two masked marriages; and so on.

Yet the scenario contained a few details that the composer and the librettist decided to change immediately: Ford's jealousy monologue was originally to begin II.ii, and Verdi suggested that it conclude II.i instead; Pistola originally did not reappear in III.ii; Fenton and Nannetta were to sing a *duettino* in III.ii that Boito first suggested be put at the end of III.i and then proposed omitting altogether; and the opera was to end with the masked marriages, not the final fugue.

Verdi and Boito were most concerned with the third act, which they quite accurately perceived would be of less dramatic interest than the preceding two. In order to fortify the close of the opera, Verdi suggested some concluding lines in his letter of 11 July 1889:

[At the end of your sketch] the marriages interrupt the attention that ought to be completely returned to Falstaff, and the action is chilled. With regard to this there would be a ready-made musical piece in Sha[k]espeare:

| | |
|---|---|
| MISTRESS PAGE: | Let's not push the jest any further. |
| FALSTAFF: | And these are the fairies? |
| MISTRESS FORD: | And do you believe that if we wanted to sin we would have chosen a man like you? |
| FORD: | A whale! |
| FALSTAFF: | Fine! |
| ANOTHER: | A man of cream! |
| FALSTAFF: | Fine! |
| ANOTHER: | An old, withered man. |
| FALSTAFF: | Very fine. |
| ANOTHER: | As accursed as Satan. |
| FALSTAFF: | Fine again. |
| OTHERS: | As poor as Job. |
| [FALSTAFF:] | Excellent. |
| ALL: | And devoted to fornication, to taverns, to wine, to debauchery, swearing, lying, and cursing God . . . |
| FALSTAFF: | Amen . . . and so be it. |

MISTRESS [PAGE]:    And now, Sir John, how do you like the wives
of Windsor?
FALSTAFF:    I now begin to perceive that I am an ass.
ALL:    Bravo! Well said! Well said! Viva viva viva!
*Applause and the fall of the curtain.*

(*Carteggio Verdi–Boito* 1978: I, 148-50)

This is the only extant letter in which Verdi proposes that a substantial number of lines be versified and inserted into *Falstaff*. He derived most of them from the final scene of Carlo Rusconi's Italian translation of Shakespeare, *Le allegre comari di Windsor* (1838; 3rd ed. with small revisions, *Le allegre femmine di Windsor*, 1852-3), and not from the other Italian translation that he owned, that of his friend Giulio Carcano (*Le donne allegre di Windsor*, 1881). Boito accepted Verdi's suggestions and the provisional ending on 12 July but insisted that the wedding between Fenton and Nannetta be retained. He would be ready to begin work, he wrote, in fifteen days.

On 1 August 1889 Boito requested that the scenario (of which the composer, surely, had made a copy) be returned to him. Verdi complied the following day and probably spent the next two weeks thinking about his new opera. By 18 August he had another suggestion: 'You are working, I hope? The strangest thing of all is that I am working too! I'm amusing myself by writing fugues! Yes, sir; a fugue . . . and a *comic fugue*, which would be in place in *Falstaff!*' (Walker 1962: 497). On the basis of this letter Frank Walker has suggested (p. 498) that the final fugue was the first portion of *Falstaff* that Verdi composed and that it was therefore written before he had received its text. Walker may well be correct – and it is a happy suggestion indeed – but there is no supporting evidence to link the fugue mentioned on 18 August with the one that now concludes the opera. The letters of 11 July and 18 August do reveal, however, that the present ending – nearly everything, in fact, after the masked marriages – was Verdi's idea, not Boito's.

Working in Ivrea, Milan, and Nervi (and with his Rusconi and Carcano translations of Shakespeare close at hand), Boito continued to write the libretto for more than six months. The almost complete lack of correspondence between Verdi and Boito suggests that they saw each other frequently during this period. One meeting can be documented. On 30 October 1889 Boito wrote from Milan: 'I shall arrive next Monday (4 November), and if the second act is not yet finished, I'll finish it during the week I stay at Sant'Agata . . . I sketched the scene with the laundry basket, and it seems to me to have much promise. But there is still much to do!' (*Carteggio Verdi–Boito* 1978: I, 155-6). Moreover, Verdi, as usual, spent the winter in Genoa, while Boito took up residence in the neighbouring town of Nervi. They undoubtedly met often to discuss the nascent libretto.

Boito had nearly completed the text by 1 March 1890. On that date he announced: 'Within three or four days at the latest I shall have finished *Falstaff*. The third act is turning out to be less brief than I had hoped, but it's the most varied of all' (Ibid. I, 158). Verdi responded the next day: 'So Big-Belly is almost finished! Hurrah! ... I'm not afraid of the length, because I am certain that there won't be anything useless in it. You said that you would be in Genoa Wednesday [5 March]. Delay a few days. I'm leaving for Sant'Agata tomorrow morning [3 March] and I won't be back until Saturday [8 March]' (Ibid. I, 159).

Boito, then, might have brought the libretto to Genoa on 8 March, or, more likely, he might have sent it earlier so that the composer could have it on his return. On 8 March Verdi sent Boito a sum of money for the libretto: 'Accept ... not as payment, but as a sign of gratitude, for having written this stupendous *Falstaff* for me. If I do not manage to finish the music for it, the poetry of *Falstaff* will remain your property' (Ibid. I, 160). Boito replied with a letter of great modesty: 'Now, Maestro, again in the name of Shakespeare, give Art and our country another modern victory' (Ibid. I, 160).

By this time, of course, the libretto contained few surprises: Verdi had been acquainted with it as a work in progress. Indeed, he had probably added and rejected lines of text throughout the winter of 1889-90. Certainly he did not hesitate to request or ratify textual changes after receiving the libretto: slight modifications, for example in the Honour Monologue, the text of 'Quand'ero paggio', the '-elli' rhymes in the middle of Alice's 'Avrò con me dei putti', the '-on' rhymes hurled at Falstaff in III.ii ('Cialtron!/Poltron!/Gorgion!' etc.), and the final fugue (see Luzio 1935-47: II, 154, IV, 49; *Carteggio Verdi–Boito* 1978: I, 205, 214-15). The libretto, from its inception, was the product of a collaboration. There is no reason to suppose that Verdi did not begin to consider – either in his mind or actually on paper – a number of musical ideas for the opera before receiving the libretto on 8 March 1890.

Boito's text blends Shakespeare's *The Merry Wives of Windsor* with several Falstaff passages from the two parts of *Henry IV* and other, non-Shakespearean ideas. *The Merry Wives* was the fundamental source for the story, but it had to be simplified and tightened to serve as an operatic plot for a work lasting only two hours. This affected both the number and the quality of Shakespeare's characters. Of Falstaff's original three henchmen, only Bardolph and Pistol remain, Nym and his 'humour' being, presumably, untranslatable into operatic language. Likewise totally absent are George Page and his schoolboy son William, Sir Hugh Evans, Caius' servant John Rugby, and Slender's servant Peter Simple. Four of Shakespeare's characters are given only mute roles in the opera: the Host of the Garter Inn, Falstaff's page Robin, and two of Ford's servants, John and Robert (who become four for the sake of rhyme and metre: Ned, Will, Tom, and Isaac).

Boito's Dr Cajus is primarily a telescoping of the country justice Robert Shallow and his nephew Abraham Slender. There is, in fact, very little besides hot temper, a fierce desire to marry Anne (Nannetta), and an eventual false marriage to a boy (to Bardolfo in the opera) that links Shakespeare's French physician to the Cajus of *Falstaff*. Not a line of the original Caius is transferred to the opera. (This is not surprising, since much of the humour of the character lay in his extravagant French accent.) Thus, in the opening scene of *Falstaff* Dr Cajus accuses Sir John of breaking into his lodge and beating his servants. These were originally the charges made by Robert Shallow (*The Merry Wives* [*Wiv.*], I.i, 104-5).* Dr Cajus' origins here in a country justice are even more apparent a few lines later: 'M'appellerò al Consiglio Real' ('The Council shall know this': *Wiv.*, I.i, 110). Here, the legalistic language involving an appeal to a higher court (Cajus actually specifies the 'Royal Council', while Shallow, in the opening lines of the play, threatens to 'make a Star-Chamber matter of it') makes no sense in the mouth of a physician, even though his exact profession is never clarified in the opera. Shortly thereafter, Dr Cajus turns on Bardolfo and Pistola for picking his pocket the day before. Just as he had earlier been Shallow, now he becomes Slender. It is the latter who demands recompense for an emptied pocket in the play (*Wiv.*, I.i, 118-74).

Other characters also undergo transformations from play to opera. Quickly is no longer Dr Cajus' servant; she loses many of her scheming ways and addle-headed malapropisms and becomes merely a willing neighbour who enjoys a good joke. Shakespeare's Anne Page becomes Boito's Nannetta Ford — the necessary result of omitting Master Page, as well as an opportunity to focus even more attention on Master Ford, who now also has to contend with his daughter's marriage. Fenton's character, by no means complex in the play, is even less so in the opera. We never learn, for instance, that he is a peer who has earlier squandered

---

* Line references and quotations are from *The New Shakespeare,* ed. John Dover Wilson and Sir Arthur Quiller-Couch. Cambridge, 1968-9.

his wealth in carousing and whose original interest in the middle-class Nannetta was to obtain a large dowry. Boito's Fenton is more of an operatic type, the youthful, lyric-tenor lover, whose purity of ardour is self-explanatory and untainted by such admissions as Shakespeare gives to his Fenton:

> Albeit I will confess thy father's wealth
> Was the first motive that I wooed thee, Anne:
> Yet, wooing thee, I found thee of more value
> Than stamps in gold or sums in sealéd bags. (*Wiv.*, III.iv, 13-16)

In the play Anne's father's antipathy to Fenton is understandable; in the opera it is a postulate of the plot but remains largely incomprehensible. One can only presume that Ford sees more economic gain in Nannetta's eventual marriage to Dr Cajus, although we are never told so.

As Boito simplified the characters, so too he streamlined Shakespeare's sprawling plot by cutting out everything that could be considered unessential: Caius' discovery of Simple in his closet, the Caius–Evans duel, William's Latin lesson, the stealing of the German duke's horses, etc. Even three humiliations for Sir John at the hands of the wives were too many. Boito retained the first (the laundry basket) and the third (Windsor Forest) but omitted the second entirely, in which Falstaff is lured back into Alice's home but is compelled to flee disguised as an old woman, the witch of Brainford, as Ford pummels him out of the door.

Individual speeches, too, show evidence of Boito's masterly concision. For example, in Ford's monologue 'È sogno? o realtà', at the end of II.i, he condensed and fused two separate speeches from *The Merry Wives*, the conclusions of II.ii and III.v. Moreover, Boito's thirty-one lines are beautifully shaped and proceed more dynamically and consistently than do Shakespeare's, from the opening with its imagery of dreams, through a recitation of Ford's fears, to the powerful resolution contained in the final seven lines.

But nowhere is Boito's talent more apparent than in his brilliant interweaving of words, lines, and speeches from the *Henry IV* plays. The most obvious inclusion is Falstaff's Honour Monologue at the end of I.i, the heart of which ('Può l'onore riempirvi la pancia?') is derived from the famous Honour Catechism in *Henry IV: Part I* [*1H4*], V.i, before he enters the Battle of Shrewsbury. This explains the rather surprising references to the loss of limbs, to surgeons, and to dead men, which might otherwise seem overworked in the context of Falstaff's amorous plottings in the Garter Inn. Boito surrounds the catechistic core of the monologue with ten preceding lines from *Wiv.*, II.ii, 18ff (beginning

'You stand upon your honour! Why, thou unconfinable baseness, it is as much as I can do, to keep the terms of my honour precise') and four concluding lines from *Wiv.*, I.iii, 79-80 ('Rogues, hence, avaunt, vanish like hail-stones; go!'). Only once in the monologue does one sense an awkward joint between the various sources: the contrived initial line of the final quatrain, 'Ma per tornare a voi, furfanti' ('But to return to you, you rogues').

Boito's decision to have the knight chase out the two thieves by smacking at them with a broom is his own, although he may have had the witch of Brainford episode (*Wiv.*, IV.ii) in mind. In any event, that Falstaff relies on such a commonplace item as a broom seems tame and contributes to the conclusion that the Falstaff of the opera lacks much of the roughness of his counterpart in the plays. One need only recall his swordplay in *Henry IV: Part II* [*2H4*], II.iv, to clear the Boar's Head Tavern of swaggering Pistol.

Other significant passages sung by Falstaff are likewise based on the *Henry IV* plays. Sir John's evocation of his slender youth, 'Quand'ero paggio' in II.ii, intertwines 'When I was about thy years, Hal, I was not an eagle's talon in the waist, I could have crept into any alderman's thumb-ring' (*1H4*, II.iv, 325-8) with Shallow's 'Then was Jack Falstaff (now Sir John) a boy, and page to Thomas Mowbray, Duke of Norfolk' (*2H4*, III.ii, 25-7). His brilliant monologue at the beginning of III.i in praise of the trilling effects of hot wine is built from three Shakespearean passages: the aftermath of the Gad's Hill trick and Sir John's discovery of lime in his sack, *1H4*, II.iv, 114-15, 128 ('Is there no virtue extant?' ... 'A bad world, I say', etc.); Falstaff's meditation on being dumped into the Thames, *Wiv.*, III.v, 3-17 ('Go fetch me a quart of sack – put a toast in't' ... 'I had been drowned, but that the shore was shelvy and shallow ... a death that I abhor; for the water swells a man', etc.); and Sir John's praise of sack on the battlefield, *2H4*, IV.iii, 93-113 ('A good sherris-sack hath a two-fold operation in it').

Even more fascinating are the individual lines from the *Henry IV* plays that flash forth in new contexts to enrich the *Merry Wives* source. To enumerate them all here would be tedious, but a selection of particularly subtle or provocative examples will illustrate the point:

The limed sack mentioned above (*1H4*, II.iv, 121) also appears in *Falstaff*: 'Ho l'intestino/Guasto', etc. (I.i, 9 bars after no. 2).

Bardolph asks Prince Hal to consider his face, 'My lord, do you see these meteors?' (*1H4*, II.iv, 315-16); similarly, indicating his glowing nose to Dr Cajus in the opera, 'Vedi questa meteora?' (I.i, 13 bars after no. 2).

Falstaff's remark to Pistol in the Doll Tearsheet scene, 'No more, Pistol. I would not have you go off here' (*2H4*, II.iv, 131-2) is transferred (and hence bowdlerized) to Pistola's wrath at Cajus, 'Non scaricarti qui' (I.i, 6 bars before no. 5).

Poins's reading of the knight's expenditures while he sleeps behind the arras, 'Item, A capon', etc. (*1H4*, II.iv, 526-30), becomes the Host's bill that Falstaff cannot pay (I.i, no. 7).

Falstaff's sarcastic praise of Bardolph's torchlight nose, 'thou art the Knight of the Burning Lamp . . . Thou hast saved me a thousand marks in links and torches' (*1H4*, III.iii, 26-7, 41-7), becomes a cause of his financial ruin in 'So che se andiam, la notte' (I.i, 19 bars after no. 7).

His lament 'Do I not bate? Do I not dwindle?' (*1H4*, III.iii, 2), the result of humiliation and debauchery, is turned into a monetary complaint with 'Mi struggete le carni! Se Falstaff s'assottiglia' (I.i, 2 bars before no. 8).

His confirmation of his identity on the battlefield to the newly surrendered enemy, Sir John Coleville, 'I have a whole school of tongues in this belly of mine, and not a tongue of them all speaks any other word but my name' (*2H4*, IV.iii, 18-20), becomes, in effect, his self-introduction to the audience at the conclusion of his first *arioso* (I.i, 9 bars after no. 8).

From two lines in the *Henry IV* plays, Prince Hal's parting from Sir John, 'Farewell, All-hallown Summer!' (*1H4*, I.ii, 152-3), and Poins's question to Bardolph, 'And how doth the martlemas, your master?' (*2H4*, II.ii, 99-100: Martlemas refers to St Martin's Day, 11 November), comes Falstaff's 'Io sono ancora una piacente estate/Di San Martino' (I.i, 7 bars before no. 12).

Originally referring to his skill as a thief and pickpocket, Falstaff's remark to Prince Hal, "tis no sin for a man to labour in his vocation' (*1H4*, I.ii, 102-3), is used to justify his attempted seduction of Alice (II.ii, 4 bars before no. 42).

On Gad's Hill Falstaff fears to lie down to place his ear to the ground: 'Have you any levers to lift me up again?' (*1H4*, II.ii, 33); in the final scene of the opera the prostrate knight calls frantically for a crane: 'Portatemi una grue!' (III.ii, 9 bars before no. 39).

Falstaff's soliloquy 'Men of all sorts take a pride to gird at me . . . I am not only witty in myself, but the cause that wit is in other men' (*2H4*, I.ii, 6-10) becomes his moralizing comment after his punishment that helps to elevate the whole opera from the particular to the universal (III.ii, no. 49).

After the Gad's Hill episode, Prince Hal's comment about the fled Falstaff, 'Were't not for laughing, I should pity him' (*1H4*, II.ii, 107-8), is given, with an added touch of violence, to Ford near the end of the opera to comment on Falstaff's moralizing: 'Se non ridessi ti sconquasserei!' (III.ii, 2 bars after no. 50).

Certain passages or events in the opera are traceable neither to *The Merry Wives* nor to the two parts of *Henry IV*: Quickly's narrative in

II.ii, 'Giunta all'Albergo della Giarrettiera'; the hiding of Fenton and Nannetta behind the screen in II.ii; the marrying of Cajus to Bardolfo, not merely to 'un garçon', as in *Wiv.*, V.v; and Ford's and Falstaff's overcourteous deference to each other before exiting at the end of II.i ('Prima voi . . . Passiamo insieme'), which may well have its source in the concluding lines of *The Comedy of Errors* (but cf. a similar problem of courtesy between Anne and Slender in *Wiv.*, I.i, 289-96). The text of the final fugue, with its opening line 'Tutto nel mondo è burla', is surely an intended reminiscence of Jaques' bitter 'All the world's a stage,/And all the men and women merely players' in *As You Like It*, II.vii (although Boito and Verdi seem to have interpreted the line as festive, not cynical; one wonders whether the sentiment of alienation inextricably embedded in the text is appropriate at the end of *Falstaff* – if so, we might reopen the question of the opera's meaning); and its final line is surely taken from the proverb 'He who laughs last laughs best'.

Most of the lines illustrating Fenton and Nannetta's love are either original to Boito or have their sources in non-Shakespearean literature. Andrew Porter has recently pointed out (1979: iv) that their recurring couplet, 'Bocca baciata non perde ventura. / Anzi rinnova come fa la luna', is a quotation from the conclusion of the much racier Seventh Story of the Second Day of Boccaccio's *Decameron*. Giuseppe Petronio, in his edition of the *Decameron* (Turin, 1950), identifies the couplet as a proverb (see also Osthoff 1977: 160) – and in another tale in the volume (Second Story, Eighth Day, II, 122, n. 20) he identifies *la ventura* as a slang expression for *membro virile*. It is possible that Boito knew the couplet principally as a proverb, for it is listed as such in the 1883 proverb collection of Strafforello, *La sapienza del mondo* (*The Wisdom of the World*, I, 183). And the couplet certainly could not have been obscure: Dante Gabriel Rossetti's 1859 portrait of Fanny Cornforth was entitled *Bocca baciata* and carries the two lines on the back of the picture. Yet the claim of a Boccaccian source seems unassailable, particularly in light of Boito's letter to Bellaigue before the Parisian première of *Falstaff* in early 1894: 'Come, come, dear friend, come and hear this masterpiece; come and live for two hours in the gardens of the *Decameron* and breathe flowers that are notes and breezes that are timbres' (Boito 1932: 317-18).

Porter finds additional evidence (1979: iv) for the influence of Boccaccio in Boito's selection of archaic or difficult words throughout the libretto: he cites words such as *nacchere, cozzare, aizzare, strozzare, ruzzare, rintuzzare, scrollare*, and *punzecchiare*, which are all words used in the *Decameron*. This is impressive evidence. The richness of the vocabulary is probably the most distinctive feature of the libretto, a fact that was evident at its première. On 10 February 1893, the day after the first performance, the critic of *La sera* complained: 'Boito has collected and jumbled together obsolete and old-fashioned words that are horrifying, such as *ciuschero, cerèbro, pagliardo, sugliardo, scanfardo, scagnardo, falsardo, castigatoja, crepitacolo, assillo, guindolo*, and a hundred other words that not even Ruscelli dared to put into his famous rhyming dictionary.' Although some of Boito's words may be found in Alfredo Barbina's *Concordanza del 'Decameron'* (Florence, 1969), including the phrase *sozzo can vituperato* (employed in two different *Decameron* stories, III.vi and IX.v), several of the uncommon *Falstaff* words are not in the concordance and are hence non-Boccaccian. These include *orticheggiare, spilluzzicare, crepitacolo, cialtron, malvisia, gagliofferia, scanfardo, falsardo, acceffare, arroncigliare*, and *guindolo*.

Besides its quotation of the Boccaccian couplet, Fenton's Sonnet in III.ii, as Wolfgang Osthoff has pointed out (1977: 161-3), may well be indebted to a complex of Shakespearean sources: Romeo's and Juliet's first words to each other, which form a 4+4+4+2 sonnet ('If I profane with my unworthiest hand', I.v), in which the imagery of a kiss is prominent (Boito had probably translated *Romeo and Juliet* for his mistress, Eleonora Duse, in early 1889); and Sonnets 8 and 128, both of which contain musical imagery that associates, for example, 'the concord of well tuned sounds' with the concept of the lovers' union. (Osthoff, pp. 176-81, also detects here a touch of the atmosphere of Manzoni's *I promessi sposi*.) Another source, undetected by Osthoff, is a fragment from an uncompleted expansion of *Le grazie* by the nineteenth-century poet Ugo Foscolo. The resemblance, first noted by Raffaello Barbiera (1893: 87), involves a line from the 'Venere' section of the lengthy poem, in an episode with the subtitle 'Calliroe e Ifianeo'. The line had been published in a critical edition of Foscolo's poems prepared by Giuseppe Chiarini (Livorno, 1882, p. 80), and Boito could well have known it: 'Su' labbri il canto le rompea co' baci' ('He broke the song on her lips with kisses').

Nannetta's song in III.ii appears to be largely Boito's invention, although certain sources for individual lines can be traced. The song is quite unrelated to Quickly's (!) Song as Fairy-Queen in *Wiv.*, V.v, 55-76, except for the correspondence of a single line: 'Fairies use flowers for their charáctery' becomes 'Le Fate / Hanno per cifre i fior' (cf. the Carcano translation 'Delle Fate i fior son cifre'). Roy Aycock's suggestion (1972: 604) that a dash of the flavour of *A Midsummer Night's Dream* is present in the final part of *Falstaff* seems particularly appropriate here.

It is easy for the listener not acquainted with Italian poetics to overlook the importance of purely literary structures in *Falstaff*. Boito distinguishes different situations or characters, for example, by differing poetic metres. Fenton and Nannetta usually sing to each other in *quinari*, five-syllable lines:

> Labbra di foco!
> Labbra di fiore! (I.ii, no. 30)

This metre returns, for example, with their love-lyrics in II.ii, as they hide behind the screen, as in Nannetta's

> Tutto delira,
> Sospiro e riso. (no. 63)

Falstaff himself slips into this love-metre when beginning his amorous serenade to Alice, 'Alfin t'ho colto' (II.ii, 10 bars after no. 38).

The wives in scheming mood are given *senari*, lines of six syllables, in their unaccompanied quartet:

> Quell'otre! quel tino!
> Quel Re delle pancie. (I.ii, no. 25)

The metre returns for the women's lines during the laundry-basket ensemble, as in Quickly's

> Facciamo le viste
> D'attendere ai panni. (II.ii, 8 bars after no. 59)

Falstaff, the victim of the wives' plot in this scene, now shares their six-syllable metre.

The pursuing men characteristically sing verses of *ottonari*, eight-syllable lines, in their quintet that follows the women's quartet. Thus, Dr Cajus sings:

> È un ribaldo, un furbo, un ladro,
> Un furfante, un turco, un vandalo: (I.ii, no. 26)

and the *ottonari* return for the four enraged men in the laundry-basket scene — sometimes even divided between different characters, as in the beginning of the ensemble:

> Se t'agguanto!
>                    Se ti piglio!
> Se t'acciuffo!
>                    Se t'acceffo! (II.ii, no. 59)

Boito wrote many of Falstaff's lines to match his girth. Both in soliloquy and in dialogue Sir John often declaims in *settenari doppi*, fourteen-syllable lines, typically with witty enjambment to produce unexpected rhymes in the middle of the logical sense, as in these lines from the Honour Monologue:

> Il vostro Onor! Che onore?! che onor? che onor? che ciancia!
> Che baia! Può l'onore riempirvi la pancia?
> No.                                             (I.i, 5 bars before no. 15)

The 'proper' pieces, or those delivered as if in quotation marks, are either in formal *endecasillabi* (eleven syllables), as in Falstaff's love-letter to Alice, the beginning of Quickly's 'official' report about her interview with Sir John, the tale of the Black Hunter, Fenton's Sonnet, and the text above the nuptial minuet; or in equally formal *settenari* (seven syllables), as in the Song of the Queen of the Fairies and the concluding fugue.

A number of important solo pieces display freely alternating, rhymed lines of five, seven, or eleven syllables – the metres that, minus the rhyme, provided the *versi sciolti* typical of recitatives in most of Verdi's earlier operas. Such mixed metres are found in Falstaff's 'Va, vecchio John'; Ford's Monologue 'È sogno? o realtà'; Falstaff's 'Quand'ero paggio' (the protagonist finally breaking free – youthfully? – from his characteristically stout, fourteen-syllable utterance); and Alice's 'Avrò con me dei putti'. Alice's 'Gaie comari di Windsor! è l'ora!' in II.ii exemplifies a particularly flexible mixed metre, since besides *quinari* and *endecasillabi* it also contain several lines of *senari*, the six-syllable metre established earlier as appropriate to the wives' scheming.

As if all of this were not brilliance enough, in certain passages Boito employs rhymed submetres tucked into different metrical forms. Much of the Falstaff–Alice duet in II.ii, for instance, is written in the usual alternating, rhymed *settenari* and *endecasillabi*:

> Ogni più bel gioiel mi nuoce e spregio
> Il finto idolo d'or.
> Mi basta un vel legato in croce, un fregio
> Al cinto e in testa un fior.

But, as Boito indicated in the manuscript libretto, the passage rhymes equally well in *novenari* (nine syllables):

> Ogni più bel gioiel mi nuoce
> E spregio il finto idolo d'or.
> Mi basta un vel legato in croce,
> Un fregio al cinto e in testa un fior

or in *quinari* (five syllables):

> Ogni più bel
> Gioiel mi nuoce
> E spregio il finto
> Idolo d'or.
> Mi basta un vel
> Legato in croce,
> Un fregio al cinto
> E in testa un fior.

A similar instance involves a hidden five-syllable submetre within much longer lines beginning with Bardolfo's 'Assottigliam' (I.i, no. 9) and going consistently through to 'Io son di Sir John Falstaff' (I.i, 4 bars after no. 11).

Surely one of the functions of this playful manipulation of traditional Italian metres, as well as the references to such native writers as Boccaccio and Foscolo, was to insist on the essentially Italian character of *Falstaff*. For Boito, and probably for Verdi as well, the opera was at least partially an aesthetic statement, in many ways a counterthrust to the main operatic directions of the time, that is, the immediate association of 'progress' with German Wagnerianism and the recent vogue of *verismo* in Italy. (Curiously, this aesthetic counterthrust was largely misunderstood: see Chapter 8.)

It is well known that Verdi had been alarmed for some time by the rise of Germanic influence on Italian composition. In a letter of April 1878, for example, he had maintained: 'Nobody knows better than I that art is universal, but still, individuals create it, and just as the Germans have different means from ours, so too there is also something different inside of them. We cannot – rather, I will say we ought not to – write like the Germans, nor the Germans like us' (Cesari and Luzio 1913: 626). His comment about the young Puccini in June 1884 had reflected the same attitude: 'It seems, however, that the symphonic element predominates in him: nothing bad. Only one must proceed cautiously here. Opera is opera and the symphony is the symphony, and I don't think that it is beautiful to create a symphonic piece in an opera' (Ibid. pp. 629-30).

Such clearly articulated suspicions of the seemingly irresistible Wagnerian formulas allied Verdi and Boito with conservative critics throughout Europe. Camille Bellaigue, a close friend of Boito, and the musical journalist for the Parisian *La Revue des deux mondes*, seems to have been particularly well attuned to this aspect of *Falstaff*. The anti-

Wagnerian posture is certainly the tacit content of Bellaigue's comment to Verdi on 12 February 1893, his initial reaction to the *Falstaff* score: 'What verve and what clarity! What a masterpiece of *Latin*, classical genius!' (Abbiati 1959: IV, 477).

For Boito, the final justification of this attitude lay not only in the *Decameron* borrowings but also in the fact that Shakespeare himself seems to have based *The Merry Wives* on an Italian tale from Ser Giovanni Fiorentino's 1558 collection *Il pecorone* (Second Story, First Day). This defused the only major non-Italian aspect of the libretto, and he made certain that Bellaigue realized it in a letter of April (?) 1894:

You say 'Here is the true, modern, Latin, lyric drama (or comedy)'. But what you cannot imagine is the immense intellectual joy that this Latin lyric comedy produces on the stage. It is a real overflowing of grace, force, and gaiety. The miracle of sounds guides Shakespeare's sparkling farce back again to its clear Tuscan source, Ser Giovanni Fiorentino.

(Boito 1932: 317)

Boito had clarified the intended anti-Wagnerian role of *Falstaff* in the aesthetic battles of the late nineteenth century in two slightly earlier letters to Bellaigue from April of the same year:

Ah, this *Falstaff*! How right you are to love this masterpiece. And what a boon for art when everyone manages to understand it. We'll do everything we can [in Paris] to arrive at this goal. The human spirit must be 'Mediterraneanized'; only there is true progress.     (Ibid. pp. 315-16)

The phrase 'to Mediterraneanize music' is not mine, but Nietzsche's. You are as well acquainted as I with the Bohemian philosopher, and I thought while writing to you that you would have recognized the phrase.

(Ibid. pp. 316-17)

Today's audiences do not feel the acute aesthetic tensions that bore so strongly on the consciences of composers and librettists during the late nineteenth century. But by no means did Boito and Verdi conceive *Falstaff* as an abstract work of art apart from the stresses of its time. With all the integrity and talent they could muster, they produced, in effect, a textual and musical manifesto by example, a work of art that, it was hoped, could redirect the course of music by what it was, rather than what it preached.

# 3 *The composition of the opera*

On 17 March 1890, nine days after having received the completed libretto, Verdi wrote from Genoa to Boito:

The first act is finished without any changes in the poetry: just as you gave it to me. I think that the same will happen in the second act unless some cuts are made in the *concertato* [i.e., in the laundry-basket scene in II.ii], as you yourself said. Let's not talk of the third now, but I believe that there will not be much to do, not even in this.

*(Carteggio Verdi–Boito* 1978: I, 163)

What astonishing facility in a man of seventy-six years! Even when one admits that Verdi must have known the libretto well before Boito formally delivered it to him, and that he could therefore have already sketched a number of important musical ideas, his achievement is extraordinary and shows with what vigour he greeted his new task. Because of the current inaccessibility of his sketch and draft material, few details are known about his compositional process. It seems clear, however, that he was announcing the completion of an unorchestrated draft (or 'continuity draft'): a *particella* containing the voice part along with, usually, the principal instrumental bass and/or treble, with only a few of the harmonizations supplied – the sort of draft that we know he composed for *Rigoletto* and that we presume he wrote for all of his mature operas following an extended period of more fragmentary sketching.

Whatever the circumstances that led to Verdi's astonishing burst of creativity in March 1890, his initial eagerness came to a nearly complete halt when Boito wrote to him in mid-March about the incurable illness of their mutual friend Franco Faccio, the composer, conductor, and director of the Parma Conservatory, who had conducted the first La Scala performances of *Aida* and *Otello*. Verdi was deeply shocked. His sorrow pervades many of his letters to Boito and Ricordi from March 1890 to 21 July 1891, the date of Faccio's death.

Moreover, since late 1889 he had been unwillingly embroiled in a prolonged legal battle. Both the firm of Bénoit, the recipient of much of the material once owned by the publisher Escudier, and the firm of Ricordi claimed the exclusive rights to *Le trouvère* (the French version of *Il trovatore*). Verdi was caught in the middle of this dispute, for his memory of the events of 1855-7, and of 1882, when he voluntarily ceded to the translator Pacini what he still believed to be his rights to *Le trouvère*, was of critical importance. Throughout much of 1890 and 1891 he was obliged to write statement after statement recounting in detail what he remembered of these events. In nearly every letter, particularly as the litigation progressed, he showed considerable annoyance at being distracted. In order to gain time he repeatedly counselled his editor to cede victory to Bénoit. Ricordi refused to yield, and the struggle pressed on until 1893, when Bénoit finally won. There is little doubt that at various times from 1890 to 1893 the Bénoit affair was directly responsible for delaying the composition of *Falstaff*.

Verdi returned to Sant'Agata from Genoa in early May 1890. For a few weeks Boito seems to have been unaware of the composer's inactivity. On 21 May 1890, for instance, he wrote to suggest a definitive text for the fugue (*Carteggio Verdi–Boito* 1978: i, 173-4). Verdi's response of 23 May clarified the new state of affairs: 'With regard to Big-Belly, Alas! Alas! I have done nothing . . . except for a few full stops and commas added or changed in what was already done. But we'll talk about everything in person at Sant'Agata' (Ibid. i, 175). Boito visited Verdi in late May or early June 1980. The summer passed with little work on *Falstaff*, still a secret between them.

Verdi's depression worsened in the late summer after he learned that two more friends, Giuseppe Piroli, the Italian patriot, statesman, and senator, who had known Verdi since 1859, and Emanuele Muzio, the conductor, who had been a student of the young Verdi in the 1840s, were very ill. Nevertheless, he turned momentarily back to *Falstaff*, and, in anticipation of a visit from Boito, he wrote to him on 6 October:

I haven't worked very much, but I have done something. The sonnet of the third act [the opening of III.ii] was tormenting me; and to get this nail out of my head I put aside the second act, and, beginning with that sonnet, gradually one note after another I arrived at the end. It's only a sketch! And who knows how much will have to be redone!

(Ibid. i, 176)

Shortly thereafter two blows descended: Piroli died on 14 November, Muzio on 27 November.

At this saddest of times Verdi prepared for his customary winter move to Genoa. On the way he stopped for a few days in Milan, and on 26 November he invited Boito and the Ricordi family to dinner at the Hotel Milan – the editor was still unaware of the existence of the half-sketched opera. During the dinner, according to the most complete contemporary account (in the Milanese *La Lombardia* of 28 November 1890), Boito suddenly proposed a champagne toast, perhaps to enliven Verdi's spirits, or perhaps according to a prior agreement: 'I drink to the health and triumphs of Big-Belly!' Amid general surprise he announced again: 'I drink to the health of Falstaff!' Ricordi did not yet understand, until his wife turned to Giuseppina Verdi and asked 'A new opera?' Giuseppina nodded assent.

Giulio Ricordi, the editor who would surely publish the new work, was elated. In the next two days several Milanese newspapers published the report of Verdi's new opera and included many accurate details about it, information probably supplied by Ricordi. *Falstaff* was now public knowledge. The Italian musical world was exultant. Within a few weeks Verdi and Ricordi had received a flood of mail about the new opera from friends and interested impresarios.

Few realized that at this time the composer felt more than ever the weight of his own mortality and could not envisage the completion of *Falstaff*. His letter of 6 December 1890 to Maria Waldmann is deeply revealing:

In around fifteen days I have lost two of my oldest friends! Senator Piroli . . . Dead!! Muzio . . . Dead! And both were younger than I!
All is over!! Life is a sad thing! I leave it to you to consider the pain I have felt and still feel! And so, I have very little will left to write an opera that I have begun, but haven't got very far with. Don't pay any attention to the gossip in the press. Will I finish it? Won't I finish it? Who knows! I am writing without plans, without a goal, solely to pass a few hours of the day.                                    (Abbiati 1959: IV, 408)

From this period on he became apprehensive about *Falstaff* and maintained that he might not finish it at all, that he was writing it for his own amusement, not for performance, and so on. This is a distinctly new attitude, and it must be directly related to the illnesses and eventual deaths of his close friends. Certainly from the opera's exuberant beginnings in July 1889 ('What joy, to be able to say to the public: *Here we are again!! Come and see us!*') to the rapid drafting of March 1890 *Falstaff* had been planned for public performance. Now, fearing that his project would never be finished, he tried to lower the public's expectations by assuming a defensive modesty.

On 1 January 1891 he wrote to Ricordi about his problems with the opera:

I told you that only about half of the music had been done [I.i, I.ii, and, one presumes, parts of II.i and III.ii] . . . but let's understand well, 'half-sketched', and in this half the greater labour remains, the putting together of the parts [*concerto delle parti*, presumably the vertical expansion of the draft], the redoing and retouchings, besides the orchestration, which will be very difficult. Finally, to sum up: all of 1891 won't be enough to bring it to completion. (Ibid. IV, 414-15)

To add to his distress in early 1891, the Bénoit affair grew more complex and demanded much of his time. It seems likely that he considered abandoning *Falstaff* during this period. Certainly he did no work on the opera for several months. After Boito sent him an aquarelle of Falstaff for his name day (19 March), Verdi wrote to Ricordi: 'Ha! Ha! Ha! What a surprise! *Big-Belly*? I haven't heard news of him for more than four months. Meanwhile he, blind drunk, was probably asleep the whole time! Let's let him sleep! Why awaken him? He might commit some great knaveries of a magnitude to scandalize the world! And then? Bah! Who knows?' (Ibid. IV, 418). But the aquarelle reawakened his interest. Two days later, on 21 March 1891, he wrote to Boito to inquire whether the word 'Windsor' was accented on the first or the second syllable. On the first, replied Boito the next day, believing this to be true of all English bisyllables (although he admitted that in writing the song 'Quand'ero paggio' he intended 'Norfolk' to carry an accent on the second syllable). But to Boito the big news was that Verdi was gradually turning back to *Falstaff*. And so the librettist urged him on: 'Ahead! *At full steam*! And then the four lost months will be regained in one week. I am quite certain of it' (*Carteggio Verdi–Boito* 1978: I, 180-2).

It was not until 2 June that Verdi could write to Ricordi that he had made some progress on the score, and not until 12 June that he reported his activity to Boito: 'Big-Belly is on the road that leads to madness. There are days that he doesn't move, sleeps, and is in a bad humour. At other times he howls, runs, jumps, and kicks up a rumpus . . . I give in to him a bit, but if he continues, I'll muzzle and strait-jacket him' (Ibid. I, 190). Boito responded with enthusiastic encouragement and even mentioned that he had just heard a good voice for Quickly.

Verdi probably spent much of the summer preparing a draft of II.ii. He and Giuseppina made their usual summer visit to the baths of Montecatini in early July and returned to Sant'Agata on 22 July to discover that Franco Faccio, after his long illness, had died the day before. We hear nothing from Verdi for a month after this. Finally, he wrote to

Ricordi on 23 August with an invitation to Sant'Agata that included the news: 'Ah! Big-Belly? Even he [like Peppina and me] has weak legs, and he moves very slowly, and I'm afraid that he sings like a drunk! [a reference to the opening of III.i?]' (Abbiati 1959: IV, 424).

By the time of Ricordi's three- or four-day visit beginning on 11 September, Verdi had entered a new stage of compositional activity. Until September 1891 he had been preparing a short score, or draft, probably with few indications of instrumentation. On the basis of still rather fragmentary evidence it would seem that he had written the draft in the following order: the fugue (perhaps as early as August 1889; at present one cannot reject the possibility that it might have been orchestrated shortly thereafter); I.i and I.ii (very rapidly from 8 to 17 March 1890, with later revisions); the beginning of II.i (spring and summer 1890); Fenton's Sonnet in III.ii (6 October 1890); the remainder of II.i, all of II.ii, and the remainder of III.ii (March – September 1891). Only the first part of the third act, or at least a large portion of it, remained to be drafted.

Although the core of the music for *Falstaff* was not complete, the task of orchestration still lay ahead. In early September Verdi began to write the autograph orchestral score. His letter to Boito on 10 September 1891 not only documents this crucial move to instrumentation but also contains a pointed barb at the Wagnerians:

Just one word: let me correct this: it's not true that I have finished *Falstaff*. I'm now working to put into score everything that I have done, because I fear I may forget certain passages and instrumental combinations. I'll do the first part of the third act later . . . and then Amen! This part is shorter and less difficult than the others.

It's necessary, however, to pay attention to the first recitative of Falstaff [in III.i] and the passage [at the end] where the wives depart . . . Here one would need . . . I have to say it – a *motive*, that would progress *diminuendo*, dying away in a *pianissimo*, perhaps even with a solo violin on stage. Why not? If they now put orchestras in the cellar, why couldn't one put a violin in the attic?!! If I were a prophet my apostles would say 'Oh, what a sublime idea!' Ha, ha, ha, ha! How beautiful the world is!!                                    (*Carteggio Verdi–Boito* 1978: I, 196)

Verdi worked on the autograph score from early September 1891 to mid-October 1892, when he gave the last portion of it to Ricordi for piano-reduction and engraving. The manuscript score itself, now located in the archives of G. Ricordi & C., Milan (Casa Ricordi published a facsimile of it in 1951), furnishes a great deal of information about how Verdi wrote it. It is clear, for instance, that he consistently followed a two-step procedure in filling up the multistave music paper, before he submitted the 'completed' work to even further, usually smaller, polishings and revisions. In the first step he copied the few lines of the existing draft onto the appropriate orchestral staves – perhaps a voice part, a violin line, and a bass line for cellos or contrabasses – thus leaving most of the page blank for later harmonization and coloristic instrumentation. It is this 'skeleton score' (to use Andrew Porter's descriptive term) that Verdi wished to set down in September 1891. The differing inks present in the autograph manuscript today suggest that he completed the skeleton score of Acts I and II at Sant'Agata in September and November 1891 (Hepokoski 1979: 277-98). Although this compositional layer must often have been a direct copy of the earlier draft, Verdi probably revised and recomposed portions of it in the act of 'copying' it onto the orchestral staves.

Verdi's second step was to return to his completed skeleton score and fill in the inner parts: the actual harmonization (which he might have already elaborated at various points during the earlier stage or shortly thereafter) and orchestration proper. During this procedure he frequently modified what he had previously written, sometimes to the point of removing an entire folio or set of folios and replacing them with new ones. The manuscript inks confirm that he was not able to proceed to this second stage for Acts I and II until the spring of 1892. His customary winter move to Genoa in early December 1891 had slowed him down, and in January and February he and Giuseppina were weakened by a prolonged bout with influenza. 'Almost two months of lost time', he groaned to Boito on 23 January (*Carteggio Verdi – Boito* 1978: I, 201).

Finally, on 15 April, he wrote again to his librettist with more cheerful news:

And now, before I lock up the first act completely orchestrated, tell me if the two lines are established from the Honour Monologue:

> Bel costrutto! – L'onore lo può sentir chi è morto?
> No. Vive sol coi vivi? Neppure, perché a torto et[c].
>
> (Ibid. I, 204-5)

Boito responded on Easter Sunday, 17 April 1892, with some variants in the lines of the monologue (Ibid. I, 205). Verdi must have completed the first act a few days later. On 2 or 3 May, probably with much of the second act orchestrated as well, he returned to Sant'Agata. In the next two months, to judge from the inks of the autograph score, he entered the skeleton score first of III.ii, then finally of III.i (the date of whose compositional draft is at present unknown).

By now, with Act I and probably most of Act II orchestrated, neither

Ricordi nor Verdi doubted that Italy would soon hear the *Falstaff* première. Accordingly, they began to discuss the details of the first performance. The composer asked three basic questions in a letter to Ricordi of 1 June: '1 Who will be the impresario? . . . 2 Which theatre? 3 Which singers?' (Abbiati 1959: IV, 441).

Within a few days Ricordi had provided acceptable, if somewhat predictable, answers to the first two questions – Luigi Piontelli (whom Verdi had originally not wanted) and La Scala – but the matter of available and appropriate singers proved to be more difficult to resolve. For several weeks Verdi and Ricordi discussed possible singers and the vocal and dramatic demands of the various roles. These letters of June and July 1892 are consequently central documents to the study of how *Falstaff* was first performed. (A summary of this information appears in Chapter 6 below.)

As Ricordi became more and more involved in the planning, Verdi slowed the process down. On 17 June: 'First of all don't think about the music of *Falstaff* either for the end of this month or the next. Even in the finished pieces I am redoing several bars here and there; even several pages, and I'm not making progress' (Ibid. IV, 444).

Still, by July Verdi, now on vacation at the baths of Montecatini, was probably beginning to orchestrate the skeleton score of the third act and continuing to plan for future performances of the opera. At this time he quite suddenly – and uncharacteristically, given his measured, methodical plan of instrumentation – decided to change the shape of II.ii radically. He inserted a major solo piece for Quickly, a narrative in which she tells the other women of her meeting with Sir John. Clearly, his decision was prompted by the visit of Giuseppina Pasqua, a mezzo-soprano/contralto and a prime candidate for the part of Quickly. Verdi's letter to Ricordi on 12 July 1892 reveals that at that time Quickly had no such solo piece at all and that Verdi had not quite decided how to fortify Quickly's part:

Pasqua has been here for two days. I read her most of the libretto and had her sing some phrases from the third act that I had with me. Perhaps secretly [*in petto*] she wanted some piece or other in which she could stand out alone; but she understood, intelligent as she is, what the situation is, and she will be content to do that part, which she will do well. Only I noticed (I alone) that at certain points in the third act Quickly has been on stage too long without saying anything, and I think that without ruining the comedy one could take away a few phrases and a few words here and there from Alice and Meg and give them to Quickly, and we won't lose anything in the performance. I'll write to Boito about it myself after I have looked over this third act again.

(Ibid. IV, 466)

Verdi, in fact, decided to go far beyond giving her a few extra lines. At the end of July 1892 in Milan, where he was involved in further negotiations about the opera – and successfully auditioned Emma Zilli for the role of Alice – he probably met Boito to request a text for a new solo piece for II.ii (for which it seems that he had already drafted at least part of the music). The result was Quickly's 'Giunta all'Albergo della Giarrettiera', a late insertion into both Boito's manuscript libretto and Verdi's autograph score (Hepokoski 1980: 240-9).

Composed, then, as a surprise for Pasqua (who was not told of the solo piece until 7 November 1892), this was the only major textual revision that Verdi had made in the opera since he had received Boito's libretto two years and four months earlier. The new *racconto* (narrative aria) changed the flavour of the opening of this scene by immediately and decisively retarding the pace of the action. In a sense, the insertion is the first violation of the principle of mercurial motion that had prevailed in I.i, I.ii, and II.i. Yet, precisely as a violation, the insertion was a brilliant idea. The compositional and dramatic difficulty inherent in setting the *Falstaff* libretto to music lay in moving from the concentrated, rapidly moving opening scenes to the nearly static third act. By adding Quickly's solo at the midpoint of the opera, Verdi gave the listener his first significant pause – a deceleration that anticipates the eventual repose and stylized formality of the closing scenes. Perhaps the only negative effect of adding 'Giunta all'Albergo' was that, in its comparatively massive proportions and highly theatrical effect, it generally upstages Alice's much smaller 'Gaie comari di Windsor', which is in almost all respects a subtler, more significant piece.

The late addition of a major solo piece geared to the abilities of a specific singer shows the flexibility of mind that Verdi had brought to all of the compositional stages. The autograph score contains hundreds of *pentimenti*, large and small second thoughts, erasures and corrections. Verdi changed something or other nearly every time that he reviewed the score. The constant struggle for increased effectiveness is manifest on nearly every page. There is nothing haphazard or hastily considered in *Falstaff*.

Three of the larger changes that Verdi made while orchestrating the opera are not widely recognized to be afterthoughts. All three are evident from the physical structure, inks, and erasures of the manuscript score.

In I.ii (orchestrated in March and April 1892) he decided to interpolate a seventeen-bar introduction to the unaccompanied women's quartet 'Quell'otre! quel tino!', an introduction employing the same text.

(The insertion now occupies all of no. 24 in I.ii.) Curiously, Verdi inadvertently erred by giving Quickly Meg's lines and vice-versa, and today, as all singers of those roles must be aware, the seventeen-bar reversal of lines still persists.

He added an orchestral introduction to III.i (orchestrated in summer 1892), based on a motive associated with the breathless pursuit of Falstaff in the preceding scene. The fifty-two-bar prelude begins solidly in E major. At present one cannot know how the earlier version of the act began, because Verdi removed the original first page of the manuscript of Act III. This page probably contained about four bars of music on each side before proceeding into the music now heard at no. 5. It would appear that the act may have begun in A minor, perhaps with the slow descending tetrachord in the low wind, now heard first at no. 6. The first appearance of this motive in the final manuscript score is otherwise inexplicably marked 'I° tempo'.

During the orchestration of III.i he changed the key of the conclusion of Falstaff's monologue from E♭ to E major. The original skeleton-score ending had also included a slightly longer orchestral codetta (Ex. 1). The half-step upward shift had occurred precisely at the words 'Accende l'occhio e il pensier' (5 bars before no. 10). It seems to have been motivated by Verdi's desire to avoid writing a low D♭ – C♮ trill in the third flute below the word 'brillo', 3 bars after no. 10. After the semitone transposition the trill became the far more possible D♮–C♯. If the hypothesis presented above about the opening of the act is correct, i.e., if the early version had begun in A minor, the beginning and conclusion of Falstaff's monologue would originally have been a tritone apart: A minor to E♭ major, with a considerably different effect on the macrotonality of the act.

Certainly by late summer 1892 Ricordi's principal concern was to receive the completed *Falstaff* manuscript with time enough to have a piano-vocal reduction prepared and corrected, the plates engraved and proofs checked, an orchestral score and parts copied for the first performance, and, ultimately, the first vocal score produced for sale in time for the eventual première. Verdi, on the other hand, was reluctant to hand over his autograph score until he had made certain that everything was as he wanted it. After several weeks of gentle coaxing about the manuscript, Ricordi visited Sant'Agata on 27 August, and there he finally received the first act. Upon his return to Milan he immediately assigned the task of preparing the vocal score to his most reliable reducer Carlo Carignani, a 36-year-old composer and conductor who had already produced reductions of Catalani's *Loreley* and *La Wally*, Franchetti's *Cristoforo Colombo*, and Puccini's *Edgar*. Individual manuscript fascicles of Carignani's *Falstaff* reduction were sent to Verdi for his approval beginning on 2 September. Ricordi realized from the outset that

Ex. 1

FALSTAFF

e il gio-con - do glo - bo squi ~ li ~ bra u-na de-men - za tril -

lan - te e il tril - lo_in-va - de il mon - - do

[vln 1]

dim.

QUICKLY *interrompendo come prima*

Re -ve - ren - za!    la bel-la_A - li - ce

Verdi's consent would be necessary at every stage in the preparing of the edition.

While inspecting Carignani's reduction of Act I, Verdi was working on his own autograph of Act II and putting the final touches to Act III. He completed the third act in the first two weeks of September and delivered it on the 15th to Tito Ricordi, Giulio's son and eventual heir to the firm, at the Piacenza railway station. The exact date when he gave Act II to the editor is uncertain. We know that Giulio Ricordi visited Sant'Agata again on 4 October, probably with Boito and Adolph Hohenstein, the artist responsible for the costumes and scenery (see Chapter 6 below). Ricordi could well have received the second act at this time. If not, he must have been given it in Milan between 13 and 16 October during the composer's visit to examine and correct the score. Whatever the precise date of the actual consignment, Verdi's letter to Ricordi of 21 October 1892 (misdated in Abbiati 1959: IV, 430) makes it clear that Act II (and hence the entire manuscript score) was then in Milan, not Sant'Agata.

On 24 October Verdi moved to Genoa and finally handed over the last fascicles of Carignani's reduction of Act II when Ricordi visited him four days later. With the arrival of the printed proofs of somewhat less than half of the vocal score (all or most of I.ii, III.i, and III.ii) on 4 November, Verdi turned his attention to proofreading. As he combed through this material in November and December – he received the final set of proofs, those of II.ii, on 17 November – he altered over 300 passages and kept Ricordi informed of these changes in almost daily correspondence. His work on the score during these two months may be followed and dated with precision. Not only do we have the highly informative (and still largely unpublished) letters of Verdi and Ricordi, but the proofs themselves, with Verdi's corrections, are also available for study in the library of the Milan Conservatory. Only slightly over half of the revisions are simple corrections of printing or reduction errors. Well over 100 were compositional revisions of either text or music.

Ricordi felt continually thwarted by the *maestro*, who almost every day threw sand into the machinery by uncovering more errors in the proofs, deciding to revise a phrase here or there, or even requiring a few plates to be re-engraved. Verdi's letters contain a parade of small corrections that forced Ricordi to swallow his business sense, stop the presses, and wait politely until the composer, who refused to be hurried, had finished. Verdi wrote with his final corrections on 27 December, only slightly over a week before the binding of the initial copies of the vocal score.

Although space here does not permit a detailed examination of Verdi's proof corrections – several have been treated in separate discussions by Guglielmo Barblan (e.g., *Un prezioso spartito*, [1957], and 'Spunti rivelatori', 1969) and Hepokoski (1979: 54-108) – three in particular are worthy of consideration because of their audible impact on important moments in the opera. The most thorough alterations that Verdi made in the proofs, as Barblan first pointed out, concerned two passages of Fenton's Sonnet at the beginning of III.ii. (We now know that he revised the sonnet between 12 and 17 November 1892; during some of this time he was also teaching the part to its first interpreter Edoardo Garbin.) The original opening of the vocal line, the version that Verdi found printed in the proofs, is shown in Ex. 2a; his revision, i.e., the final version, is shown in Ex. 2b.

Ex. 2a

Ex. 2b

Here Verdi clearly wished to reserve the high A♭ until line 3, 'E alfin ritrova un altro labbro umano'. The result is a pleasing and expressive linear ascent, from E♭ and F in the first line, through G in the second, and finally to the peak of the arch, A♭, in the third, before the gentle descent to the lower A♭ tonic in the fourth – a melodic curve whose shape mirrors the sense of the text, the upward flight of a lover's song and its gradual descent onto the lips of the beloved. Verdi's modifications must have been an attempt to weaken the powerful upward thrust of the original version. Thus he changed two ascending leaps, a seventh and a fourth, into one of a fifth. The seventh leaps found later, in lines 5 and 6, are now heard as new material – a further expansion – rather than as a development of the melodic seventh in the original line 1. With this small revision the sonnet grows more consistently from the unassuming, lyric *naturalezza* of the opening line to the intense ardour of the middle and end of the piece. (See also the discussion in Osthoff 1977: 169-75).

Verdi's most radical change in the sonnet, however, is found in lines 9-10 ('Quivi ripiglia suon'). Up until the time of the proofs the solo piece had been composed without any exact reprise of the music of the opening phrase. Except for sequential or similar members of the typically Verdian phrase pairs, the piece was through-composed. Now, while correcting the proofs, he decided to rewrite the printed beginning of the first tercet of the sonnet (Ex. 3a, inaccurately transcribed in Budden 1981: 512) to include a reminiscence of the opening tune on the English horn (Ex. 3b).

Verdi's revisions throughout the proofs often show a remarkable instinct for striking harmonization at critical moments. The original climax of Falstaff's Honour Monologue in I.i, beginning 1 bar after no.

Ex. 3a

FENTON

Ex. 3b

16, restricted itself to tonic and dominant harmonies (Ex. 4a). Between 29 November and 2 December the composer pasted new slips of music paper over these bars (Barblan, *Un prezioso spartito*, p. 10; Hepokoski 1979: 97-8). The new version (Ex. 4b) was not only a bar longer and provided a rhythmically more athletic vaulting to the high G, but it also contained an emphatic, prolonged Neapolitan-sixth chord. No better

Ex. 4a

Ex. 4b

Ex. 4c

example could be found of Verdi's genius for turning the relatively commonplace into an extraordinarily theatrical event. Although the reading of Ex. 4b was printed in all subsequent editions and is the version nearly always performed today, it is not the final version. Partially on the newly pasted slip and partially on the original page of the proofs Verdi entered in pencil the necessary elements of a third version (Ex. 4c). It is this definitive version, along with the accompaniment of the second, that he wrote into the autograph score in Milan in January 1893, the period of the rehearsals, during which he transferred most of his proof corrections to the autograph score. That it never appeared in any edition is probably the result of an oversight at Casa Ricordi, not a later reversal of Verdi's opinion.

Perhaps the most vivid example of Verdi's acute harmonic sense is to be found in his proof revision of the thirteen chords that accompany Falstaff's counting of the hours as he enters Windsor Forest in III.ii (no. 28). The compositional problem involved producing a series of chords to weave around a tonic pedal F below middle C: the twelve bell-strokes and Falstaff's counting. Curiously, a version even earlier than that of the proofs may be recovered by restoring erased notes in the autograph score. This earliest available reading (Ex. 5a, the string parts plus added

F pedal to represent the persistent pitch of bell and voice) was to be performed in 'tempo doppio', an extremely rapid $\;\;$ = 144 if one accepts $\;\;$ = 72 as the prevailing tempo up to that point, although the metronomic indication may belong to a later layer of composition. The restoration of the viola part in the sixth bar must remain conjectural, as the erasures there are not completely legible.

Verdi saw greater possibilities for this passage. He changed it some time before Carignani's reduction: the version printed in the November proofs is shown in Ex. 5b (again with added pedal F). This proof version is much more harmonically adventurous than the original. Its bass line, for example, is less prosaically regular, more 'irrational'. Both the leap in the bass in bar 3 of the proof version and the subsequent unorthodox

Ex. 5a

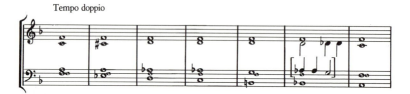

Ex. 5b

Ex. 5c

reharmonization of bars 3-5 come as unforeseen, rich surprises. Their
effect rests not only on Verdi's refusal here to resolve augmented sixths
and diminished thirds in an academically 'proper' manner, but also on
the chromatic voice-exchange in bars 3-4. The harmonic intensification
of the second half of the passage in Ex. 5b is perhaps less drastic but no
less telling: the suspension of the viola G from the sixth to the seventh
bar; the marked improvement in sonority because of the respacing of
the final five bars; and the reharmonization of bars 11 and 12, which
include a different (and unorthodox) augmented sixth as the penultimate
cadential chord (the same augmented sixth is found with different
spacing in bar 4).

Rhythmic intensification is no less important. The inner-voice motion
in Ex. 5a, bar 6, is expanded in Ex. 5b throughout the remaining seven
bars, first through the suspension of bars 6-7, then through the syncopa-
tions of the F pedal in the viola (a syncopated reflection of the first
violin's F in bars 1-7) and the accent in the second violin, bar 7, beat 4,
which furnishes an anacrusis to the first violin's upward leap of a fifth
in the following bar. Perhaps the increased harmonic and rhythmic
density made a slower tempo more appropriate: the speed of the proof
version is 'più mosso ♩ = 100'.

Verdi, however, saw still further possibilities for enrichment. While
correcting the proofs in Genoa he modified the passage one last time
and reported his correction to Ricordi on 14 November 1892. The final
version is shown in Ex. 5c. The changes, in bars 5-8, again provide added
harmonic and rhythmic intensification. The new suspension and resulting passing-note in bar 6 introduce a brief imitative passage in the inner

voices, and the inner-voice change in bar 8 produces the dissonance of a major seventh, which gives an extra shudder to Falstaff's anxiety.

With the correcting and revising of the proofs in November and December 1892 Verdi had, in a sense, finally completed *Falstaff*. By the end of December, at any rate, Ricordi had acquired his permission to print and bind the first edition of the vocal score. A few copies of the first edition (pl. no. 96000, 474 pp.) were available by 4 January 1893. On that date Casa Ricordi sent three scores to a certain Jean Lobel in Paris to initiate the process of obtaining an American copyright (Hepokoski 1979: 113). Despite the existence of hundreds of copies throughout January, Ricordi refused to release them for sale until after the actual date of the première, 9 February 1893. Nevertheless, the massive scale of the printing and binding (which continued into March) rendered the insertion of any further Verdian changes or corrections impractical. *Falstaff* was, at least for its first purchasers, a finished product.

Yet Verdi, who arrived in Milan on 2 January to supervise a month of intense rehearsals, must have continued to alter the opera in the weeks before its première. In the first place, we know that he transcribed many of the November—December proof corrections into the autograph score at this time. Corrections and revisions, that is, were on his mind. Second, a strong tradition persists that Verdi did in fact change several portions of the opera during the rehearsals. Ricordi, for instance, maintained (1893: 23) that from 9 o'clock until 10.30 every morning Verdi was involved in 'revision of the score, parts, and reductions'. A perhaps separate, and clearly false, tradition is that Verdi corrected the piano-vocal proofs during the January rehearsals. The story seems to be traceable to the faulty memory of Edoardo Mascheroni, the first conductor of the opera and an early owner of the proofs: it began to appear, at any rate, shortly after he donated them to the Milan Conservatory in 1923. Nevertheless, the account helps to confirm the idea that Verdi did indeed correct *something* during the rehearsals.

The early vocal scores help to clear up some of the mystery. There are, in fact, approximately forty minor but telling discrepancies between the first and second vocal scores — alterations that do not appear in the proofs and that doubtless testify to Verdi's *incontentabilità* during rehearsals. He insisted, for instance, that the men re-enter a few bars earlier at the very end of II.ii; originally they had been instructed to remain offstage until the women (alone) have sung 'Patatrac!', an obviously impractical situation. Similarly, he added two bars to the instrumental transition from Nannetta's solo to Bardolfo's 'Alto là!' in III.ii, making four bars in all (20-3 bars after no. 38). And — a rather important change — he added Ford's solo line 'Se parlaste uno alla volta' to the men's quintet in I.ii (7 bars before no. 28). This filled in the earlier, four-beat silence: one of those comic moments where amid a general hubbub all participants suddenly cease speaking at the same time, are perplexed by the silence, and begin again as noisily as ever. The joke apparently failed during rehearsals, and this addition for Ford neatly balanced Pistola's outburst three bars earlier (see also Dallapiccola 1970).

Beyond these small modifications (some of which Verdi never entered into his autograph score) the *maestro* probably also worked with some documents that have yet to turn up, or have perhaps been destroyed: the manuscript copy of the conductor's score and the manuscript parts of the performers. If so, this may help to explain the vexing problem of why the first edition of the orchestral score (finally printed in July 1893, months after the première) differs so radically from the autograph score in dynamics, phrasing, articulation, and even a few notes. That Ricordi would have issued such a conflicting edition without Verdi's consent seems unthinkable, and yet there is no clear evidence that Verdi was ever concerned about the printed orchestral score. Given the tradition of Verdian correction during the rehearsals, it is a convenient — and, I think, probable — hypothesis that in January Verdi laboured on an orchestral conductor's score and parts, all of which had been previously prepared (and probably 'standardized') by copyists and key members of the La Scala orchestra. In all likelihood the conductor's score, with Verdi's corrections and ultimate approval, became the model for the eventual printed score that appeared in July (Hepokoski 1979: 67-8, 219-26).

Whatever one's conclusions, it is clear that the first vocal score very nearly approaches the version premièred at La Scala (except, of course, for small details that Verdi changed in January). Much larger changes, including the thorough rewriting of two major sections, would come in the months following the première. But by the 9 February première *Falstaff* was already the product of almost three years of composition, most of it having occurred in brief, intense spurts of creativity. Verdi had considered or rethought almost every phrase of the opera dozens of times. *Falstaff* was created in sudden flashes of inspiration followed by agonizing doubts and struggle, ultimately resolved — as in the Neapolitan-sixth chord at the climax of the Honour Monologue or the unforeseen revisions of the 'midnight' chords — by sudden inspiration again.

# 4 *Milan, Rome, and Paris: three versions of 'Falstaff'*

The première of *Falstaff* on 9 February 1893 was an enormously important event to Verdi, and he was well aware that this attempt to close his
career with a comic opera involved a measure of risk. His criteria for
determining success or failure were deeply rooted in the operatic culture
in which he had matured. The chief standard, quite simply, was instant
success at the box office. Operas that failed to impress at their premières
or very shortly thereafter – notwithstanding the *La traviata* fiasco – had
a difficult time surviving at all. The hope of creating masterpieces for
posterity and the increasing suspicion of widespread public success
(characteristic of the greatest German and Austrian composers throughout the century and on the rise in 'modern' France in the 1890s) were
alien ideas.

This is surely one reason why Verdi felt compelled to revise, correct,
and recompose from 1890 to 1893. His first concern was to create a
work that would engage the spectator by being constantly vivid, fresh,
and inventive. He consequently changed whatever he found commonplace or stale, conventional or repetitious. As the acknowledged Italian
*maestro* he wanted his opera to avoid sounding dated; yet it was to
approach the modern style while still conserving the vocal primacy of his
earlier works. His revisions of *Falstaff* can be seen as a continuing search
for an increasingly effective set of emphatic statements, whether climactic, lyrical, seductive, mysterious, or witty. No evidence suggests that he
actively sought a new form for Italian opera or aimed for philosophical
truth or formal profundity. Instead, he wanted to produce a work whose
musical and dramatic qualities would lead to a genuine, ongoing success
in the practical theatre – not so much for the sake of his own pocketbook but for the sake of his reputation and that of the music of his
country, ever more under attack by northern styles.

However cautiously musical Italy might have treated this complex
work in the immediately subsequent years, its La Scala première was a
triumph. The boxes, filled with the aristocracy and officials of Milan

and neighbouring cities, were 'a veritable orgy of colours, reflections, and splendours' (*L'Italia del popolo*, 10 February 1893). Dazzling diamonds and the sparkle of jewels flashed through the hall. The higher-ranking nobility – at least on the female side – were strikingly present: stunningly attired countesses, duchesses, and marchionesses, and even the Princess Letizia Bonaparte. Critics from all over Europe attended this first performance. Nor did the house lack artistic celebrities, such as the composers Pietro Mascagni, Giacomo Puccini, and Alfred Bruneau, and the writers Giosuè Carducci, Giuseppe Giacosa, and Enrico Pan-zacchi. By now the première was as much a social as an artistic event.

Much of the general Milanese public – those who could not afford boxes during the season but could usually expect to purchase an ade-quate place in the *platea* (main floor)–felt excluded by the exceptionally high prices. The management had received special permission from the city, which carefully regulated such matters, to raise the prices for the first performance to an extraordinary level. The normal price of 5 lire for a reserved place in the *platea* was elevated to a radically unprece-dented 150 lire. Seats in the boxes sold for as high as 250 lire, and even the poorest places in the gallery commanded an extravagant 30 lire. Still, every seat in the theatre was taken. Queues began to form in front of the entrances to the *platea* and gallery as early as 9.30 in the morning. Crowds of good-natured opera lovers waited for hours, entertaining themselves and purchasing bread, meat, cheeses, and fruit to eat from makeshift newspaper-tablecloths. *L'Italia del popolo* reported on 11-12 February that the management took in an astounding 86,000 lire that evening; on 21 February *La sera* reported that the actual figure was 89,000 lire, and that the following four performances, with prices much closer to normal, raised the total of receipts to 140,000 lire.

The performance itself could not fail to impress: with Adolph Hohenstein's magnificent scenery and costumes, picturesque and histor-ically accurate to the last detail; with a carefully prepared cast headed by the famous Victor Maurel as Falstaff, Antonio Pini-Corsi as Ford, Emma Zilli as Alice, and Giuseppina Pasqua as Quickly; with an effective staging supervised by Verdi; and with the composer himself present for the occasion and appearing repeatedly at the end of each act to receive tumultuous cries of 'Viva! Viva Verdi!' Two pieces were encored: the women's quartet in I.ii, 'Quell'otre! quel tino!', and Falstaff's 'Quand'ero paggio' in II.ii (see Chapter 6 below). Throughout the performance a crowd persisted outside the theatre to wait for news and gossip from inside and to see the *maestro* emerge after the opera. An even larger crowd of three or four thousand awaited him at the Hotel Milan only a few blocks away. There Verdi's arrival with his wife and Boito was greeted with a huge and gratifying ovation. Once in the hotel Verdi acknowledged the shouting crowd three times from the second-floor balcony, the third time holding Boito's hand.

In the following two months *Falstaff* received twenty-two performances in Milan, from 9 February to 2 April 1893. The La Scala company then travelled to Genoa and performed *Falstaff* four times (twice with Verdi attending) at the Teatro Carlo Felice from 6 to 11 April. From Genoa the opera moved to Rome, where it was given five performances (with the original cast and conductor, Edoardo Mascheroni, but with a Roman orchestra) from 15 to 25 April, four at the Teatro Costanzi and one (22 April) at the Teatro Argentina. The complete La Scala company then continued their tour with four performances in Venice, 2-7 May; four performances in Trieste, 11-16 May; two performances in Vienna, 21-2 May; and four performances in Berlin, 1-*c*.6 June 1893, for which last productions Ramon Blanchart substituted for Victor Maurel. The La Scala tour ended in Berlin, and the original cast never again performed the opera as a group.

During the course of these initial performances it would seem that none of the critics noticed that Verdi had made two major changes that were probably first performed together in Rome. In the first of these he replaced sixteen bars near the end of the ensemble in II.ii (first edition, no. 63) with six; in the second he discarded the final 111 bars of III.i and rewrote a new conclusion of eighty bars. For neither version is an orchestral score extant, because he removed the corresponding pages from the autograph score and replaced them with the newly composed material. The earlier versions may be found only in the proofs and in copies of the first edition of the Ricordi vocal score.

Certainly neither Verdi nor Ricordi did anything to publicize the new, post-première revisions. Ricordi's second vocal score of June 1893 included them without comment along with several smaller modifications that Verdi had probably made during the January rehearsals. The changes even made the second edition twelve pages shorter than the first (462 pp. as opposed to 474) — and still nobody seemed to notice it. Finally, in 1941, Hans Gál printed the essence of the virtually unknown earlier version of the II.ii ensemble; Guglielmo Barblan later sketched the outlines of the original ending of III.i in his monograph on the *Falstaff* proofs (1957).

Fig. 1 (pp. 57-65), taken from the first vocal score, shows the bars that Verdi removed from the II.ii ensemble. The revised version is readily

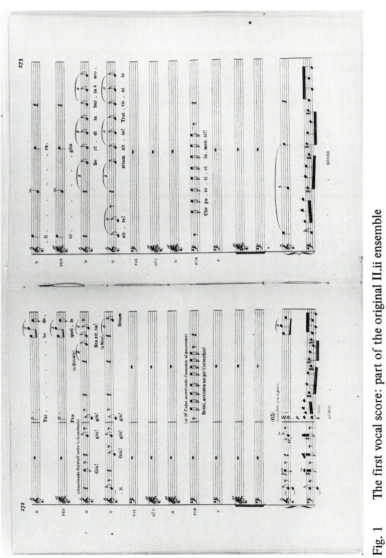

Fig. 1    The first vocal score: part of the original II.ii ensemble

58

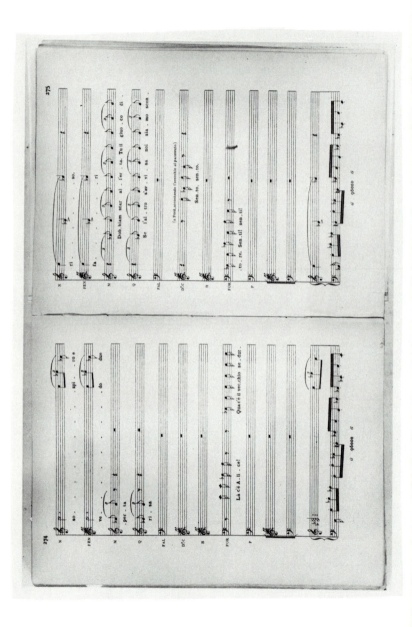

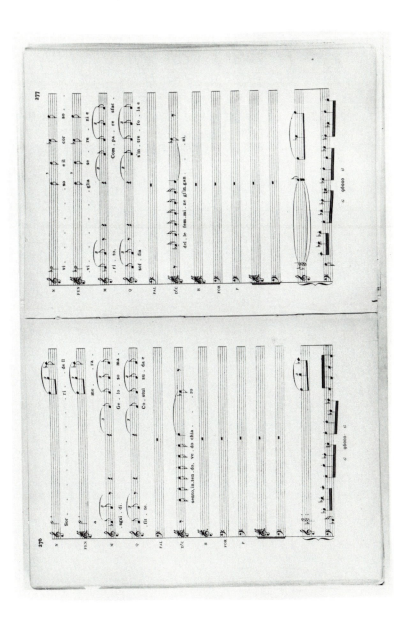

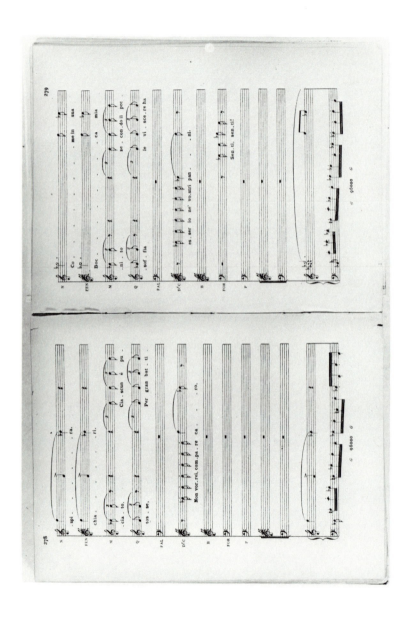

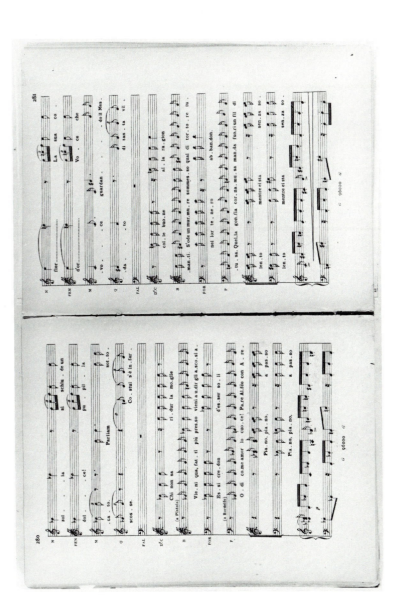

62

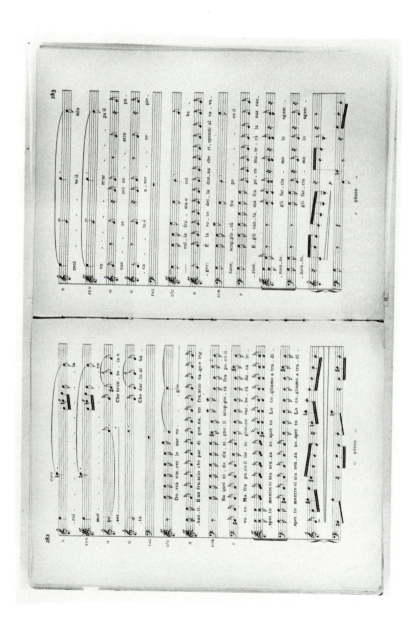

63

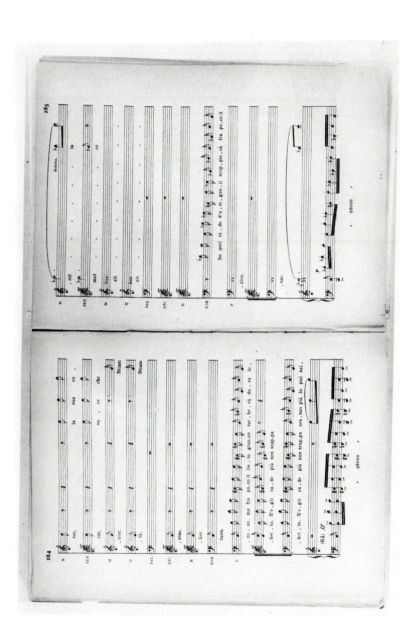

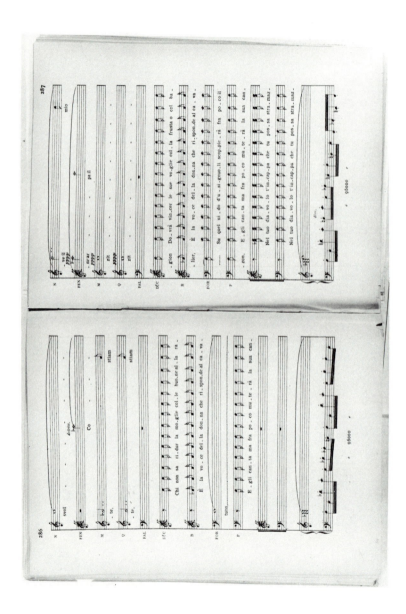

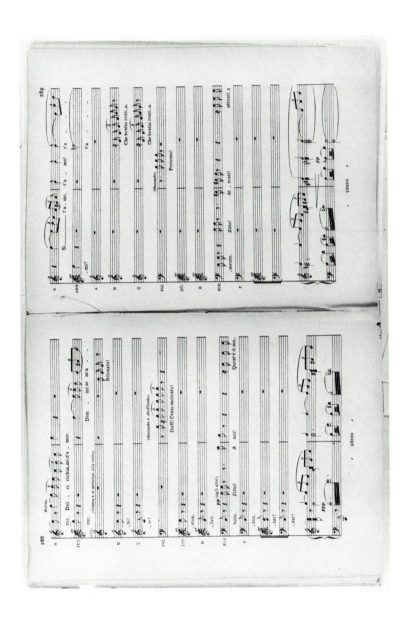

available and is not reproduced here; its corresponding melodic line, however, appears in Ex. 6.

The aesthetic significance of this change can scarcely be overstressed. The ensemble is the dramatic climax of the opera. Here one arrives at the resolution of the intrigue of the first two acts: Falstaff is humiliated, the wives triumphant. The passage that Verdi so radically altered is nothing less than the extended climax of that ensemble, its highest lyrical point and most memorable moment.

Ex. 6

Both the original version and the revision begin with the same C major cadence on the words 'Giù! giù! giù!' and conclude with a similar (but not identical) passage that prolongs C major and begins with Nannetta's 'Dolci richiami d'amor'. Between these two points the music differs markedly. The earlier version (Fig. 1, bars 2-17) moves leisurely into remote chords on the flat side of C major: from C (bars 2-3) the chords descend by thirds to A♭ (bars 4-5), F minor (bar 6), D♭ (bar 7), B♭ minor (bar 8), and G♭ (bars 9 and 10, beats 1-2). An upward sequence of dominant-seventh chords, $C^7$, $D^7$, and $E^7$ (bars 10-11), then leads back to a cadence in C major (bars 12-14); and a bar-by-bar descent by thirds through the flat side, C, A♭, F minor, half-diminished $d^7$ (bars 14-17), ultimately reaffirms C major for the 'Dolci richiami d'amor'. With its luxurious suspension of time this version is a splendid example of the 'static' music so characteristic of the slow portion of the *ottocento* operatic ensemble.

By contrast the revised version (Ex. 6) is brief indeed. It is ten bars shorter and, except for a lowered seventh in the bass (under bar 5) it avoids the flat side of C major in favour of more conventional harmonies. The ensemble gains in dramatic speed but loses its earlier musical richness. Verdi insisted on preserving the effective conclusion of the ensemble, beginning with 'Dolci richiami', and it is evident that he wrote the new version specifically to retain this conclusion. Nevertheless, he also changed the inversions and spacings of the chords of the last four bars shown in Fig. 1, for reasons that are not apparent.

Verdi first indicated a desire to modify this passage in a letter written to Ricordi from Genoa on 7 March 1893, almost a month after the première (the opera was still being performed — with the music of Fig. 1 — at La Scala):

I don't know whether you know that at an orchestral rehearsal at which I went back into the seats to hear the opera I was so dissatisfied with the ensemble finale that I told all the artists gathered together: 'This piece doesn't work this way; either perform it more softly, totally *sotto voce* and standing apart from one another in groups, or it will have to be cut or changed.' Nobody breathed, but the impression of these words was not good, as they may have told you.

The next evening they performed better and nothing more was said. But at the performances I saw that on the stage this passage is long and resembles an ensemble piece too much.

I wanted to change it in Milan, but I never had an hour of complete peace. I say to change it, because I am an enemy of cuts. To cut a passage is like cutting an arm, the stomach, the legs, etc. etc., from a body. In pieces conceived too broadly a cut is sometimes necessary, but it is always a monstrosity; it is a body without a head or without legs.

For the *Falstaff* ensemble it was easy to cut and jump in immediately at 'Dolci richiami d'amor', but it wasn't the same piece of music any more, lacking the stomach. I redid six bars and the piece remains shortened by ten bars. I'll send it to you tomorrow. I would like it to be performed before the performances at La Scala are finished. And for you, are we in time for the second edition?

To teach it is very easy. A little gathering of the singers for a half-hour (instead of taking a walk), and when the orchestra joins them for another rehearsal five minutes will be enough. It can be done without Maurel, i.e., if he comes too those *parlanti* can be redone — they are not in time any more and by now are no longer music.     (Abbiati 1959: IV, 499)

Verdi might have sensed that the La Scala audience was uncomfortable at this point in the opera. Moreover, he must have been dissatisfied with the performers. The two most reliable singers, Emma Zilli (Alice) and Victor Maurel (Falstaff), did not participate in this passage at all, and the two remaining singers in whom he had the most confidence, Giuseppina Pasqua (Quickly) and Antonio Pini-Corsi (Ford), did not have parts here that could rescue bad singing by the others. Nannetta and Fenton had to make this passage effective, and, although we know little of Verdi's attitude towards Adelina Stehle, we know from the Genoese rehearsals of late 1892 that he had no faith whatever in Edoardo Garbin (Ibid. IV, 466-9). Verdi probably decided that the original passage simply required too much singing ability from secondary characters.

He sent off his revision to Ricordi the next day, 8 March: 'For the action this is better; for the music I don't know . . . Do with it as you please. Look it over with Mascheroni and Boito' (Busch 1981: 347). At this point, however, the trouble began. Ricordi wrote to Verdi on 9 March that Boito did not like the revision, that somehow it seemed a bar too short (Hepokoski 1979: 134-5). Verdi was stunned by the criticism. He rewrote the last two bars of the revision and testily mailed them back to the editor on 10 March: 'Try it with the singers, and if you still have the impression that a bar is lacking after you have tried it, well, let's not talk about it any more and leave it as it has been until now' (Busch 1981: 349-50, where it is probably misdated; for the 10 March dating see Hepokoski 1979: 134-6).

When Ricordi received Verdi's letter, he was alarmed by the suggestion that the composer was not going to come to Milan to hear the passage and that he was prepared to leave the decision whether to accept it to Ricordi, Boito, and Mascheroni. During the next week Ricordi, unwilling to bear the responsibility for the decision, pleaded with Verdi to come to Milan. But the proud *maestro* refused to leave Genoa (Busch 1981: 348). On 16 March he complicated the whole question by announcing his plan to make another major change in the opera:

Looking at that passage of the finale again and again I saw other bars that one might retouch [these are surely the chords under 'Dolci richiami d'amor' and the following bars]. Moreover, I never liked that sort of mazurka that ends the first part of the third act . . . and then there was right there under one's eyes a motive ('Avrò con me dei putti') that, played and modulated well, would have been more effective; and it was also more appropriate and more musical. It was the continuation of the masquerade scheme

   . . . *che fingeran folletti*
   *Spiritelli*
   *Farfarelli*, etc. etc.

It was such an easy thing to do! Ah, what poor heads we have!!! It would be better to throw them against a wall . . . and so long . . .

   P.S. *Torno all'assalto.* For now let's not make changes in *Falstaff*. Later, who knows. Maybe in another production.

   (Misdated in Abbiati 1959: IV, 501, and misdated in Busch 1981: 348; the 16 March date above is taken from the postmark on the envelope.)

Thus, the ensemble revision was not to be publicly performed in Milan. Even more significant, Ricordi now realized that Verdi was contemplating another large revision. It would become, of course, the second major revision to be printed in the second edition: the rewritten conclusion for III.i, beginning with Meg's cadence on 'Rincasiam' (23 bars after no. 19).

In the first vocal score (Fig. 2, pp. 70-4) the music continued at this point with declamation over an orchestral restatement of the 'Avrò con me' melody. As Alice, Nannetta, Meg, and Fenton exited slowly, the orchestra began the 'sort of mazurka' that continued until the end of the act: a reprise of Alice's 'Fandonie che ai bamboli' from earlier in the scene (Fig. 2, 11 bars after no. 20). It is this passage that Verdi replaced in the final version with orchestral music from 'Avrò con me'. When Ford and Cajus entered in the original version, they formed their plans for disguise over fragments of the mazurka, instead of the 4/4 march of the final version. The earlier version proceeded through a beautifully expansive phrase for Ford as he explained to Cajus about the monk's disguise and his eventual blessing of his wedding (Fig. 2, beginning 11 bars after no. 21). This led to a descending chain of seventh chords in 3/4 (before no. 22) that Verdi retained – in 4/4 – in the final version. The final bars of the early setting died out in D major to echoes of the mazurka theme, not, as now, the 'Avrò con me' melody.

Verdi may have been long dissatisfied with the earlier version. It was the last section of the opera that he had composed, and prior to its composition he had minimized the difficulty that he expected to encounter in creating it (see his letter of 10 September 1891, p. 39). One wonders whether Verdi had composed this passage too hastily in his eagerness to arrive at a drafted conclusion.

One fact, however, is clear: the original ending of III.i suffered from redundancy. In the first place there is no dramatic reason why the 'Fandonie' motive should have reappeared here at such length. Its original text (11 bars before no. 15) refers to the foolishness of superstition and has nothing to do with the action at the end of the scene. The composer tacitly acknowledged this in his letter of 16 March by saying that the motive to be used in his revision would be 'more appropriate'. Second, and more important, the motive is repeated too often without significant variation. No other portion of the score dwells upon such an elementary motive in this manner. The result, except for a few striking moments, is a passage outstanding only by its surprising lack of invention.

Finally, Verdi was undoubtedly aware that the La Scala audience found the music of III.i to be weaker than that of the first two acts. It was a bold critic indeed who dared to criticize *Falstaff* in those early

70

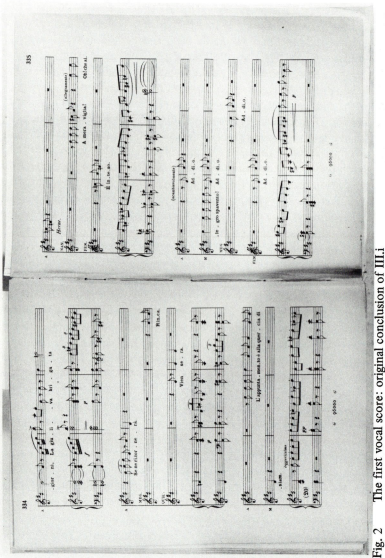

Fig. 2    The first vocal score: original conclusion of III.i

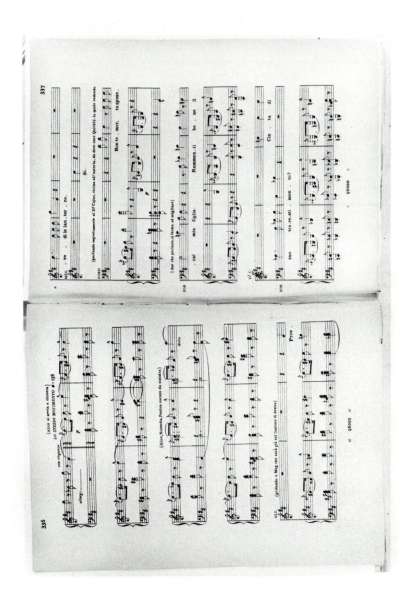

71

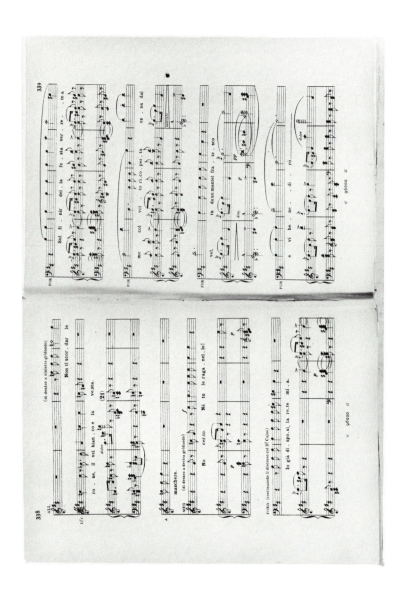

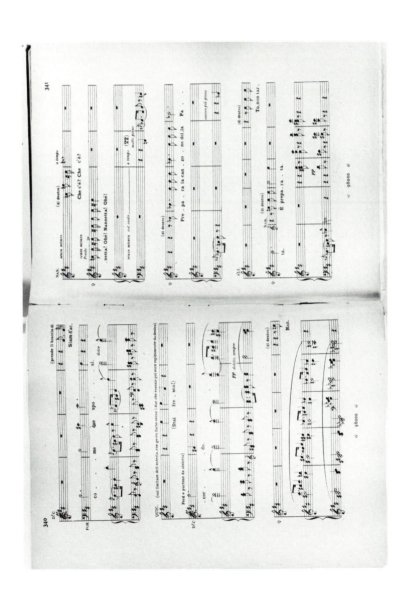

74

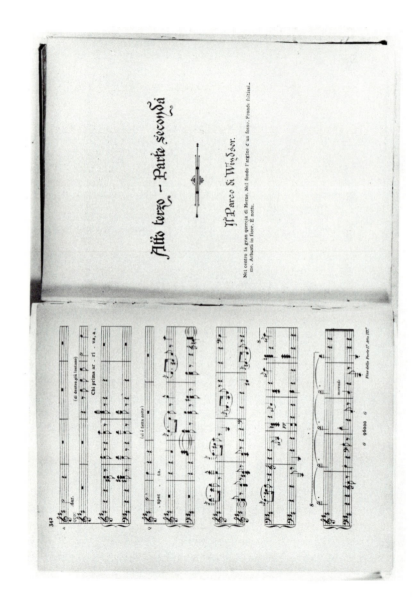

Atto terzo ~ Parte seconda

Il Parco di Windsor.

Nel centro la gran quercia di Herne. Nel fondo l'argine d'un fosso. Fronde foltissime. Arbusti in fiore. È notte.

days; and yet Verdi could read in *La Lombardia* after the première: 'The second visit of Quickly brings nothing new, and in the planning of their nocturnal masquerade the wives are not able here and there to find the mood of the preceding acts, although they often do have accents of humour and subtle gaiety.'

Two weeks passed after his letter of 16 March before Verdi mentioned this last alteration again. By this time the La Scala performances were drawing to a close. Plans had been made to bring the opera to the Teatro Carlo Felice, Genoa, where the *maestro*, then residing in the city, would be obliged to make an appearance. Perhaps the prospect of meeting the artists again prompted him to compose the revision at this time. On 1 April, the day before the last Milanese performance, he wrote to Ricordi:

For a long time since the first orchestral rehearsals in Milan I had determined to make two changes. Many nuisances distracted me. This morning, enraged by the most recent events [with regard to the forthcoming Roman productions of *Falstaff*] I threw myself down to write. I'm sending the passage (I don't know what it might be). Have the little vocal parts copied immediately, and I'll rehearse them here with the artists, not so as to have it done at the theatre either here or anywhere else at least for now, but for my own artistic satisfaction.

(Abbiati 1959: IV, 503)

At last he was consenting to hear not only this second revision but also, implicitly, the first, written nearly a month earlier. The La Scala orchestra and cast left for Genoa on 4 April. Verdi probably rehearsed the two new passages with the singers on 5-6 April. In all likelihood, only the II.ii ensemble revision was performed in Genoa at that time, for the orchestral parts of the III.i revision were probably not yet available. We may be certain, however, that Verdi approved both of his modifications in Genoa in early April 1893, and that they were first performed together in Rome: four unpublished telegrams from Ricordi to Mascheroni, the conductor, of 9 to 11 April make it clear that the two variants were to be inserted into the Roman score (Hepokoski 1979: 158-9). Verdi attended two performances in Rome, on 15 and 20 April, and undoubtedly gave the revisions his final approval at that time.

The parts, however, may not yet have assumed their definitive form, nor had Verdi entered the changes into the autograph score. Ricordi sent him the relevant fascicles of the manuscript to correct in the middle of May, but Verdi did not remove the old passages and insert the new until 23 May, when he wrote to the editor: 'I sent you this morning the last notes of *Falstaff*! Peace to its soul!!' (Abbiati 1959: IV, 509). In the pages of the II.ii ensemble change he had enclosed a separate slip with his famous emotional farewell to his protagonist; the slip that was to be discovered some thirty years later by Toscanini: 'The last notes of *Falstaff*. Everything is finished! Go, go, old John. Go your way, as long as you can. Amusing sort of scoundrel. Eternally true, under different masks, in every time, in every place!! Go . . . go . . . Walk walk . . . Farewell!!!' (Gatti 1950: 746).

By late May 1893, then, Verdi had formally sanctioned a revised *Falstaff*, the 'Roman' version that would soon be transmitted in the new edition of the vocal score in June 1893, the first printed orchestral edition a month later (Ricordi pl. no. 96180, for rental only), and, quite by accident, the first orchestral edition published for sale (Ricordi pl. no. 113953, 1912). Moreover, he had removed from the autograph score much of the evidence that a first version had ever existed. It would be relatively simple today to reconstruct the music of the original, 'Milanese', *Falstaff*. One need only follow the readings of the second vocal edition (the 462-page score) – the first is inadequate because Verdi changed several of its readings during the rehearsals – substituting the original ensemble music of II.ii (Fig. 1) and the earlier conclusion of III.i (Fig. 2). These two passages, of course, would have to be orchestrated – at least until Verdi's own orchestrations turn up, should they still exist.*

It is likely, however, that neither the Milanese nor the Roman version is definitive. Soon after the printing of the Roman score Verdi was to approve still another set of variants for the Parisian première on 18 April 1894. This première, unlike, say, those in Vienna and Berlin in May and June 1893, mattered a great deal to him. All through his life Paris had been the operatic capital of Europe, the city that composers most desired to conquer. It was not a city to be taken for granted, and Verdi was particularly concerned that the quality of the French version be as high as possible.

As early as November 1892 Verdi had agreed, upon Ricordi's suggestion, that Boito himself should prepare the French translation. The less important English and German translations could be sent off to men not involved with the Italian version, W. Beatty Kingston and the conservative Viennese music critic, and future biographer of Brahms, Max

---

* Since the above was written, the two 'Milanese' passages have been orchestrated by the author and have been incorporated in a complete performance of *Falstaff* at the Oberlin College Conservatory of Music, 17-20 November 1982.

Kalbeck. The French *Falstaff*, far from being a simple translation, was to be a work of art to rival the Italian original. Boito was quite at home in French, but for assistance in translating this word-rich libretto he found a collaborator, Paul Solanges, a Parisian poet then residing in Milan. We currently know nothing about the Boito–Solanges collaboration, but the correspondence of Verdi, Boito, and Ricordi in 1893-4 suggests that Boito was the principal translator and that ultimately Verdi was the final judge of the translation.

Boito and Solanges completed their work in the first week of September 1893. On 9 September Boito brought it to Verdi at Sant'Agata. The composer was pleased with what he read. Boito returned to Milan a few days later (14 September) to give the approved text to Giulio Ricordi for engraving and printing.

Notwithstanding this activity no date had yet been established for the Parisian première. It was clear that *Falstaff* could not be premièred at the convention-bound, formal Opéra. That ornate theatre would be acceptable for a French *Otello* with new ballet (which was in fact premièred there on 12 October 1894), but not for the naturalness and wit of a *Falstaff*. The idea of a performance at the Opéra Comique had always been more attractive. When its director, Léon Carvalho, had attended the Milanese première of *Falstaff*, Verdi and Ricordi had assured him that the first French performance, with Victor Maurel in the title role, would be granted to his theatre. Final plans for an Opéra Comique production seem to have been made only in the very last months of 1893. By this time Verdi's correspondence implies that *Falstaff* had been arranged for a spring 1894 performance in Paris.

At first it was assumed that the French version would require no musical changes, except, of course, for the minor adjustments that Verdi and Boito would have to make to suit the French declamation. These small changes are generally of no significance to any Italian performance, but, strangely enough, two of them were included in Ricordi's third Italian vocal edition in 1897, although Verdi never bothered to write them into the autograph score. The first alters a single note for Alice in II.ii, sixteen bars after no. 48. The Milanese and Roman versions of her 'Che fai?' had ended on a C (Ex. 7a); the Parisian version ('Réponds?') ended a sixth lower, on E (Ex. 7b, from the 1897 Italian vocal score). The second tiny change that made its way into an Italian score occurs further into II.ii, during the ensemble, fifteen bars after no. 59. Bardolfo's seemingly insignificant 'Non si trova', four reiterated G's in the 1893 versions and the autograph score (Ex. 8a), was changed to conclude on a B, probably to reflect the accented final syllable of the French 'Disparu!'

Ex. 7a

Ex. 7b

Ex. 8a

Ex. 8b

That B was inserted into the 1897 Italian score (Ex. 8b). What astonishes here is not the two changes themselves, but that somebody – probably Verdi, or at least Ricordi or Boito with the composer's knowledge and consent – considered them significant enough to require that the engravers take the extra trouble of modifying a plate for the 1897 Italian edition.

The few copies of the French *Falstaff* score (Ricordi pl. no. 96413) that Ricordi had printed and deposited in the requisite Italian libraries in January 1894, then, contained these two small changes and several more just like them that would never, however, apply to any Italian performance. This early, and very rare, printed French *Falstaff* is essentially a Roman *Falstaff* in French, with a few, virtually insignificant, variants in textual declamation. But now in January Verdi's penchant for revision asserted itself again. Within a few weeks he had made three larger changes, all in III.ii, that would oblige the editor to re-engrave portions of his already printed French score. That Verdi considered all three to be definitive may be inferred from their inclusion in the revised, third Italian edition of 1897.

We first hear of one of them in Boito's letter to Verdi of 18 January 1894: 'I am enclosing a slip on which is transcribed the new entrance of the Fairies in the third act of *Falstaff*' (*Carteggio Verdi–Boito* 1978: I, 223). The passage in question occurs in III.ii, in Windsor Forest, immediately after Falstaff hears the fairies entering and throws himself, terrified, on the ground: 'Sono le Fate. Chi le guarda è morto.' What had followed in the Milanese and Roman versions consisted of twelve bars of untexted instrumental music (no. 34) preceding Nannetta's song 'Sul fil d'un soffio etesio'. Boito was now supplying Verdi with a dialogue to sing over this instrumental music:

| | | | |
|---|---|---|---|
| ALICE: | Par ici. | | |
| MEG: | | Doucement. | |
| ALICE: | | | Il est là. |
| NANNETTA: | | | Le bravache |
| A grand peur. | | | |
| FAIRIES: | | Il se cache. | |
| ALICE: | Avancez. | | |
| FAIRIES: | | Pas de bruit. | |
| ALICE: | | | Glissez-vous pas à pas. |
| FAIRIES: | Commençons. | | |
| ALICE: | | Ne ris pas. | |

| | | | |
|---|---|---|---|
| ALICE: | This way. | | |
| MEG: | | Quietly. | |
| ALICE: | | | There he is. |
| NANNETTA: | | | The braggart |
| Is really afraid. | | | |
| FAIRIES: | | He's hiding. | |
| ALICE: | Go ahead. | | |
| FAIRIES: | | No noise. | |
| ALICE: | | | Glide along step by step. |
| FAIRIES: | Let's begin. | | |
| ALICE: | | Don't laugh. | |

Boito and Verdi were patching a dramatic, not a musical, problem. Before the dialogue was added, Falstaff was required to lie prostrate, while the whole cast entered in disguise and assumed prescribed positions on stage. Yet nobody except Nannetta and the fairies had any lines to sing until after Nannetta's solo piece. Most of the characters were on stage for several minutes without singing or, for that matter, doing anything, a fact that Verdi must have observed painfully during the early Italian performances. Now Verdi and Boito planned to delay the entrances of everyone except Nannetta, the accompanying fairies, and, possibly, Alice and Meg (as the masterminds of the plot). But were this to be done, the original twelve bars, no longer needed to accompany the various entrances, would seem pointless. The dialogue, surely, was conceived to fill the dramatic gap. The original twelve instrumental bars became accompaniment to the new dialogue.

After receiving the 'Par ici' insertion, Verdi approved it in a letter to Boito of 19 January 1894: 'It seems to me that those few lines in French will be very fine. Translate them now into Italian without, understand, adding anything' (Ibid. I, 223). Clearly, this was a change not only for the French theatre, but also for future Italian performances. Verdi then sent the vocal settings to Ricordi on 21 January. Shortly thereafter – it is not known exactly when – Verdi modified the dialogue further (e.g., omitting Meg entirely and assigning her single line, 'Doucement', to Nannetta). Ricordi printed the revised version in the French score in March and April 1894 (pl. no. 96413), and, translated, it was included in the Italian 1897 vocal score (and has appeared in every vocal score since that time).

The second major change in the French *Falstaff* in early 1894 involved the 'Litany' section of III.ii (no. 43): sixteen bars in which the women invoke Heaven for justice ('Domine fallo casto!'), while Falstaff pleads in puns that his belly be spared ('Ma salvagli l'addomine'). In the Milanese and Roman versions this passage is a *tour de force* of ensemble writing, with the phrase endings filled in by alternate interjections from the men ('Pancia ritronfia!') and the fairies, played by children ('Pizzica, pizzica, pizzica!'). In the second French edition of 1894 – printed specifically to include the early 1894 revisions – all of the interjections are omitted. Only Alice, Meg, Quickly, and Falstaff sing these bars – no men or children. This simplification was Verdi's last word on the passage and appears in the 1897 edition as well, although, as will be discussed later, the original, fuller reading was reinstated in most of the scores published long after the composer's death.

Why might Verdi have deleted the interjections? Perhaps he had heard several poor performances of the original 'Litany': the entrances demand perfect timing from the singers, and the children, especially, may have been unable to keep up the steady rhythm. Since Verdi never included this change in his autograph score, one might be tempted to conclude that it is not his, or that he accepted it reluctantly as a compromise. Although the latter might be an alluring hypothesis, the former cannot reasonably be maintained. Ricordi's concern for the authenticity of the score throughout the entire process of publication suggests that he would never have taken such a modification without the composer's approval (Hepokoski 1979: 202).

The third change concerned the text that Ford sings above the nuptial minuet in III.ii (beginning five bars after no. 50). The early Italian versions began with four lines of *endecasillabi*:

| | |
|---|---|
| FORD: | Già s'avanza la coppia degli sposi. |
| | Attenti! |
| FALSTAFF AND CHORUS: | Attenti! |
| FORD: | Eccola in bianca vesta. |
| | Col velo e il serto delle rose in testa, |
| | E il fidanzato suo ch'io le disposi. |
| | Circondatela, o Ninfe! |

| | |
|---|---|
| FORD: | Now the wedding pair approaches. |
| | Attention! |
| FALSTAFF AND CHORUS: | Attention! |
| FORD: | Here she is, dressed in white, |
| | Veiled, and with a rose-wreath in her hair, |
| | And with her betrothed, to whom I give her. |
| | Encircle her, o Nymphs! |

Some time before January 1894, possibly during Boito's visit in early September 1893, Verdi had decided to delete most of these words. Whatever the reason, they no longer appeared in the January 1894 French score: there the beginning of the minuet proceeded largely without text. On 21 January 1894 he told Ricordi that he wished to insert a new text: 'In the Minuet I had asked for too much and it remained empty. Everything will be in place if Boito finds a way to complete the alexandrine that rhymes with *cortège*' (Abbiati 1959: IV, 530-1; Verdi's references to versification and rhyme are unclear). Boito did indeed give him a new text. Ricordi printed it in the March—April 1894 French score:

| | |
|---|---|
| FORD: | Le cortège s'avance, |
| | C'est elle. |
| FALSTAFF AND CHORUS: | Silence. |
| FORD: | Elle cache son fin minois. |
| | Nymphes, formez le cercle. |

| | |
|---|---|
| FORD: | The procession approaches, |
| | It's she. |
| FALSTAFF AND CHORUS: | Silence. |
| FORD: | She hides her fine features. |
| | Nymphs, form the circle. |

Translated into Italian, this new text and its musical setting – evidently Verdi's preferred version – were printed in the 1897 score: the vocal parts above the minuet are shown in Ex. 9.

How should these revisions – Roman and Parisian – affect modern performances in Italian? Can one accept any single version as definitive, even with regard only to the text and notes? One thing is certain: sim-

Ex. 9

plistic reliance on a single source is unwise and creates more problems than it solves. Placing his faith, for example, on what would seem an unimpeachable document, the autograph score, Denis Vaughan (1958: 11-15) has denounced the currently available Ricordi orchestral scores (e.g., the 'nuova edizione riveduta e corretta' of *c*. 1954, pl. no. P.R. 154) for containing an estimated 27,000 differences from Verdi's manuscript, mostly in matters of phrasing, dynamics, and articulation. Yet Verdi never intended the manuscript to be the final judge on all *Falstaff* matters. As mentioned earlier, he failed to enter many of his proof corrections into it; and now in 1894 he similarly neglected to amend it by failing to include his latest Parisian revisions. Moreover, Verdi probably expected some of the first-desk players at La Scala to adjust his phrasings, dynamics, articulations, and so on, prior to the first performance – to the point where the autograph score was probably no longer relevant to the engraving of the orchestral score (see p. 53 above).

The first step in deciding among the variants is to realize that the opera was performed in three versions in Verdi's lifetime: the Milanese, with its longer II.ii ensemble and III.i conclusion; the Roman, with the rewritten, shorter versions of these sections; and the Parisian, with its five variants that were carried over into the 1897 Italian vocal score. One often hears today the Roman version with only the first three of the Parisian revisions: the two tiny changes and the added 'Inoltriam' dialogue (i.e., the 'Par ici' insertion, translated into Italian). Occasionally, as with Mario-Parenti's 1964 edition for G. Ricordi & C., the shorter minuet text is offered as well (and, curiously, Parenti reinstates the C♮ in Alice's 'Che fai?'). Most modern performances, however – certainly those currently available on recordings – retain both the full Litany and the longer, original text above the wedding minuet. The editorial confusion began in the early twentieth century. In 1912 Casa Ricordi released the first publicly available orchestral score. It was, through a series of apparently inadvertent errors, virtually identical with the Roman *Falstaff*, although the 1897 vocal score available at the same time contained the Parisian version (Hepokoski 1979: 206). Vocal and orchestral scores have not been in complete agreement since, and conductors have been left to sort out the differences for themselves.

At this level of discussion only one difficulty remains. Not all of the revisions are obvious improvements. Although most would probably prefer the Roman ending of III.i, they might also find the Roman II.ii ensemble musically inferior to its earlier version. Hans Gál (1941: 266-72), for instance, has called for the reinstating of the Milanese ensemble as common practice. Even more difficult, many might well prefer the new Parisian staging and added text of the 'Inoltriam' dialogue, but fewer would be eager to embrace the simplified Litany, and some might balk at the abbreviated text above the minuet. The concern for historical accuracy or Verdi's 'last word' may lead to the excision of some beautiful settings.

The question of which *Falstaff* to perform, and the question of the depth of commitment Verdi might have had to each of the three versions, will probably always be controversial. The evidence is insufficient to permit one to assert that Verdi strongly preferred the Parisian to the Roman, although he clearly preferred the Roman to the Milanese − at least with that staging, that audience, and that cast. As usual, the burden of aesthetic judgment will continue to rest exactly where it belongs: on individual conductors and performers.

# 5 *Musical technique and structure*

Most discussions of *Falstaff*'s music centre on 'progressive' qualities: its avoidance of square-cut, predictable formulas, its spontaneity and uninterrupted musical flow, its reliance on evanescent orchestral motives, its masterly iridescent orchestration. For a half-century Verdi had been gradually, but inexorably, modifying many of the ground rules of *ottocento* opera to suit his demands for increased realism, breadth, and power. Surely in 1871 many must have considered *Aida* the *ne plus ultra* of his stylistic development. Here he had skilfully interwoven Meyerbeerian eclecticism and grandeur with the traditions of Italian opera. Moreover, *Aida* was Verdi's first opera not divided into explicitly numbered sections. It did contain a series of pieces recalling the old 'numbers', but, more often than before, these pieces ended by merging directly into bridge passages or transitions.

Yet Verdi's growth away from the standard Italian formal procedures did not stop here. It continued into the 1880s and 1890s with spectacular results. This final period – essentially one of intensification and recompression after the expansion of *Don Carlos* and *Aida* – saw three stylistic 'experiments', each more far-reaching than its predecessor: the *Simon Boccanegra* revision (1881), *Otello* (1887), and *Falstaff* (1893). With *Falstaff* Verdi seems as liberated from habit as he could ever have wished to be. Compositional surprises, unexpected turns of phrase, sudden bursts of athletic energy – all these wink playfully from nearly every corner of the score, as if the composer had feared the charge of predictability.

So remarkable is the suppression of traditional operatic structures here that one risks overstressing it. Yet, for all its apparent novelties, *Falstaff*'s roots are anchored in the soil of earlier values. In an increasingly Wagnerian, symphonic, and intellectually sceptical age Verdi surely believed that he was upholding the primacy of the voice, the dominance of diatonic melody, the direct outpouring of elemental, instantly communicable emotions, and the attracting of as large a public as possible (see pp. 33-4). Except for the now outgrown, conventional formal shells, the 'standard' Verdian techniques are anything but absent in *Falstaff*; rather, they have been intensified, enriched, and emphatically confirmed with more skill than ever. And although the traditional forms are shattered nearly to the point of irrelevance, a few fragments and contoured edges remain, pushing through the otherwise continuous and fluid texture. Thus, while it is true that many critics in the 1890s misconstrued *Falstaff* as Verdi's surrender to Germanic techniques (see Chapter 8), other, generally more conservative men like Arthur Pougin and Camille Bellaigue hailed it as an antidote to what they feared were the more virulent microbes of the modern temper. Paradoxically, *Falstaff* is both formally progressive and profoundly traditional.

### Formal design

The typical Verdi opera from the 1840s to the 1860s consisted of a succession of closed (or, more rarely, semi-closed) musical units separated from one another by silence – pearls on a string. Especially in Verdi's non-Parisian operas, each closed form (introduction, aria, duet, ensemble, chorus, etc.) implied more or less standard formal expectations which he might tease for heightened expression, but which would persist as a contextual background for whatever music suited the dramatic moment at hand. For instance, the formal aria (or 'cavatina', if it happened to be an introductory or entrance aria) usually proceeded through four stages: a dramatic introduction, customarily dominated by recitative in blank verse; a *primo tempo* or *cantabile*, i.e., a lyrical formal song (*AABA'* or *AABC*) in rhymed regular verse, usually six, eight, or ten lines long; a dramatic interlude to introduce a new emotional situation by means of another recitative, or perhaps a dialogue, chorus, or *parlante* (declamation over an orchestral melody); and a standardized, usually vigorous cabaletta, the second formal song, again in rhymed regular verse and characterized above all by being literally repeated after a brief retransition.

The conventional duet offered slightly more freedom. Here, in brief, one generally expected to encounter dialogue and recitative leading to at least two, and possibly three, formally closed songs, the last of which was a cabaletta with vigorous rhythms and some sort of literal repetition as part of its internal form. The customary procedure in writing the formal songs was to make each into a kind of double solo-song: a statement by one singer and a confirming or contrasting response (*risposta*) by the other, before both join in a relatively free codetta. Another, less frequent, method — most typically found in the middle song of a tripartite duet — presented both voices together simultaneously, frequently singing nearly parallel melodic lines. (For more on the forms and their possible variants, see Budden 1973: 14-19).

Considerable variation, expansion, and contraction were possible, and as Verdi matured he boldly changed the conventions into more supple background principles to be manipulated for his own dramatic needs. His contraction (and eventual elimination) of the stiffest part of the older aria, the repeated cabaletta, is a case in point. He accomplished most of this in the operas of the 1860s, although, as Philip Gossett has demonstrated (1974), cabaletta forms still persist to conclude several of the *Aida* duets. Little, if anything, remains of the repeated form in *Otello*, but here and there Verdi evokes the conclusive vigour and decisive texture of the earlier cabaletta.

In *Falstaff* such gestures towards the earlier forms become far less evident. The forward thrust of the plot is so great that, by and large, with the exception of the ritualistic last scene, there is no time for immobile reflection. More than once characters appear to begin formal songs that the onrush of events then deflects from symmetrical closure. (Of course, Boito had built a series of such deflections into his libretto.) Still, although *Falstaff* avoids the formalism of mid-century Italian opera, it is nevertheless a spatial arrangement of *ad hoc* solo pieces, duets, ensembles, introductions, transitions, interruptions, and the like, which flow into one another or, at least, are neatly juxtaposed.

Ignoring for the moment the exceptional Windsor Forest scene, we may group most of the solo pieces into two broad categories. The first comprises the larger solos, which resemble free monologues or soliloquies. Falstaff sings two of them, 'L'onore! Ladri!' near the conclusion of I.i and 'Ehi! Taverniere!' at the beginning of III.i. Ford sings one, 'È sogno? o realtà' near the end of II.i. Verdi constructs all three along similar lines. Each begins with loose, but vividly dramatic, recitative or *arioso* declaimed over a spare, rapidly changing motivic accompaniment; and each pushes to a powerful final line of resolution and summary, followed at once by a *fortissimo* explosion and a rapid *diminuendo* to less weighty music. The pattern is not new to this opera. It has, for example, an immediate predecessor in Iago's 'Credo' in the second act of *Otello* (although the *arioso* section of the 'Credo' is more obviously patterned, reflecting the anaphora in the text) and less developed, more distant ancestors in such dramatic monologues as Rigoletto's 'Pari siamo'.

The second category consists of brief, sharply characterized solos, many of which are a mere two- or three-dozen bars long. Typically, each is cast in a concise, easily grasped form. Falstaff's 'Va, vecchio John' (II.i) consists of only four phrases, *ABCA'*, suggesting a ternary form (see the discussion of II.i below). His 'Quand'ero paggio' (II.ii) is shaped into a simpler, continuous ternary form, *ABA'*. Alice's 'Gaie comari di Windsor! è l'ora!' (II.ii) is binary — not rounded, but elaborated as two periods with similar beginnings. These three songs represent the purest types. Alice's 'Avrò con me dei putti' (III.i) has a more progressive design, but it is tonally rounded in D and quite clearly belongs in the same category. Her earlier 'Fandonie che ai bamboli' might be included here as well, although it may be merely a stylized, asymmetrical period that all three women join voices to conclude. (It seems unnecessary to consider, as does Andrew Porter in the *New Grove* article on Verdi, the 'Fandonie — Avrò' pair as a residual aria with cabaletta.) Alice's Song of the Black Hunter 'Quando il rintocco' encloses the 'Fandonie' phrase. Although more of an inset tale than a 'normal' solo piece (Quickly, after all, is telling the same story to Falstaff), this narrative belongs to the second category, because of its melodic character and rounded, *ABA'* form (the return to *A'* is momentarily interrupted by Nannetta's and Meg's fears and the 'Fandonie' quatrain). Slightly more problematic, but at least a satellite of the present grouping, is Falstaff's 'Ogni sorta di gente dozzinale', just before the nuptial minuet in III.ii. Here we find not a compact rounded melody, but a representative of the first category (loose declamation leading to a strong final line with emphatic cadence) shrunk to the miniature dimensions of the second.

Two other solo pieces present some difficulties in classification. Falstaff's 'So che se andiam, la notte' in I.i begins something that pushes towards the stressed conclusion 'Quest'è il mio regno. / Lo ingrandirò.' This procedure suggests the first category (its final line, for instance, could scarcely be more typical), but the 'solo' is less a reflective mono-logue than a brief lecture. Moreover, it includes participation by other singers, is generally more lyrical than the purer examples of the first group, and leads to what seems yet another beginning, 'V'è noto un tal, qui del paese'. But this new beginning has no formally closed end. Instead, it is eventually pulled apart by the undercurrent of the plot, as Bardolfo and Pistola encroach more and more on Falstaff's plans.

The second problematic case is Quickly's 'Giunta all'Albergo della Giarrettiera', a late addition to II.ii. This approaches the style of the first category in its length and motivic variety, but it is an evocation of past events, not a soliloquy revelatory of character. Nor does it move towards a climactic final line. The solo does blossom at the end with a sparkling melodic gesture ('Infin, per farla spiccia'), but this conclusion, while

not rounded in design or tonality, evokes the flavour and melodic styliza-
tion of the second category, not the first.

I have omitted Fenton's Sonnet and Nannetta's Song as Queen of the
Fairies from the above generalizations because they are unlike any other
solo songs in the opera. Mirroring their ceremonial context, they exude
a more leisured lyricism. They are extended character pieces, and their
underlying mood is one of wistful conclusion, if not valediction.

Fenton's is the more closely integrated into the substance of the
opera's music. With its quotation of the 'Bocca baciata' couplet it alludes
to the lovers' *duettini* in I.ii, melodic fragments of which constitute
part of its introduction. Smoothly through-composed, the vocal line
proceeds largely (as so often in Verdi) by tracking its course along a
chain of paired, symmetrical phrases. It contains a wealth of subtle detail.
Notice, for example, how in the second line, 'Pe' silenzi notturni e va
lontano', the rhythmic values become increasingly longer to evoke the
'distancing' of the sung melody from the lover's lips. The sonnet does
not reach a final cadence. Alice breaks it off, *entrando improvvisamente* —
for this is *Falstaff*, after all, and the demands of the plot have been
delayed too long! But the effect of the sonnet is that of a closed piece,
and in January 1894 Verdi did not hesitate to write a few extra bars for
use in the *pezzo staccato* (the 'detached' music sold separately) to conclude it gently in Db major.

Little need be said here about Nannetta's complementary song,
except that its employment of strophic form (two stanzas, each with a
choral response — Boito had originally written three) is unique and that,
unlike Fenton's sonnet, it is formally closed within the opera itself.
Clearly, such solos as these help to introduce the ensuing chain of equally
stylized pieces: the 'Pizzica, pizzica' chorus in a neatly shaped, G major,
*ABA'B'* form (nos. 40-2); the sixteen-bar, closed Litany (no. 43); the
*ABA'* instrumental minuet with miniature trio (five bars after no. 50 to
no. 52); and the concluding fugue. That Verdi reaches beyond the standard *ottocento* genres into an 'archaic' past at the end (litany, minuet,
fugue) only heightens the valedictory flavour of the entire scene.

The duets and ensembles resist easy generalization. Each deserves
close, individual analysis, but space does not permit that here. The most
extended duets, however, Sir John's conversations first with Quickly
and then with Ford, will be treated at length below in the discussion of
II.i. Nannetta and Fenton's compact duets in I.ii belong by analogy in
the second category of solos in their sense of refuge from the plot's
momentum and their concise form (a non-rounded binary structure, in
which the second half — beginning 'Labbra leggiadre' in the first duet —

veers from closure as intruders approach and leads to the 'Bocca baciata' refrain as an appended codetta). The varied repetition of this duet and refrain foreshadows the strophic form of Nannetta's song in III.ii.

The Falstaff–Alice wooing duet in II.ii is similarly terse. After dashing off some florid *arioso* introductions (e.g., the serenade at no. 38 and 'Ed or potrò morir felice' at no. 39), Falstaff proceeds to the business at hand as though he were beginning a formal song ('T'immagino fregiata del mio stemma' at no. 40). He even receives a delicious phrase from Alice as a quasi-formal *risposta* of the contrasting type ('Ogni più bel gioiel mi nuoce' at no. 41). But at this point, as is typical in *Falstaff*, the plot takes over and destroys the conventional form: Alice admonishes Sir John, he responds with the glib 'Quand'ero paggio', and before long Quickly rushes in with her terrifying news. Falstaff, that is, begins his duet (and his seduction) conventionally, but the machinations of the wives' intrigue turn it topsy-turvy. Here (and elsewhere) disintegration of a standard form becomes a 'formal' device to drive to the core of the plot.

Besides shaping the individual arias, duets, or ensembles, Verdi patterns this continuous music by using motives or thematic reminiscences. The most obvious are the 'Bocca baciata' couplet; 'Reverenza', an identifier of Quickly (Janos Kovács has argued that the contours of this motive give rise to many others, for example, the fugue subject); 'Povera donna', an ironic reference to Alice as the intended 'victim' (probably borrowed from Violetta in *La traviata*, Act I, five bars after the conclusion of the *primo tempo* of her aria 'Ah, fors'è lui'; one wonders whether Verdi intends the 'Povera donna' motive to identify a victim elsewhere in *Falstaff* where the music, but not the text, recurs, as in Nannetta's 'Eccoti avvinto' and 'Ma tu sei vinto' in I.ii after no. 35, in Falstaff's 'Certo affogavo' from his III.i monologue, seven bars before no. 7, and in several other places); 'Dalle due alle tre', the symbol of the presumed assignation; and 'Caro signor Fontana', an emblem of the man Falstaff believes Ford to be.

Occasionally, Verdi seems to have ordered sections along abstract designs. The most celebrated such pattern, first pointed out by Kovács (1969), is the overall arch form of I.ii. The whole scene can be heard in the form *A B C D E E D+C B A* – where *A* is the *brillante* introduction associated with the wives' briskness; *B* is the conclusion of Falstaff's letter 'E il viso tuo'; *C* is the women's quartet; *D* is the men's quintet; and *E* is the Nannetta–Fenton *duettino*. Here the chiasmus is one of design, not tonality: the scene begins in G and ends in E.

The structure of the opera's first event (which lasts until Cajus' exit,

five bars after no. 6) is perhaps more controversial. Kovács hears it as a
rondo with two orchestral themes (bar 1, and 8 bars after no. 1, 'Ho
fatto ciò ch'hai detto'). More recently, David Linthicum (1978) and
Julian Budden (1981: 445-9, a discussion based on 1974 observations
by Pierluigi Petrobelli) have argued that the passage is best heard as a
sonata form, since the second theme occurs first in the mediant, E major,
and is 'recapitulated' in the C major tonic four bars before no. 5 ('Bardolfo! Chi ha vuotate le tasche a quel Messere?'). This certainly fits the
facts, and Budden, in particular, turns the observation into an attractive
point: 'As in *Otello* the music [of the *Falstaff* opening] plunges *in
medias res* without prelude or overture – or so it appears. But in fact
the opening scene reveals itself to the attentive listener as its own overture, constructed thematically while at the same time giving point to
the stage action at each moment' (Ibid. 445-6). It is far from clear,
however, that Verdi actually intended to begin the opera by evoking a
symphonic technique. As an essentially 'Germanic' principle, sonata
form occupied a minimal (perhaps non-existent) role in his operatic
thinking. Such 'sonatas', like the apparent one in King Philip's 'Elle ne
m'aime pas' ('Ella giammai m'amò') in *Don Carlos*, may (or may not)
be coincidental.

### Harmonic practice

Whether experienced in musical analysis or not, every listener surely
hears a distinctly Verdian 'sound' that colours the entire opera (and,
for that matter, many of his other late works). One prominent quality
of that sound is the tension generated between the melodies and the
chords that support them. With very few exceptions the melodies of
*Falstaff* are diatonic. Considered alone, they generally imply tonal clarity
and standard diatonic harmonizations. Time and again, however, Verdi
colours them with richly chromatic harmonies that momentarily stress
otherwise unimplied tonal areas. Consider, for instance, the concluding
couplet of Falstaff's love-letter. The melody articulates an unequivocal
E major (as is common in nineteenth-century operas, the melodic lines
frequently overshoot their chord-note goals). Conceivably, one could
harmonize the phrase by using only conventional, diatonic chords –
perhaps even as blandly as in Ex. 10a (a purely hypothetical harmonization). The actual harmonization (Ex. 10b), to which I shall return later,
surprises us with functionally superfluous, but intensely evocative,
chromaticism. The first harmonization (Ex. 10a) does not sound at all
Verdian. The second (Ex. 10b), which freely explores coloristic possibil-

ities under a sturdily diatonic melody that guarantees ultimate tonal stability, is at the core of the late-Verdi sound. Verdi's use of striking harmonic colour, here and elsewhere, differs greatly from, say, Wagnerian chromaticism, partly because of the firm tonal anchor provided by the melody and frequent emphatic cadences, and partly because the actual chord-choice stresses quite different colours, spacings, and textures. There exists a typically Verdian chordal palette, a preferring of certain harmonic colours over others.

Verdi, for example, does not favour the half-diminished seventh (consisting of minor third, diminished fifth, and minor seventh), a chord which Wagner (and others) used so recurrently to evoke pain, loss, the yearning of love, etc. The chord, of course, is not absent from *Falstaff*, but, apart from its usual functional contexts, Verdi restricts its coloristic use to passages of irony or outright bluster. Thus, he underscores Cajus' initial sputtering, 'Falstaff! Sir John Falstaff!', with close-position half-diminished sevenths in rising sequence: an extreme 'hue' to depict the doctor's clashing rage. On the other hand, the coloristic half-diminished seventh does not appear in the Nannetta—Fenton *duettino* 'Labbra di foco': this, certainly, is one of the many things that set this love-music

Ex. 10a

Ex. 10b

apart from that of Wagner. Similarly, outside of its normal functional uses or its appearance as a passing chord, Verdi usually holds the fully diminished seventh in reserve for moments of perceived or actual calamity, at which time he is likely to unleash its full force, as throughout much of Ford's outburst in his II.i monologue at 'Svegliati! Su! ti desta!' (four bars after no. 20).

But Verdi does rely heavily on secondary dominant sevenths. For instance, in Ex. 10b we find $V^7$ of IV (bar 2), $V^7$ of V (bar 3), and $V^4_2$ of vi (bar 4), before the chords progress normally to an E major cadence — a cadence that emerges all the more emphatic because of the purity of its constituent chords in contrast with the preceding coloristic sonorities. Because the chromatically altered chords are functionally unessential, they lend an unforeseen glow to the text — a kind of harmonic surplus spilling out of creative abundance. Verdi seems especially fond of the secondary dominant seventh in second inversion, the $\frac{6}{4}\frac{}{3}$ position. Thus, in bars 3-4 of Ex. 11, the chords underlying the young lovers' *duettino*, we encounter three dominant sevenths (two of them secondary domi-

Ex. 11

Ex. 12

nants) in second inversion – and the passage sounds recognizably Verdian. As so often in this opera, the chord-sevenths connote a sensuous intimacy, a richness of sound almost tactile in its effect – especially when the notes of the chord 'touch' one another in close position, as on the first beat of bar 3 and in the upper three voices on the last beat of bar 4.

Verdi frequently surrounds the stressed second inversion with major–minor seventh chords in other positions. The fourth entry of the concluding fugue's subject, for instance, introduces a series of 'coloristic' secondary dominant sevenths, including a prominent $V_3^6$ of V on the accented third beat of the bar (Ex. 12). The close juxtaposition of $V_2^4$ of

IV, with its subdominant, flat-side connotations (beat 2), and the bright, sharp-side $V^6_3$ of V (beat 3), while not unique to Verdi, is particularly characteristic (cf. bars 13-14 of Alice's 'Gaie comari di Windsor' in II.ii, and notice an analogous situation − but without inversions − in bars 2-3 of Ex. 10b). Such harmonic activity normally produces a chromatically descending inner voice, along with sudden bursts of flat- and sharp-side colour. The result is a richly inflected music, tonally rooted by the rock-solid diatonicism of the melodic line − a technique of harmonic *chiaroscuro* contrasting brightness and shadow and resulting in astonishing emotional subtlety and depth.

Another clearly recognizable colour in the Verdian palette is the juxtaposition of chords or keys a third apart, frequently contrasting a major tonic and its major mediant (e.g., the opera begins in C major, but its second 'theme' 8 bars after no. 1 is in E). As will be seen in the discussion of II.i below, third-relations permeate both local contexts and long-range tonal activity. For the moment I might simply mention the often unorthodox linkings of third-related chords. A memorable instance occurs in a climactic line of I.i, in which Falstaff pats his stomach and sings 'Quest'è il mio regno. / Lo ingrandirò' (Ex. 13). Here, in an unequivocal context of D♭ major (the preceding six bars have given us two bars each of the chords I, vi, and IV), Verdi colours the word 'regno' not with the expected cadential $^6_4$ (the typical, proclamatory chord that he uses so often to signal the triumphant reaching of a goal), but with a surprising substitute: an altered 'III$^6_4$'. This then proceeds to the expected $V^7$ of D♭ major − exactly as if we had heard the 'proper' $^6_4$ under 'regno'. The chordal succession (and part-writing) defies the traditional logic of harmonic progression, but it is typical of the late-Verdi style. In one sense the altered $^6_4$ functions psychologically like the anticipated, conventional $^6_4$ − i.e., as the antepenultimate sonority in an emphatic cadence − but its most immediate goal is to intensify the cadential experience. By coloristically embellishing the *fortissimo* mediant in the voice part, it provides a dazzling, if ephemeral, flood of light on the climactic note.

Other harmonic devices are perhaps less spectacular, but no less a part of the colour-scheme. Chromatic harmony often gives way to largely diatonic passages, although even here one is likely to encounter frequent transient modulations around an unquestionably stable central key. Emphatic cadences, and clear progressions leading up to them, are frequent. This, too, differentiates Verdi's music from the progressive music of Germany or France: in *Falstaff* the chromatic or modulatory haze quickly disperses for decisive cadencing.

Ex. 13

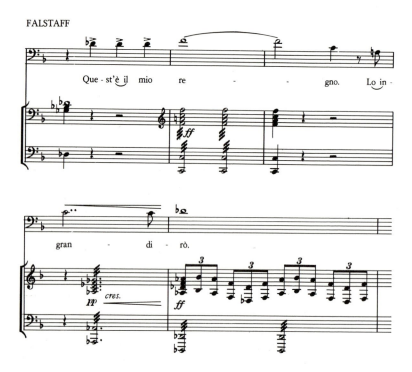

Ultimately, however, Verdi's uniqueness lies not so much in his consistent employment of a set of particular harmonic devices, but in his sense of each procedure's suitability to the given dramatic situation. He unerringly colours each incident with the proper harmonic spotlight — chromatic or diatonic, decisive or evasive, conventional or unusual. The power of his music derives from his power of selection.

To what extent do long-range (or 'background') tonal plans play a significant role in *Falstaff*? The possibility of such plans at work throughout an entire Verdi opera (often cutting across the more obvious divisions into closed pieces) has been much discussed recently. One's decision to affirm or deny such planning seems more an article of faith than anything else. *Falstaff* is less of a problem than some of the earlier operas. It at least begins and ends in the same key — C major — and contains several prominent passages in that tonic throughout (including the important laundry-basket ensemble that concludes II.ii). Each of the six individual parts, however, shows a quite different approach to tonality. I.i begins and ends in C and is the only major subdivision to be tonally closed; I.ii begins in G and ends in E. II.i begins in F and ends in E♭; II.ii begins in G and ends in C (the tonic of the opera, thus seeming to close at this point; notice how, except for the initial F of II.i, all of the beginning and ending keys in I and II form a C major or C minor triad – the third-relationships once again). III.i begins in E and ends in D; and III.ii begins in A♭ and ends in C.

How is one to make sense of the tonal arrangements within each of the six parts? Nobody would argue that Verdi selected his keys at random, but, on the other hand, there is no clear evidence that he intended his tonal plans to be as rigorous as those found in a Beethoven quartet or Wagner music drama. Moreover, keys that recur here do not always have the same symbolic significance: Falstaff's Honour Monologue is in the same G major as the music for the bustling of the wives at the beginning of I.ii and the nuptial minuet in III.ii; the women's quartet in I.ii is in the same E major as the conclusion of Falstaff's Trill Monologue in III.i, Nannetta's Song as Queen of the Fairies, and Falstaff's important pro-nouncement 'Ogni sorta di gente dozzinale' near the end of III.ii; the same D major colours the beginning of Falstaff's letter to Alice and the tale of the Black Hunter; and so on.

These keys are best understood as deriving from the interaction of two considerations, whose interests do not always coincide: a local tonal context (this can be as large as an entire scene or part); and a conceptual relationship (e.g., closely related, remote, sharp- or flat-side) that each key might have to the C major that is understood to represent a point of equilibrium in the opera as a whole – but not necessarily, as we shall see, within each scene. This interaction produces strong relationships in the shorter contexts of individual scenes, but it is less likely that Verdi methodically applied these relationships over the span of the entire opera (as claimed, for instance, by Daniel Sabbeth in his work on the tonal 'psychology' of *Falstaff*: see Chapter 8).

Perhaps the most important point is that keys aim to clarify the drama with which they are linked. Surely Verdi did not conceive his tonal arrangements as an abstract grid that follows its own, purely harmonic, logic. He binds the keys closely to the dramatic situation; they cannot be understood apart from it. Just as the text brims over with asides, mercurial changes of mood, sly innuendos, non sequiturs, and the like, the music includes purposeful discontinuities, interruptions, parentheti-cal interpolations, etc. – things that make little sense on an abstract tonal graph. Tonality does have some powerful claims of its own, and

Verdi does not select his keys without reference to them. Those claims, however, are not absolute. Verdi is perfectly willing to disrupt traditional tonal logic if the dramatic situation demands it.

### The structure of II.i

In its broadest outlines II.i consists of a brief introduction and conclusion enclosing two duets, each of which in turn produces a solo response. The shorter duet (Quickly–Falstaff) generates the shorter response: 'Va, vecchio John', a trifle. Correspondingly, the longer duet (Ford–Falstaff) generates the more complex solo piece: 'È sogno? o realtà'.

Table 1 shows the main structural and tonal divisions of the scene. It is readily apparent that Verdi's choice of keys was fluid, but not at all haphazard, even though the scene itself is not tonally rounded. From the beginning of II.i to no. 12 the only significant keys visited are F, A, A♭, and C: the constituents of the F major and minor triads. Clearly, F dominates this entire section as the fundamental tonic. Equally clearly, Verdi is manipulating his beloved mediant relationships.

With Ford's 'C'è a Windsor una dama' at no. 13 a new constellation of keys emerges that lasts until no. 16: E, A♭ minor (= G♯ minor), G, and B. These are the elements of the E major and minor triads. (The A♭ minor of 'L'amor, l'amor' does not evoke the earlier A♭ major of 'Va, vecchio John'; each belongs to a different system, and their surface similarity is coincidental.) The (transitional) D minor of 'Quella crudel beltà' at no. 16 leads to the final constellation, composed of the elements of the E♭ major triad, beginning with 'Ma se voi l'espugnate' after no. 16.

This E♭ section is freer than its predecessors. Its modulations are more transitory, its keys less emphatically stressed (probably to mirror the phantasmagoria in Ford's brain). The tonal constituents of this section are E♭ (E♭ minor), G minor, A♭, B♭, C♭, and C♮ : steps 1, 3, 4, 5, ♭6, and ♮6 of the tonic major–minor. Its underlying triadic basis, however, remains clear. The pitch levels A♭, C♭, and C♮ are secondary; they function to converge actively on the dominant, B♭.

Finally, the E♭ section also contains an interpolation of the pitch levels from the F section. This occurs at the conclusion of the Ford–Falstaff duet, from 'Io son già molto innanzi' through the 'Te lo cornifico' section. This F interpolation interlocks with the earlier, Quickly–Falstaff F area, because Falstaff refers here to the results of that prior conversation: his assignation (the revelation of which interrupts Ford's tonal 'progress').

Table 1: The broad tonal patterns of *Falstaff*, II.i

| Prevailing keys | Passage | Location |
|---|---|---|
| F | INTRODUCTION | bar 1 |
| | QUICKLY – FALSTAFF DUET | |
| C | Reverenza | 10 bars after no. 2 |
| F→C | Madonna Alice Ford | no. 3 |
| F→C | La bella Meg | 4 bars after no. 5 |
| C | Saluta le due dame | 9 bars before no. 7 |
| | FALSTAFF: SOLO | |
| A♭ | Alice è mia/Va, vecchio John | no. 7 |
| | FORD – FALSTAFF DUET | |
| A→V of A | Signore, V'assista il cielo | 6 bars after no. 9 |
| A | In me vedete un uom | no. 10 |
| C | Caro signor Fontana | 13 bars before no. 11 |
| C | (Attento! Zitto!) | no. 11 |
| F→V of E | Si suol dire che l'oro | 8 bars before no. 12 |
| E | C'è a Windsor una dama | no. 13 |
| (c♯)→V of g♯ (=a♭) | Io l'amo e lei non m'ama | 10 bars after no. 13 |
| a♭ | L'amor, l'amor | no. 14 |
| B | Ma infin, perchè v'aprite a me? | no. 15 |
| G | Spendetele! | 14 bars after no. 15 |
| d | Quella crudel beltà | no. 16 |
| E♭ | Ma se voi l'espugnate | 18 bars after no. 16 |
| E♭ | Prima di tutto | no. 17 |
| V of F→F→C | Io son già molto innanzi | 16 bars after no. 17 |
| a | Il diavolo se lo porti | no. 18 |
| F | Te lo cornifico | 9 bars after no. 18 |
| | FORD: SOLO (see also Table 2) | |
| (F)→modulatory | È sogno? o realtà | 12 bars before no. 20 |
| e♭ | L'ora è fissata | 7 bars before no. 21 |
| g | Già dietro a me | 6 bars after no. 21 |
| (A♭) (B♭) | O matrimonio: Inferno! | no. 22 |
| C | Nella lor moglie abbian fede | 9 bars after no. 22 |
| (A♭) | O laida sorte | 4 bars before no. 23 |
| (b♭) | Bue! Capron! Le fusa torte! | 3 bars after no. 23 |
| (C♭)→V of E♭ | Prima li accoppio | 13 bars after no. 23 |
| E♭ | Laudata sempre sia | no. 24 |
| | CONCLUSION | |
| E♭ | Eccomi quà. Son pronto | 16 bars after no. 24 |

There is obviously a logic at work here. We confront three broad areas, F, E, and E♭, none of which dominates the whole scene. The F triadic area circumscribes the planning of Falstaff's rendezvous with Alice: the situation that he apparently (only apparently) controls. He is gradually distracted from these events by Ford and his E major area, which finally works its spell by no. 13. Ford's ultimate tonal goal, virtually coinciding with his proposal that Sir John try to seduce his wife, is the E♭ area, which he leeringly attains shortly after no. 16. At this point Falstaff turns the tables on Ford by reasserting his own area of control, F major, to describe a scheme which, if carried out, will result in Ford's cuckolding. This shatters Ford, and he is left alone with his E♭ area, now a horror to him. This has now become the key of his plans gone awry. For this reason the E♭ area turns explicitly minor ('L'ora è fissata'), the first principal area in this scene to do so at the foreground level. The keys perfectly underscore the dynamics of the plot.

The sequence of tonalities can be understood in two differing ways. First, the above discussion has implied a gradual semitonal descent throughout the scene, from F to E♭, as in Ex. 14a. Such a plan reflects the descent of Ford's fortunes. On a larger scale, with reference to the C tonic of the whole opera (and hence much more riskily), one could hear the F area as an appoggiatura to the mediants E and E♭, the lowered mediant being appropriate to the grave news that Ford receives.

A second interpretation, one which I find preferable, construes the tonal areas of II.i as articulations of a chain of rising thirds, as in Ex. 14b. This implies an increasing mediant tension – an inexorable stretching towards the tense, sharp side. (The E♭ conclusion in this scheme is thus a D♯ conclusion enharmonically respelled.) Far from suggesting a gradual descent or settling into a key, this interpretation insists on continual ascent and intensification to correspond to the winding-up of the mainspring of the plot. That the mainspring never releases its tension here (i.e., does not 'resolve') is immaterial. The point is to continue the

Ex. 14a

Ex. 14b

process of intensification throughout the scene in as effective a way as possible.

This propensity of tonics to gain energy and rise to their mediants is evident from the very beginning of the scene. The twenty-nine-bar orchestral introduction takes the shape of a symmetrical, two-phrase period, in which the antecedent moves from the tonic F to an A major chord (as V of vi) and the consequent reasserts the original F tonic. The *allegro vivace* tempo, 6/8 metre, insistent iambs, and touches of major–minor fluctuation evoke a saltarello. (One might even hear the ecstatic rattle of tambourine simulated in the trilled cadences.) Quite apart from the question of the propriety of an Italian dance at the Garter Inn, this introduction conjures up the image not of Falstaff, who is merely relaxing and drinking his sherry, but of the high-spirited Bardolfo and Pistola, eager to set their revenge-plot in motion. The music appropriately recalls the conclusion of the prior scene, Alice's promise of revenge 'Vedrai che quell'epa / Terribile e tronfia / Si gonfia' (I.ii, 18 bars after no. 39).

Bardolfo's and Pistola's pseudo-penitential opening lines (they are pretending to reverence Falstaff as an ecclesiastical superior) retain the melodic outlines of the preceding instrumental consequent, confirm the solid F tonic, and plunge into more *allegro vivace* scurrying, as Bardolfo announces the presence of Quickly. The accompaniment whisks through A minor (no. 2, the mediant relationship again) on its way to the dominant, C; as Quickly enters, the rising C major scale refers to the motive of the wives' bustling that began and ended I.ii. This whole introductory passage, then, contains motivic links with the past scene. They function as 'inside' jokes – winkings of the eye – that the audience, but not Falstaff, can recognize.

Quickly begins the duet with affected C major courtesies in courtly-smooth, minuet style (but notice the leering promise implied by the chromatic inner voices at 'Vorrei, segretamente') before attempting to launch her first 'formal' section in F major at no. 3. Playing her role to the hilt, Quickly feigns hesitancy and delays the actual beginning of her story until 10 bars after no. 3, 'Alice sta in grande agitazione d'amor per voi'. Thus, bars 4–9 after no. 3 are – formally speaking – an interruption. The humour of the crude C major cadence 'Povera donna' is that here and elsewhere it occurs out of context. In this case it is preceded by an explicit promise of F major ('Ahimè!'), not C.

The quasi-formal sections of the duet consist of the two 'official' messages, one about Alice, the other about Meg. In each Quickly begins with the prevailing tonic, F, and shifts it to the dominant, C. The first message closes neatly in C, 4 bars before no. 5. The second (after an A minor transition 'Ma c'è un'altra ambasciata') begins in F, 4 bars after no. 5 ('La bella Meg'), closes in the dominant, 12 bars after no. 6 ('Non temete'), and is followed by an 8-bar C major codetta that again suggests the bustle of the wives at the end. The entire conversation concludes as it began, with over-elaborate C major politeness, 'Saluta le due dame'.

Up to this point the scene has presented the same harmonic motion, F to C (always touching the mediant, A, along the way), three times: in the introduction and 'Reverenza' passage and in each of Quickly's two reports. This is the harmonic equivalent of setting the springs of three identical mousetraps – a triple stretching of Falstaff's apparently secure F to an expectant dominant. Each snare is set cautiously by approaching Sir John in what is temporarily his own key, F, winning his forgiveness or attention in that key, baiting the trap in C, and returning to F to do the same thing all over again.

The point is worth stressing, because although C is the tonic of the opera, one experiences it here as a dynamic, unstable key, threatening to 'snap back' to the local tonic, F. The F–C motion of the II.i opening is unquestionably the movement of a tonic to its dominant, not a plagal gesture of relaxation (IV–I). This latter misinterpretation would not only contradict the growing intricacy of the plot but also ignore the frequency with which the mediant, A, divides the F–C fifth. Thus, we are reminded how difficult it is to assert that any given key in *Falstaff* – even the 'tonic' – evokes a consistent response. The effect of C major here depends on its local context, its position within the orbit of the prevailing tonality, in this case F.

The first duet is devoted almost exclusively to Quickly and her two messages. Falstaff reacts to interpolate a comment at various points, but he never begins anything like a semi-formal *risposta*. For this reason the whole passage is less a typical 'duet' than a free contralto solo with occasional baritone comments. Falstaff postpones his true response until after Quickly leaves (a distortion of the standard form for reasons of plot) and then bursts out with 'Alice è mia!' and 'Va, vecchio John' in A♭ major (the lowered mediant of F). This brief solo consists of four clearly separated phrases, *ABCA'*. The strong cadence in the dominant at the end of *B* ('Qualche dolcezza a te') at first suggests a medial division, producing a rounded binary form: *AB/CA'*. *B* and *C*, however, should probably be heard as a unit. The two phrases set a self-sufficient poetic 'quatrain' (rhymed *abab* and scanned as 11, 7, 11, 7 – the seven-syllable lines being, of course, *versi tronchi*), and together they form a balanced musical period in which the antecedent moves to the key of the dominant and the consequent returns to the tonic. The song, then, is best heard as ternary: *A/BC/A'*. Considered with its identical orchestral introduction and conclusion, the entire structure approaches that of a chiasmus or arch. This, too, reflects the underlying poetic structure.

The orchestral conclusion, as is typical in *Falstaff*, does not close with a clear V–I cadence. Instead of the expected full tonic A♭ triad, we are given only its mediant, a unison C (5 bars after no. 8). Bardolfo's ensuing recitative, delivered *prestissimo* and nearly *recto tono*, again evokes the flavour of the Church in its ironic evocation of recitation-tone style – as if Sir John's wine-soaked quarters were sacred space.

What follows in the transition to the Ford–Falstaff duet is one of the best examples of purposeful discontinuity in the score. Falstaff has had his swaggering triumph in A♭. Now he bids his guest to enter ('Entri') on the dominant of a new key, A major (which is associated with the arrival of 'Fontana'). Before Ford actually steps inside, however, Falstaff swerves from the dominant of A as his thoughts return to the A♭ of 'Va, vecchio John', which now receives a four-bar fragmentary reprise. Such a tonal lurch (from a dominant to the key of the leading-note, or lowered tonic) is difficult to explain in terms of abstract harmonic motion. In its dramatic context it is virtually self-evident.

The *sostenuto* at no. 9 gradually brings Falstaff from his private, A♭ world to the originally promised A major, which makes its appearance 4 bars before Ford's first words, 'Signore, V'assista il cielo', although we are not given a cadence in that key until 24 bars later (5 bars after no. 10). This whole passage resembles the beginning of the Quickly–Falstaff conversation as a rite of social courtesy, without real substance. The music parallels Ford's pose of mincing hesitancy. All delicacy and tact, it gingerly touches its way around the fringes of A major, modulates cautiously to the dominant, E major (even temporarily cadencing on it at no. 10), and finally gets to the point by moving directly to A major four bars later.

Ford 'identifies' himself with a rounded, two-phrase period in A major, whereupon Falstaff takes the bait in C (the key, one recalls, of the set traps), 'Caro signor Fontana!' Bardolfo and Pistola are whisked out of the room in the same C major at no. 11 (another interruption). Ford now turns to Falstaff and, after momentarily adopting Bardolfo's recitation-tone style, leaps into his main topic with one of the most outrageously witty lines of the opera: 'They say that gold will open any door' ('Si suol dire / Che l'oro apre ogni porta'). Apart from its earthy metaphor, the line hits its mark because it concludes with a recognizable variant of the 'Povera donna' motive, which clearly identifies the guardian of the 'porta' in question; and because it decisively modulates to F (by now the key of the anticipated snapping of the trap), stressing the aggressiveness of the move by a *fortissimo* F major exclamation point. This return to F also rounds off the first part of II.i – that part which until now has been ruled by the F tonic. The immediately succeeding lines, with first their military and then their money-jingling imagery, move from this tonic into a new area: the E major–minor region, the area of Ford's fictitious proposal.

The dramatic and tonal ground for Ford's real business with Falstaff has now been cleared. Accordingly, he now begins what corresponds to the first 'formal' section of a standard duet, 'C'è a Windsor una dama' (no. 13). This opens lyrically in E major but becomes more troubled as 'Fontana's' emotions get more and more out of hand. At 'Io l'amo' (10 bars after no. 13) he initiates a series of histrionic ascending sequences (beginning in C♯ minor, the relative minor) that discharge in the extravagant outburst 'Per lei sprecai tesori', which represents the 'squandering' mentioned in the text by its erratic bass line and harmonic wandering that refuses to approach anything like a traditional cadence. The first part of Ford's 'performance' ends with a hyperbolic parody of vocal ornamentation ('madrigale', 1 bar before no. 14) on the dominant of G♯ minor. Since Ford is acting the role of Fontana, Verdi has used this portion of the duet – roughly equivalent to the first section of the *primo tempo* – to satirize the conventional operatic treatment of emotion.

At no. 14 Falstaff begins a *risposta*, 'L'amor, l'amor', in the lugubrious A♭ minor (the enharmonic equivalent of G♯ minor). Although Ford intrudes into this response, it belongs essentially to Falstaff. It is shaped into a brief *AA'BA* form, in which the contrasting *B* section borrows Ford's earlier 'squandering' music but gives it the cadence it had lacked by pushing it powerfully into C♭ major. In this manner Falstaff turns the lover's plight into a moral lesson: 'Such is the fatal destiny of the unfortunate lover' ('Quest'è il destin fatale', 12 bars before no. 15). As usual, the final, A♭ minor section does not cadence but is interrupted ('Essa non vi die' mai luogo a lusinghe?'), as the demands of the plot again supersede those of symmetrical closure.

Ford now moves into the second section of the duet. Dramatically, he informs Falstaff that he is to be employed as a seducer. Musically, he passes through four stages, any of which may be considered to begin a free equivalent of a duet's *secondo tempo*: 'Voi siete un gentiluomo' in B major (4 bars after no. 15); 'Spendetele!' in G major (14 bars after no. 15): 'Quella crudel beltà' in D minor (no. 16); and 'Ma se voi l'espugnate' in E♭ major (18 bars after no. 16). Here one sees the degree to which Verdi has liberated himself from the demands of traditional form. It is clear that we have arrived at a second section (this is no longer a basic exposition of 'Fontana's' situation but the beginning of the Ford–Falstaff pact), but that second section refuses to be shaped into anything like a recognizable rounded 'song'. Each of the four stages veers away from symmetry as Ford's explanation becomes more intricate.

Such formal ambiguity closely follows the text. Falstaff awaits his visitor's main point (the expected *secondo tempo*), but Ford insists on circumlocution. He arrives at the puzzling heart of the matter only at the end of the second stage, 'Chiedo che conquistiate Alice!' (6 bars before no. 16), and finally provides the requisite explanation in stages three and four. Once Falstaff grasps the situation, he seizes Ford's proffered dominant of E♭ ('Che ve ne par?') and plunges headlong into a short *risposta* of eager acceptance, 'Prima di tutto' (no. 17). Falstaff's E♭ cadence 14 bars later seals the agreement and closes the second section of the duet.

So far, all has proceeded according to Ford's plans. In purely musical terms he has dominated the vague outlines of two sections of a quasi-tripartite duet and has wheedled Falstaff from his F area (introduction) through an E area (the first section) and into the region of E♭ (the pact: conclusion of the second section). But Falstaff rules the final section. In a transitional passage he blithely returns to his secure F tonic to shatter Ford's peace of mind: 'Within a half-hour she'll be in my arms' ('Fra una mezz'ora sarà nelle mie braccia', 20 bars after no. 17). Here, 'nelle mie braccia' provides an almost perfect musical rhyme with Ford's earlier line in the duet's introduction 'Si suol dire / Che l'oro apre ogni porta' (with its evident allusion to the 'Povera donna' motive). Structurally, this cadence signals the beginning of Sir John's mastery, just as Ford's earlier, corresponding line had initiated his proposal. Falstaff's flippant inclusion of the 'Dalle due alle tre' motive brings this transition to a close in C (4 bars before no. 18). This horrifies Ford, of course, but it also reminds us of the trap set for Falstaff earlier in the scene.

The third formal section begins in A minor with Falstaff's 'Il diavolo / Se lo porti all'inferno' at no. 18. Its principal element, the mocking 'Te lo cornifico', quickly establishes the true key of this section, F major. One may discern here the rough outlines of an *ABA'* design. The *A* areas are those concluding with the 'Te lo cornifico' motive: in each case the motive is introduced by propulsive material ('Vedrai') that sets it off as a cadential release. The *B* section (moving briefly to the relative minor) begins with 'Se mi frastorna', 12 bars after no. 18. After his *ABA'* 'song' Falstaff takes Ford's money and exits to an exultant orchestral codetta (based on 'Te lo cornifico') in his own key, F, thus bringing a very complex duet to its end.

Ford has been silent throughout the duet's abusive third section. Just as Falstaff had delayed his *risposta* in the Quickly–Falstaff duet in order to turn it into a solo piece, so now Ford postpones a response until after Sir John's departure. This is one of the major solo pieces of the opera, 'È sogno? o realtà', a monologue which is constructed from brief orchestral motives developed in an almost symphonic manner, as Edward Cone has pointed out ('The Old Man's Toys', 1954).

Its opening six lines are introductory, as the bewildered Ford tries to regain some kind of tonal balance. Much of this music recalls that at the beginning of I.i. It seems that Verdi is drawing a parallel between Ford and Cajus (both duped by Falstaff). We find, for example, the device of an agitated accompaniment ascending to a climactic high note in the monologue at 'Due rami enormi' (5 bars before no. 20) and 'Mastro Ford! Mastro Ford! Dormi?' (no. 20), corresponding to I.i, bars 14-16; Ford's Cajus-like sputtering of repeated notes on such lines as 'Tua moglie sgarra e mette in mal'assetto' (cf. Cajus' delivery of lines in I.i up to 6 bars after no. 1); the textual reference to a disordered 'casa' (cf. I.i, bar 16); and at 9 bars after no. 20, immediately after 'Ed il tuo letto!', the rhythmic motive of four descending sixteenths, two slurred and two staccato, which had depicted Cajus' rage in the earlier scene (first sounded in the opening bars of the score). Moreover, the notes on the first and third beats of the agitated accompaniment of no. 20, bars 1-2 ('Mastro Ford!'), outline the four-note motive of Falstaff's unconcerned responses to Cajus' accusations (I.i, 8 bars after no. 1, the 'second theme' of Linthicum's and Budden's presumed sonata).

The remainder of the monologue, although fluid in mood and texture, suggests an overall arch structure, as shown in Table 2. At the first section of the arch, 'L'ora è fissata' (7 bars before no. 21), Ford recovers his earlier tonic, E♭, which will prevail over this monologue. Appropriately, this is the key of the duet's pact, but it is sounded here in the minor mode with shuddering 'what-have-I-done?' implications. The accompaniment outlines Ford's fears: the cuckold's horns and the triplet bass cadences with their ominous allusions to the 'Dalle due alle tre' rhythm. This first section closes with a memorable outburst in the tonic major, 'E poi diranno / Che un marito geloso è un insensato!' (3 bars after no. 21).

The second and fourth sections (6 bars after no. 21 and 4 bars before no. 23) are dominated by two motives that the accompaniment develops as goals: 'Te lo cornifico' and the triplet knock of 'Dalle due alle tre'. Both form the core of Ford's terror. Their persistent appearance here reflects his gnawing agony. (Notice also his employment of the music of Falstaff's earlier 'un bue' − 19 bars after no. 18 − for his own outcry 'Le corna!' in the fourth section, 2 bars after no. 23.) The fourth section, much larger than the second, proceeds in two halves divided by a brief resolution 'Ma non mi sfuggirai! no!' (7 bars after no. 23). This shifts the textual emphasis away from the fears of ridicule that dominate sections 2 and 4 and prepares for the final resolution of section 5. The continued presence of 'Te lo cornifico' in the second half of section 4 ('Prima li accoppio'), however, shows that Ford is still grounded in fears rather than in true resolution: this is why the music and text break off in near collapse six bars later.

Table 2: The arch form of Ford's monologue

| | *Introduction*: 'È sogno? o realtà' |
|---|---|
| e♭ →E♭ | *Situation*: 'L'ora è fissata' (concluding with 'E poi diranno') |
| g→modulatory | *Fears of ridicule*: 'Già dietro a me' (with the 'Te lo cornifico' and 'Dalle due alle tre' motives as goading accompaniment) |
| (A♭)→modulatory | *Curses*: 'O matrimonio: Inferno!' |
| (A♭)→V⁻ of E♭ | *Fears of ridicule*: 'O laida sorte!' (again with the 'Te lo cornifico' and 'Dalle due alle tre' motives as goading accompaniment) |
| V of E♭ →E♭ | *Resolution*: 'Vendicherò l'affronto!' and 'Laudata sempre sia' (concluding with an orchestral reprise of 'E poi diranno') |

The central section of the arch, beginning 'O matrimonio: Inferno!' (no. 22), comprises curses and scorn for his wife. Here the 'reminiscence motives' in the orchestra are more subtle, but no less present. A touch of the 'Cajus' colour re-emerges: the descending sixteenths, two slurred and two staccato, 4 and 7 bars after no. 22; the threatening 𝅘𝅥𝅯𝅘𝅥𝅯𝅘𝅥𝅯 | 𝅘𝅥𝅮 bass rhythm similarly punctuating 'Inferno!' and 'Demonio!', 3 and 6 bars after no. 22 (cf. Cajus' threats at his exit in I.i, 4 and 7 bars before no. 6); and the raging half-diminished seventh tint on the stressed opening word of 'Non mia moglie a se stessa', 22 bars after no. 22 (cf. I.i, bars 7-10). At the midpoint of this section the bright, angular signals that accompany 'Affiderei / La mia birra a un Tedesco', etc., ironically recall

Ex. 15

the music with which Ford had complimented Falstaff in the earlier duet, 'Voi siete un gentiluomo' (4 bars after no. 15).

In the final section Ford devotes his entire strength to resolution. He lands on the dominant of E♭ *con violenza* with his 'Vendicherò l'af-fronto!' at no. 24. The concluding two lines are given over completely to enhancing the tension of that smouldering dominant – heard through-out as a pedal point – before resolving it (see Ex. 15). In the melodic line Ford starts from a low B♭ and climbs towards the B♭ an octave higher. This he overshoots by a whole step and lands on the appoggiatura C (Ex. 15, bar 3). Instead of immediately resolving the C downwards (the standard procedure in *ottocento* opera: see Ex. 10), he delays the resolution to augment his wrath further. In methodical, step-by-step increments he 'supercharges' the appoggiatura by expanding it to its upper fifth, high G. This stretches the bow to its point of highest ten-sion – a terrible, grim maximizing of a now burning rage. He then returns to the appoggiatura (in bar 5), resolves it on the now correspondingly supercharged dominant, B♭ (bar 6), and finally releases the energy powerfully into the E♭ resolution (bar 7).

The chordal support for this extraordinary passage supplements the force of the melodic line. The harmonic supercharging is accomplished, as so often in late Verdi, primarily by secondary dominant sevenths. After the cadential $^6_4$ of Ex. 15, bar 2, one finds above the tonic pedal (ignoring inversions) a V of ii (bar 3), a V$^7$ of V (bar 4), a V$^7$ of IV (a momentary substitute for a cadential $^6_4$) passing to vi (bar 5), and finally the dominant itself (bar 7). A good share of the force that accumulates in the harmony is due to the chromatic chords that blur the solid B♭ pedal point during the melodic ascent from C. Still, there is never a moment of doubt that all of this enhances the B♭ pitch level as dominant: the pedal point and emphatically diatonic structure of the melody ensure that. The chromatic chords, however, do multiply the tension remarkably, and when the melody and harmony finally come again 'into phase' with the dominant in bar 7 (which sounds all the more forceful for lacking a seventh), one experiences an awesome sense of harmonic potency.

The resolution itself, of course, leads directly to an orchestral reprise of the 'E poi diranno' idea first stated at the end of the first section. Its harmonic force now spent, II.i concludes with a reaffirmation of the E♭ tonic (see Table 1). Falstaff returns, the two leave the Garter Inn ('Passiamo insieme' is clearly a distorted echo of the 'E poi diranno' motive), and the orchestra sounds a mocking reprise of the boisterous laughter that had earlier enclosed 'Va, vecchio John'.

A close examination of this entire scene, then, demonstrates that although Verdi wrote continuous music and avoided the rigours of the standard aria and duet forms, the opera is still very much contoured, shaped, and sectionalized, even though each section is likely to resist closure in order to move directly into the next. In small and large sections Verdi shows a distinct liking for rounded binary, ternary, and five-part symmetrical structures. These structures, however, are not omnipresent, nor are they strongly emphasized within the ongoing flow of the work. Without question one can find references to (or residues of) earlier operatic procedures, such as the subtle tripartite quality of the Ford–Falstaff duet. But more often than not, Verdi evokes these formulas primarily to demonstrate their inadequacy to his broader thought and the demands of the plot. He evokes them to shatter them for dramatic reasons. One can scarcely conceive of a more surprising, and yet strangely inevitable, conclusion to his entire career of formal experimentation.

# 6 The interpretation of 'Falstaff': Verdi's guidelines

Of all the conditions that a composer might set for an operatic production, those affecting the style of performance and the staging are the least likely to survive into succeeding generations without substantial change. Today's conductors, performers, and critics put a high premium on the demonstrable validity of the text and the notes. Advertisements catch the eye with formidable claims to textual and musical reliability: 'original version', 'including the recently discovered aria', 'first uncut performance', and so on. But few are currently prepared to insist that the original manner of performance of nineteenth-century operas is something to be taken seriously. Today the notions of historical staging and 'performance practice' tend to conjure up things Renaissance and Baroque, not Romantic or modern. Thus, Bayreuth now customarily abjures original staging and costuming as outdated and impractical and has moved into staging that underscores the 'timeless message' of the Wagnerian music dramas by being symbolically abstract or offering trenchant social commentary. Similarly, the details of Verdian staging and performance are relegated to museums and archives, left to rest as historically quaint and irrelevant to the sophisticated demands of modern producers and audiences. Few have suggested that early recordings be studied as practical stylistic models — not to be slavishly imitated, but to initiate one into a different way of thinking about performance. And the whole question of the employment of appropriate and 'authentic' nineteenth-century instruments is so obscure that one has yet to find the subject broached in operatic literature.

There are, of course, positive reasons for this. Staging and performance cannot, and should not, be fixed as rigidly as note-choice. An opera remains alive by reinterpretation, new insights, and the unique personalities of individual theatres, producers, and performers. Verdi, of course, never conceived his operas as works that would resist fresh staging and interpretation. He was well aware that conventions and tastes change. Indeed, he had helped to change them in the 1840s. By the end of his

110

life he had unquestionably accepted as natural various stagings of *Rigoletto, Trovatore*, and *Traviata* that must have been radically different from the first few productions that he had heard. This is not to say that Verdi was infinitely tolerant. He was not. He had concrete, strong preferences rooted in his own conceptions of his operas, and he had frequently written individual roles or passages with these performance intentions in mind. Nevertheless, within a relatively broad range of mid- to late nineteenth-century conventions Verdi was prepared to admire and embrace individual creativity, so long as it did not grossly violate the original dramatic conception of the score or ride rough-shod over its details.

The fact that he thought within nineteenth-century conventions is worth stressing. Verdi could not have envisaged the radicalism and brilliance of the twentieth-century creative mind or its continual thirst for uniqueness and originality. Surrealism, abstraction, the unit set, the mechanical marvels of modern lighting and stage illusion, the conscious violation of original dramatic intent to smooth over uncomfortably old-fashioned ideas or to suggest peculiarly modern, perhaps psychologically compulsive, motivations for the characters: all these were foreign to his thought. How he might have reacted to them we cannot know, nor would everyone agree that his reaction would be relevant. Modern operatic productions are often extended, provocative glosses on the thought of an earlier age; frequently it is the gloss that one wants to see, not so much the original thought.

This is a perfectly defensible aesthetic, one that has produced many evenings of satisfying modern theatre. As one proceeds further into creative reinterpretation, however, the original conventions, performance, and staging become more unfamiliar and, hence, attractive. This attraction may well lead in certain instances – surely not in all – to a new regard for Verdi's own traditions and theatrical concerns. However one regards the issue, it is not without value to review here what we do know about how Verdi conceived the original *Falstaff*, and what his suggestions were for its interpretation. The summary that follows, then, is not a prescription, but a description of Verdi's dramatic intentions, some of which it might be appropriate to consider today.

Scholars have now begun to examine the recently discovered production books (*disposizioni sceniche*) that Ricordi printed for most of the Verdian operas from *I vespri siciliani* onward. These were manuals of performance instructions prepared in order to suggest a proper staging (usually, the original staging at a major theatre like the Opéra or La Scala) to provincial theatres that had also rented the score and parts. With varying degrees of explicitness, they describe what stage apparatus is required, where to stand, when to move, where to enter and exit, what emotional expressions to convey, and so on. The degree to which these manuals are historically binding or 'authentic' is a complex issue and is still being debated. Yet it is clear that they do document certain performances that Verdi had seen. He certainly knew of the manuals and often read them over before Ricordi released them. In many instances they describe staging that he must have suggested as he participated in rehearsals, although in certain cases, such as *Otello*, he later expressed regrets about the original staging.

Unfortunately, the list of production books – *I vespri siciliani*, *Un ballo in maschera*, *La forza del destino*, *Don Carlos*, *Aida*, the revised *Simon Boccanegra*, and *Otello* – does not include *Falstaff*. At one time Giulio Ricordi had planned to publish the *Falstaff* production book; in mid-1893 he even assigned it a plate number, 95685. The manual, however, has not yet turned up. Considering the attention and wide distribution that Ricordi would surely have given it, it now seems likely that it was never printed, perhaps never even written.

Nevertheless, a wealth of information exists about the first *Falstaff*, principally because Verdi insisted on supervising it. While he was willing to delegate certain decisions to others, ultimately he had to approve everything before the opera could be premièred. The classic, but not the earliest, formulation of this demand is found in his letter to Ricordi of 18 September 1892:

With regard to *Falstaff* I do not wish to incur obligations to anyone, but *I promise the editor Ricordi* to give *Falstaff* at La Scala in the 1892-3 Carnival season if the cast we have been discussing is completed, reserving for myself the right to replace anyone whom I find inadequate during the rehearsals. The *Falstaff* première can take place in early February, provided that I have the theatre completely at my disposal on 2 January 1893.

With regard to the rehearsals we'll do them as we always have before. Only the dress rehearsal must be done differently from before. I have never been able to obtain a dress rehearsal at La Scala as it ought to be done in that theatre. This time I will be implacable. I won't complain, but if anything is lacking, I'll leave the theatre, and then you will have to withdraw the score.                    (Cesari and Luzio 1913: 381)

Throughout the long planning for the première Verdi strove to shape a believable, realistic production. Music or stunning vocal technique alone would not suffice. He persistently urged that the word– Boito's intricate text – and the stage action be treated as equals, if not superiors, to the music. He realized from the start that *Falstaff*, his most intimate opera, could not rely on broad stage gestures. On the contrary, the production was obliged to emphasize delicious detail, for therein lies the essence of the opera. At first the composer was suspicious about La Scala's vast stage. On 2 June 1891 he shocked Ricordi by suggesting that Italy's foremost theatre was probably 'too large to hear the words well and to see the faces of the artists' (Abbiati 1959: IV, 421), and that he was considering the Teatro Carcano, a much smaller, less prestigious Milanese theatre. A few days later he even suggested (surely not seriously) that the opera be premièred at Sant'Agata.

Ultimately, of course, he agreed to La Scala. Adolph Hohenstein, the set and costume designer, helped to create the illusion of a slightly smaller stage with scenery that framed the action near the centre or front of the performing area. The quest for a smaller stage, however, did have its practical limits. In a review of the first French performance at the Opéra Comique, Giovanni Pozza, writing in the *Gazzetta musicale di Milano* of 29 April 1894, noted that the restricted stage area harmed the effect of the opera: in the II.ii ensemble the laundry basket had to be too close to the screen; and, similarly, most of the action of III.ii seemed too crowded – especially the dancing.

Hohenstein's goal with the costumes and scenery was literal, historical fidelity. On Ricordi's insistence (Verdi approved, but thought it a financial extravagance) Hohenstein travelled to London, Windsor, and the libraries of Paris in mid-1892 to copy not only fifteenth-century buildings and clothing, but also historically authentic tables, chairs, bottles, glasses – even the masks to be donned in the final scene. The result of his efforts may be seen today in his *bozzetti* – oils and watercolours – that provided the models for the 1893 La Scala première, now preserved in the Casa Ricordi archives (see Figs. 3-7).

We may be quite certain that these *bozzetti* satisfied Verdi. He had had the opportunity to approve or modify Hohenstein's work when the artist, along with Ricordi and Boito, came to Sant'Agata for a day or more in the autumn of 1892 (probably on 4 October; the dating derives from letters from Boito and Ricordi to Verdi, some of which are still unpublished; see *Carteggio Verdi–Boito* 1978: I, 213, and Hepokoski 1979: 256). The visitors brought with them a small replica of the La Scala stage: a half-metre-square *teatrino* fitted out with Hohenstein's proposed sets and doll-like figurines to represent the characters. Here the four men determined the main lines of the staging. Clearly, Verdi must have assumed the major responsibility for positioning the objects about the *teatrino*. Anyone else's suggestions were at least subject to his

Fig. 3    Adolph Hohenstein's original set for I.i and II.i (1892)

Fig. 4    Adolph Hohenstein's original set for I.ii (1892)

Fig. 5    Adolph Hohenstein's original set for II.ii (1892)

Fig. 6    Adolph Hohenstein's original set for III.i (1892)

Fig. 7    Adolph Hohenstein's original set for III.ii (1892)

approval: that was why the apparatus had been brought to Sant'Agata in the first place. These primarily verbal decisions probably incorporated aspects of Verdi's more 'abstract' drawings and staging suggestions in his letters of only a few weeks before: for example, to Ricordi on 18 September 1892 (reproduced in Cesari and Luzio 1913: 379-80, and Chusid 1979: 173). Today one should treat these letters and drawings with caution. They document only an early point in the planning: by early October 1892 they were no longer actively relevant to the première.

When it came to selecting and preparing the cast, Verdi's insistence on credibility led him to stress dramatic characterization and clear textual delivery. He filled his letters of June 1892 and subsequent months with references to the implicit subordination of musical to dramatically realistic values. The sweeping lyricism and traditional stylized exaggerations typical of earlier comic opera were to be sacrificed in favour of a more natural delivery. 'The music is not difficult,' he wrote to Ricordi at the conclusion of a long letter about performance on 13 June 1892:

but it must be sung differently from the other modern comic operas and the older *opere buffe*. I wouldn't like it to be sung, for example, as one sings *Carmen*, and not even as one sings either *Don Pasquale* or *Crispino* [*e la comare*, a 'comic-fantastic opera' by the brothers Luigi and Federico Ricci]. It will take study to do it, and we'll need time. In general, our singers only know how to perform with a fat voice. They have neither vocal elasticity nor clear and easy enunciation of syllables, and they lack accent and breath.                    (Abbiati 1959: IV, 444)

Verdi was preparing once again to do battle against the cult of the glorious voice and all forms of vocal affectation.

Nowhere is this more clearly seen than in his choices for the major roles of the opera. He considered Alice's part to be central. 'She must be full of the devil', he wrote on 13 June 1892. 'She's the one who leads the whole pack' (Ibid. IV, 443). Two days later Ricordi wrote back with several suggestions. Almost as an afterthought he mentioned Emma Zilli as a splendid actress rather than an admirable singer. After another month of deliberation Verdi began to consider her seriously. He auditioned and accepted her in Milan in the final days of July 1892. On 3 August he sent a request to Ricordi: 'With regard to Zilli, tell us particularly that she is not forgetting what I told her, to hold her voice steady and to loosen up her tongue and clarify her pronunciation' (Ibid. IV, 450). A week and a half of private rehearsals in Genoa with Verdi from 11 to 22 December helped to prepare her for the part, but Verdi never considered her to be perfect. Long after the première, on 2 September 1893, he wrote to Ricordi about recasting the opera:

One needs to pay a lot of attention to Alice's part. Alice is the most important part after Falstaff. Although Zilli has a great deal of talent and understands and acts well, she has neither the elastic voice nor the self-confident figure for that part. She's good, I repeat, but she doesn't deliver her part with that *brio* that's needed – I told you this, if you remember, even at the Milanese rehearsals. Alice is the most important part after Falstaff. In *Falstaff* don't encumber yourself with artists who want to sing too much and effect sentiment and action by falling asleep on the notes.                                        (Ibid. IV, 517)

Verdi's comments about Quickly's part show many of the same concerns. When Ricordi suggested the brilliant Guerrina Fabbri to him, a singer also recommended highly by Boito a year earlier, Verdi rejected her on 13 June 1892:

With Fabbri's good voice she could be successful in cantabiles based on agility as in *La Cenerentola*, etc., etc. But Quickly's part is something else. It requires both voice and acting, much stage presence, and the right accent on the proper syllable. She doesn't have these qualities, and one would risk sacrificing the most characteristic and original part of the four.                                        (Ibid. IV, 443)

At this time Verdi's thoughts were turning to Giuseppina Pasqua, a slightly aging mezzo-soprano/contralto with a fine reputation as an

Fig. 9    Costume design for Mistress Quickly (Adolph Hohenstein, 1892)

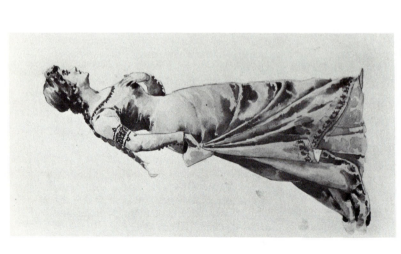

Fig. 8    Costume design for Alice (Adolph Hohenstein, 1892)

actress, who had recently sung the role of Tigrana in the revised version of Puccini's *Edgar*. Swallowing his fear that she might overwhelm Quickly's part with lyricism and force, Verdi told Ricordi on 17 June 1892 that she could be offered the role: 'That Pasqua is relying on her Puccini connections is frightening. Nevertheless, you yourself could write to her and tell her openly that here one must put nerves and sentimentalism aside. It is a matter of comedy: music, note and word, stage action, and much energy, not cantabiles' (Ibid. IV, 444-5). Verdi underscored the essential lightness of the 'Infin, per farla spiccia' core of Quickly's solo in a letter to Pasqua on 7 November: 'It would be necessary to perform it *prestissimo, a mezza voce*, with only one breath, and neat and clear syllables' (misdated in Cesari and Luzio 1913: 714). Quickly's part needed to be acted well, but not overacted. On 17 October 1894 Verdi criticized Marie Delna, the Quickly in a French *Falstaff*: 'She tends to exaggerate; and [this] may be a problem in the future. Indeed, she repeats her *racconto* three times' (Abbiati 1959: IV, 556).

Verdi's requirements for Ford similarly stressed acting ability and stage presence over purely vocal facility. Before deciding upon Antonio Pini-Corsi, a bass-baritone known particularly for his incisive characterization of *opera buffa* roles (many of which – Figaro in *Il barbiere di Siviglia*, Dr Dulcamara in *L'elisir d'amore*, the title role in *Don Pasquale*, etc. – he recorded during the first decade of this century), Verdi had rejected several of Ricordi's suggestions for the role, including Arturo Pessina, for the usual reasons: 'Pessina is a fine artist,' he wrote to Ricordi in his letter of 13 June 1892:

but he is more of a singer than an actor and a little heavy for the role of Ford, the furiously jealous man who howls, screams, jumps, etc. Without all of this the effect of the second-act finale would be lost. All the attention is turned upon him, and only here and there upon Falstaff, when he pokes his snout out of the laundry basket.     (Ibid. IV, 443)

Pessina, curiously enough, later sang the role of Falstaff in Brescia on 12 August 1893 and in the London première (Covent Garden) on 19 May 1894 (see Chapter 7).

The minor roles also had their dramatic demands. Again from 13 June 1892: 'And for Bardolfo we also need a self-confident actor who knows how to carry his nose well' (Ibid. IV, 443). And as Verdi rehearsed the future Pistola, Vittorio Arimondi, in Genoa from 1 to 11 December 1892, he complained not about the singer's vocal quality, but that his pronunciation was unclear: 'He has a huge voice and thinks only of vocal production: all of the syllables wrong, he never supports his voice, and, for example, instead of an *a* he pronounces an *i*, an *e*, an *o*, and the same

Fig. 10    Costume design for Ford (Adolph Hohenstein, 1892)

is true of the other vowels' (5 December 1892, unpublished). Since Verdi had purposely avoided explicit (and traditional) instrumental doublings of even the minor vocal lines, he demanded absolute security from his singers and was outraged to struggle with such performers as Arimondi, who were unable to follow his elementary requirement, which he despairingly underscored in the same 5 December letter: '*to deliver the word and the note in time without orchestral help*'.

Only for the roles of Fenton and Nannetta did Verdi seek the lyrical voice. Concerning Nannetta Verdi wrote on 13 June 1892: 'Nannetta must be very young and sing very well: extremely brilliant on stage, above all in the two little duets with the tenor, especially in one of these, very lively and comic' (Abbiati 1959: IV, 443). He amplified his comments on 17 June, as he considered Adelina Stehle, who was eventually offered the part: '[Stehle's] voice is too thin [for Alice], but she could perform Nannetta well if she brings the role a little sentiment besides the *brio*. In the third act there is a fantastic, misty, pathetic song that she would have to perform well' (Ibid. IV, 445).

Verdi's most concise description of Fenton's part is found in a letter to Ricordi from midsummer 1892, as he was considering Angelo Masini for the role. Here one senses the significance of the purely musical aspect of the III.ii sonnet:

It is a charming, comic, brilliant part with some singing scenes, such as the *Sonnet* that he sings at midnight in Windsor Forest. If the music succeeds there, he, Masini, would certainly benefit greatly. All in all, considered as a whole, an extremely charming, brilliant character who has a part in many scenes without being tiresome. Except for the sonnet, a part [like the others, that requires attention] *to notes, words, and gestures.*                                    (Ibid. IV, 446)

Much to his distress, Verdi could not easily obtain Masini as Fenton and had to settle for the inexperienced Edoardo Garbin. Verdi coached the young tenor in Genoa for nearly a month, from at least 16 November until 11 December 1892, and as he taught him the part he vented his frustrations on Giulio Ricordi. Again and again Verdi lamented that Garbin could not learn his part, that he could not sing a line undoubled by the orchestra, and (Verdi's *idée fixe*) that he clouded his words with incorrect vowels. Many of these complaints have already appeared in print (Abbiati 1959: IV, 466-9, Chusid 1979: 171-2), but his letter to Ricordi of 20 November 1892 is still widely unknown:

Near the end of the month [perhaps] Garbin could go to Milan, and there he would need to find not a *Maestro di Canto* but a Pedant who would teach him *notes, tempo*, and the *neat and clear word* well. And who wouldn't let him open his final vowels. For example, when he pronounces 'che gli risponde alla [sic] sua parolaaa', the *a* is so open that his voice changes and seems to be somebody else's. This is a serious defect, above all in *Falstaff*, where there are many spoken things without the support of flutes and clarinets.                           (unpublished)

Given Verdi's remarks about the other parts, it may seem surprising that he left no written advice about the major role in the opera, that of Falstaff. Clearly, the reason is that Verdi never doubted whom he wanted to sing the part: Victor Maurel, who had so strikingly brought Iago to life in the 1887 *Otello* première. For that role Verdi had prized not so much his voice, although it was generally conceded to be splendid, but his gifts of commanding the stage and projecting the text dramatically. It is characteristic of Verdi, for instance, to have written on 11 November

Fig. 12   Costume design for Falstaff, Act III (Adolph Hohenstein, 1892)

Fig. 11   Costume design for Falstaff (Adolph Hohenstein, 1892)

1886: 'Iago is not performable and is not possible without pronouncing [the words] extraordinarily well, as Maurel [does] . . . One need neither sing nor raise the voice in that part (except for a few exceptions). For example, if I were a singing actor, I would say everything at half-voice, at the tip of my lips' (Abbiati 1959: IV, 299). Maurel's talents probably account for the declamatory nature of Falstaff's part.

Since Maurel is such an important figure in the first *Falstaff* performances, both in Milan and in Paris, his 1907 recording of 'Quand'ero paggio', now available on long-playing record, is a fundamental performance document. His towering security − and vanity − are faithfully preserved. With piano accompaniment he performs the song three times, the final time in French, urged on by a seemingly insatiable claque. Just as in the drama Falstaff casually offers Alice the story of his slender youth, Maurel tosses off the song with irresistible nonchalance and self-assurance.

Still, Verdi would not have been completely pleased by the performance. Maurel's pronunciation is faulty by the composer's standards (not by his own: George Bernard Shaw's column in *The World* on 20 July 1892 tells us that Maurel had developed an elaborate, 'scientific' system of vowel substitution to enhance vocal performance); he changes a few rhythms and pitches and favours a casual legato over the crisp staccato marked in the score; and, worst of all, he takes the piece too slowly, about 88-90 to the crotchet instead of the indicated 112. His propensity to slacken Verdi's tempi was rémarked, and censured, by Ricordi in the 19 March 1893 *Gazzetta musicale*, less than a month after the première and after Verdi had returned to Genoa.

Excessively slow tempi were not the least of Maurel's documented offences. Apparently dissatisfied with the effect (or the demands) of his III.i monologue during the spring 1894 Parisian performances, he simply cut it out altogether. Bellaigue informed Verdi of the fact in late May: 'The other day he massacred the second reprise of "Quando ero paggio". . . I think that the next time he'll sing standing on his hands; next year he'll sing on horseback bursting through paper hoops . . . The whole monologue was omitted the other day . . . The curtain has scarcely gone up by the time that Quickly enters with *Révérence*' (Ibid. IV, 544). Verdi immediately denounced the cut and Maurel's impudence in making it.

The 1907 recording, then, fails to tell us much about the composer's wishes. It does, however, convey the professional assurance that was at once Maurel's glory − it was this, surely, that had attracted Verdi's attention in the first place − and, pushed too far, his principal weakness.

Modern singers should expect to find in the recording a spur to their own boldness, not a presumed 'definitive' interpretation of the role.

Verdi's interest in the performance was not limited to matters of vocal delivery. His complementary demand for flexible, realistic theatrical gestures led him to supervise the Milanese rehearsals from 4 January to 7 February 1893. *Falstaff* required about 60 rehearsals (often two or three a day): piano rehearsals until about 21 January and staged orchestral rehearsals from that date onward.

We know few details of this activity, because Ricordi and Verdi insisted that the rehearsals be closed to the press and public. Still, from Ricordi's delicately prepared descriptions, his few press releases, and a few rehearsal documents in Verdi's hand, it is clear that the composer actively suggested tempi, interpretation, stage movements, and so on. Even in matters where he willingly shared his authority with others — with Hohenstein in the scenery and costumes, with Ricordi and Boito in the staging, with Mascheroni in orchestral balance and interpretation — he still retained his right to intervene. And from all reports the fiery, 79-year-old perfectionist did precisely that every day.

Ricordi's picture of Verdi may be seen most clearly in a February 1893 article: 'How Giuseppe Verdi Writes and Rehearses'. This piece of unashamed puffery depicts the *maestro* as indefatigable, efficient, and certain about the placement of every detail. Like most caricatures, this one is probably basically true, if exaggerated. Ricordi should not be doubted, for example, when he maintains that Verdi demanded the proper pronunciation to the point of forcing the singers to repeat individual words and phrases until he was satisfied, and that he opposed the practice of holding the high notes. And, even though the advice is too vague to be of much practical value today, the editor was surely correct when he wrote that Verdi wished the gestures to arise spontaneously from an understanding of the words and music: `

All the artists remain around the pianoforte, attentively follow the *maestro*'s instructions, and seek to interpret them, while he shows at half-voice the inflections of the voice part. This is the true point of departure for the so-called staging. The singers, more secure in their [musical] parts, begin to come alive. The more intelligent try out a few gestures: Verdi observes them attentively, admonishes or encourages or praises them, or animates them even more. The parts used for study are little by little, almost unconsciously, left on the pianoforte: the artist gets away from them and begins (as Verdi says) to put on the clothes of the character. Verdi's eyes begin to flash at once and remain constantly on the performer. Then two or three form a group, and Verdi directs their steps, motions, and gestures – he suggests and corrects. Should a motion or gesture not satisfy him, he himself takes the place of the character and vigorously indicates by reciting or singing how the role must be interpreted.

In the *Gazzetta musicale* of 14 May 1893 Ricordi printed an anecdote that showed how direct Verdi's interventions could become. During a rehearsal of the love duettino in I.ii, 'Labbra di foco', Edoardo Garbin (Fenton) and Adelina Stehle (Nannetta) seemed too reserved for young lovers. After Boito's encouragement failed to resolve the problem Verdi shot up impetuously: 'Why are we daydreaming here? Make these two kisses real, and there will be the naturalness you are seeking. Here, Nannetta, I'll be Fenton for a moment: you do it like this – and like this.'

Several of Verdi's remarks during the rehearsals are preserved on small slips of paper which he used as reminders. Over two dozen are still extant, primarily in two collections: one originally owned by Edoardo Mascheroni and partially transcribed in Edoardo Susmel's *Un secolo di vita teatrale fiumana* (Fiume, 1926); and the other pasted into the proofs of the first vocal edition (now housed in the library of the Milan Conservatory). Although many slips are enigmatic, others suggest Verdi's concerns and some of the problems that he encountered. For instance, from the Mascheroni–Susmel collection:

'Quando ero paggio' too slow. [Cf. Maurel's recording.]
The finale [of II.ii] always *pianissimo* except for the phrase 'Voi sarete l'ala destra'; then the rest *ppp*, always less *marcato*; then the first time for 'affogo, affogo' and I would like to see Falstaff's snout come out of the laundry for the first time.
So the basket is prepared a little bit later, and all the men ought to come out impetuously when they say 'Patatrac' [at the end of II.ii].
'Quando il ritocco [sic] della' etc. [in III.i]: pay attention to the piccolo.
The sonnet [III.ii] ought to be delivered more *a tempo*, without haste. At the end of the sonnet they ought not to kiss because they are interrupted by Alice.
The piccolo louder in the fugue.

And from the proof collection:

Tell *Falstaff* and *Ford* to beat the sack of money in time [to its music in II.i].
Falstaff's solo 'L'amor, l'amor' [II.i] more *scherzoso*.
Bardolfo's 'Furfanteria' [III.ii] a little bit towards the public.

Two additional observations may be found in an undated note that the composer wrote to Ricordi during the period of the rehearsals:

For the staging let's not complain about every little thing. Now we should let things go as they are and not confuse our heads with observations. I ask only for a little light in Garbin's *Sonnet*. And, if possible, to find a way of avoiding the impression that the Chorus of Fairies are *Vestals* – so they seemed to me. For that matter, even this isn't very important.

(Abbiati 1959: IV, 471)

In addition, four timings that Verdi wrote into the proofs inform us about the 1893 tempi, probably during a rehearsal. According to these indications, I.i lasted 14½ minutes and I.ii 14 minutes. In III.ii Verdi timed the passage from no. 34 (after 'Sono le Fate') to no. 42 ('Cialtron!') at 5½ minutes; and from no. 42 to the bar before no. 45 ('Riconosco Bardolfo') at 1½ minutes. These timings, of course, do not necessarily imply approval; on the other hand, had he disapproved, we would expect some indication of it alongside the written timings. These durations may be supplemented by those of the virtually uninterrupted final rehearsal on 7 February 1893, as reported two days later in an *indiscrezione* in *La Lombardia*: 'The [dress] rehearsal began at exactly 9 o'clock. The first act lasted precisely one half-hour, the second and third 50 minutes each.'

Verdi's preparations for the first production seem to be dominated by a single idea: evoking a genuine, positive response from the audience. Clearly, the challenge for any *Falstaff* production is to invite the viewer into an appreciation of verbal and musical subtlety; to ensnare the audience into following a nearly constant succession of spotlighted moments. In an opera so skilfully texted, so rapid in its action, Verdi stressed pronunciation, clarity, and realistic, immediately comprehensible gestures. *Falstaff* must impress through small details, and Verdi continually took pains to illuminate them.

In the nineteenth century the audience proclaimed its enthusiasm by applauding and calling for the *bis*, or encore. Verdi hoped for such interruptions, even with *Falstaff* and its continuous music. At the première two pieces were repeated, clearly with Verdi's consent and pleasure: the women's quartet 'Quell'otre! quel tino!' and 'Quand'ero paggio'. Because the audience that first evening could not possibly have known exactly when any piece concluded, Verdi must have required the applause to be invited in one way or another. This would have been mandatory with the quartet. At its conclusion (no. 26) the women are leaving the stage, the men have just entered, and nothing separates the last note of the quartet from the opening line of the quintet. It is inconceivable that an uninitiated audience would have broken the music here, unless something provoked them to do so. The most likely provocation in this instance would be an emphatic, perhaps *poco ritardando* cadence into no. 26

followed by a *Luftpause* before Cajus begins the quintet. The only alternative is a planted claque.

However the opportunity for the encore might have been made available, Verdi must have planned it in advance. This is all the more curious, because 'Quell'otre! quel tino!' may not strike us today as the most obvious choice for a *bis*. We know that the audience asked that Nannetta's 'Sul fil d'un soffio etesio' be repeated in III.ii and that Verdi refused to grant the request. Yet the self-contained Song of the Queen of the Fairies separates much more easily from its context than does the I.ii quartet. Why did the composer have the quartet repeated and not the song? Probably because of the dramatic importance that he wished to give the quartet itself. It is an unusual ensemble, innovative in its textual chaos — and yet, as Verdi explained to Ricordi on 17 March 1894: 'that quartet must have its effect, not so much for the music as for the stage action, because it immediately reveals the character of the wives, who are ultimately the ones who accomplish the comedy' (Abbiati 1959: IV, 535). Here Verdi surely took advantage of the *bis* tradition to underscore an essential but potentially difficult part of the drama. Even within the traditions of operatic performance, his goal seems to have been comprehensibility.

After the first few performances Verdi relaxed his attitude towards the availability of the encore. In Rome from 15 to 25 April 1893 he finally added Nannetta's song to the list of repeated pieces and allowed Maurel to sing 'Quand'ero paggio' three times. Later, two other pieces were encored in performances that Verdi did not attend: Ford's monologue (Trieste, 11-16 May 1893) and, as the *Gazzetta musicale* reported on 29 April 1894, a 'phrase of Alice, 3rd act' (Florence, April 1894) — probably her 'Avrò con me dei putti'. And on 17 October 1894 Verdi saw a performance in Aix-les-Bains in which Marie Delna sang Quickly's 'Giunta all'Albergo' three times (Ibid. IV, 556). He never objected to these repetitions; rather, he seems to have been pleased by them.

At first glance, one may be surprised to discover that Alice's 'Gaie comari di Windsor' and Fenton's Sonnet were not among the encored pieces. Yet Alice's solo risks being dwarfed by Quickly's preceding narrative, and it passes so rapidly into the ensuing dialogue that it is likely to speed by the audience entirely. Fenton's Sonnet, on the other hand, does not 'end'. It has no final cadence, since Alice interrupts the music and draws Fenton into the masquerade before he can sing his concluding phrase. Although Ford's monologue did — at least once — receive a repetition, there are no documented encores of Falstaff's larger solo pieces.

And, of course, duets were sung only once, even though one would think that Fenton and Nannetta's 'Labbra di foco' in I.ii must have been a powerful temptation.

Finally, a word on translation. Verdi saw nothing inviolable about the original Italian text when performed in other countries. He expected that non-Italian audiences would want to hear the opera in their own language (again, comprehensibility was the critical issue). Ricordi issued an English—Italian and a German—Italian vocal score in 1893, only a few months after the first performance and tour. As mentioned in Chapter 4, Verdi especially prized the French *Falstaff*, and he entrusted the bulk of the work to Boito, whose translation (which might well serve as a model for modern translators of this and other operas) treated his own original with remarkable freedom. It is true that the first productions in Vienna, Berlin, and London were sung in Italian, but this was more a matter of convenience for the cast than the result of an artistic credo.

On the other hand, no translation can hope to reproduce the intricacy of Boito's text, which brims over with complex, sometimes archaic vocabulary. This explosion of language is central to the *Falstaff* experience. If one takes Boito as a guide, a translation should compensate in boldness, colour, and phonetic sensitivity for what it must inevitably remove from the original. Andrew Porter has pursued this matter further in the introductory comments to his recent translation of *Falstaff* (1979).

# 7 A brief stage history

Critical reaction to the initial twenty-two La Scala performances and the subsequent tour (Genoa, Rome, Venice, Trieste, Vienna, and Berlin, from 6 April to c.6 June 1893) was almost exclusively favourable, particularly in Italy: any major criticism in that country would have amounted to *lèse-majesté*. Nevertheless, the praise was a historical fact – and an economic one for Giulio Ricordi, whose company owned the exclusive rights to the opera. Striving to keep the 'triumph' of *Falstaff* in the Italian eye, Ricordi stuffed his *Gazzetta musicale di Milano* with performance reports for months after the première. And in April 1893, surely out of commercial rather than purely artistic motives, he had edited and printed a 296-page collection of enthusiastic reviews: *Falstaff. . . Judgments in the Italian and Foreign Press* (*Giudizî della stampa italiana e straniera*).

The positive glaze that coated the early reviews could not entirely hide the stupefaction that many felt in confronting this intricate work. T. Montefiore, in an otherwise good-humoured report on the Roman *Falstaff*, touched upon the heart of the problem (*La tribuna*, 19 April 1893):

There was considerable astonishment – perhaps even disappointment – among many of the innumerable admirers of Verdi's immortal genius ... 'Is this our Verdi?', they asked themselves. 'But where is the *motive*; where are the broad melodies that decorated his earlier operas; where are the usual *ensembles*; the *finales*? Alas, all of this is buried in the past. At the age of eighty, then, does he acknowledge having changed course? Are *Rigolettos, Traviatas*, and *Aidas* no longer beautiful and fresh?'

Although the Italian press obligingly underplayed the occasional difficulties with *Falstaff*, from time to time its troubles did surface for a sentence or two. Thus, on 18 April 1893, *La perseveranza* noted that 'although the prices for the second *Falstaff* performance had been reduced from those of the first evening, they still remained so high that the theatre was half empty. Moreover, many boxes were empty, even though Rome is now populated with many visitors'.

After the La Scala tour the opera spread at once to theatres all over Europe and the Americas. The second half of 1893 saw productions in Buenos Aires (8 July, with Antonio Scotti in the title role – a part with which he would be long identified), Rio de Janeiro (29 July), Brescia (12 August), São Paulo (24 August), Stuttgart (10 September, the first performance of Max Kalbeck's German translation), Mexico City (7 October), Bucharest (October), Prague (16 November, in a Czech translation), and Turin (23 December). In early 1894 *Falstaff* was produced in Hamburg (2 January, under Gustav Mahler), St Petersburg (29 January, in a Russian translation), Madrid (10 February), Cologne (18 February), Naples (19 February), Lisbon (27 February), Munich (2 March), Berlin (6 March), Karlsruhe (11 March), Baden (14 March), Weimar (8 April), Barcelona (10 April), and, of course, Paris (18 April: see Chapter 4).

London saw its first *Falstaff* at Covent Garden on 19 May 1894. The performance, conducted by Luigi Mancinelli, boasted two important members of the original La Scala cast, Emma Zilli (Alice) and Antonio Pini-Corsi (Ford). Arturo Pessina sang Sir John, and *The Times* found him 'a far more genial Falstaff than the gloomy cynic presented by M. Maurel, whose makeup and general appearance are exactly imitated' (Rosenthal 1958: 259). The tradition of the *buffo* Falstaff – the knight as blundering clown – may have begun here. The opera received favourable reviews for its eight London performances and returned for four more in 1895, when Pessina shared the role with its creator, Victor Maurel. But it failed to enter the repertory. It did not reappear at Covent Garden until 1914 (for only two performances), and English audiences remained cool to the work for several decades afterwards.

*Falstaff*'s early stage history at the New York Metropolitan Opera mirrors that in London. Mancinelli conducted the Metropolitan première on 4 February 1895. Victor Maurel headed the cast, which included Emma Eames (Alice), Giuseppe Campanari (Ford), and Sofia Scalchi (Quickly). Maurel probably also exercised considerable influence over the sets and stage direction (he had demonstrated his interest in staging seven years earlier in a monograph on interpreting *Otello*). The opera received five performances that season in New York and returned the following year, again with Maurel, but with Armando Seppilli conducting. As had happened in London, New Yorkers lost interest in *Falstaff* after its first two seasons. It remained absent from the Metropolitan stage until 1909, Toscanini's first season.

Public malaise with the opera was beginning to invade Italy as well. In December 1894 Toscanini conducted *Falstaff* in the Teatro Carlo Felice, Genoa. The performance seems to have been excellent; Toscanini had even consulted Verdi about the proper tempo of Ford's 'Quella crudel beltà' in II.i (Sachs 1978: 45-6). Yet the public remained uninterested. Verdi wrote to Ricordi on 30 December 1894: '*Falstaff* is a fiasco! but really, a genuine fiasco. Nobody is going to the theatre! The best part is that they are saying they have never heard an opera so perfectly performed and coordinated. So we must conclude that the music is accursed!' (Abbiati 1959: IV, 566). Nor did the situation improve. On 11 January 1895 Verdi reported further: 'Last night at the Carlo Felice a reduced *Falstaff* – not in stomach, but in price!! I dare not say it! 1.50 lire. Result? *The same*' (Ibid. IV, 566). From this point onward it was clear that audiences would need much persuasion (and education) to embrace *Falstaff* as they had embraced Verdi's earlier works.

Toscanini accepted the role of persuader and educator. As a young conductor in the 1890s, a period of intense aesthetic controversy in Italy, he markedly preferred orchestrally complex operas, particularly Wagner's music dramas and Verdi's last two operas. For the next half-century *Falstaff* was closely identified with Toscanini, who made it a key production at nearly every significant juncture in his career.

In 1898 Toscanini was appointed musical director of La Scala. He began the season with *Die Meistersinger* (26 December 1898) and pointedly juxtaposed it with *Falstaff*, which opened on 11 March 1899 and received ten performances. The *Falstaff* cast included Edoardo Garbin (Fenton) and Adelina Stehle (Nannetta) – now husband and wife – from the first production, along with Antonio Scotti (Falstaff) and Angelica Pandolfini (Alice). The very firmness of Toscanini's control provoked criticism. From Genoa Verdi soon warned Ricordi of his antipathy to conductors who behaved as tyrants. Ricordi, meanwhile, was mounting a campaign against Toscanini in the *Gazzetta musicale*. The conductor's conception was too stiff, he argued, too metronomic; it was 'metallic' and reminded one of an 'incessant pendulum'; it lacked the 'delicate shadings' and 'elasticity of movement' that Ricordi identified as characteristic of Italian orchestras (Ibid. IV, 636-7). It would appear that the Verdi–Wagner struggle lay behind much of the criticism, although Ricordi also had personal reasons for attacking Toscanini, who had recently neglected to include one of Ricordi's compositions in the Turin orchestral concerts (Sachs 1978: 69).

Ten years later, in 1908, Toscanini and Giulio Gatti-Casazza began their joint directorship of the Metropolitan Opera. Toscanini selected *Falstaff* for his first season, and it appeared for the first of three performances on 20 March 1909, with Scotti (Falstaff), Emmy Destinn (Alice), Giuseppe Campanari (Ford), Maria Gay (Quickly), Frances Alda (Nannetta), and Rinaldo Grassi (Fenton).

One provocative offshoot of the 1909 *Falstaff* (which was revived the following year and then remained absent from the Metropolitan until Tullio Serafin conducted it in 1925) is Scotti's recording (7 October 1909) of 'L'onore! Ladri!', the conclusion of I.i. The recording surely shows the influence of both Victor Maurel (whom Scotti deeply admired but who never recorded this excerpt) and Toscanini. Scotti conceives most of the monologue as song. He carefully sings the pitches as written, even in the face of such temptations as the purely declamatory 'Possiam star ligi al nostro' (13 bars after no. 14) and 'E vi discaccio' (no. 17). Only at the conclusion does he switch to the conventional shouts for 'Lesti, lesti, lesti, al galoppo' and 'Ladri!' (beginning 7 bars after no. 17). His rhythms, however, become increasingly free as the monologue progresses. Some of them seem to be unnecessary errors: 'Sì, io, io', 14 bars after no. 14, sung to quavers instead of semiquavers, but characteristically, at the proper pitches; the unfortunate misplacing of 'No!' a beat too early, 8 bars after no. 15; the borrowing of the accompaniment's triple rhythms beginning with 'perchè a torto / Lo gonfian le lusinghe', 5 bars before no. 16. Others seem to be intentional *rubati*, possibly inspired by Maurel: the free pulse of the 'Può l'onore riempirvi la pancia?' section, no. 15; the conversion of 'Una parola', 12 bars after no. 15, into a crotchet, dotted quaver and semiquaver, and two crotchets; and the slow *ad libitum* declamation at the first bar of no. 16, 'e per me non ne', before the launch into the following *poco più mosso*. Since most of these discrepancies from the score do not reappear in any Toscanini recordings of *Falstaff*, Scotti's 1909 recording with a different conductor may have reinstated some of the late-*ottocento* flexibility that Toscanini might have been denying him.

In 1913, the centenary of Verdi's birth, Toscanini contributed to the celebrations by directing *Falstaff* in the tiny theatre of Busseto, near Sant'Agata. The festivities continued with another *Falstaff* under Toscanini at La Scala: six performances beginning on 21 October, again with Scotti, in what Carlo Gatti describes as 'a great success: another step forward in this masterpiece's slow progress towards attaining the public's fully developed comprehension and love' (1964: 253).

The 1920s were decisive for *Falstaff*, and once again Toscanini led the charge. Newly appointed as the general artistic director of a completely reorganized La Scala — it was now an autonomous society (*ente autonomo*), depending less on the old elite of boxholders and more on the general public and Milanese tax money — he chose to open the first season with *Falstaff* (26 December 1921), as if to stress its significance. Toscanini subordinated virtually everything in the staging and music to the letter of Verdi and Boito's text. Apparently, he even required the

set designer, V. Rota, to remain faithful to Hohenstein's original sets:
Rota's set for I.i, reproduced in Gatti's *Verdi nelle immagini* (1941: 137),
is essentially the same as Hohenstein's. Moreover, Toscanini had personal-
ly selected Mariano Stabile as Falstaff, and had taught him the role, line
by line (Sachs 1978: 149-50). This was Stabile's début at La Scala: he
was to become one of the most prominent Falstaffs of the century, singing the part nearly 1200 times (Ibid. p. 149).

More significant than the nine *Falstaff* performances of 1921-2 was
Toscanini's decision to include it in every season for seven years thereafter. It would appear that he was counting on frequent rehearings to
break down the barriers between the opera and the public. Thus, La Scala
saw eight performances in 1923, eight more in 1924, five in 1925, four
in 1926 (with Ettore Panizza, Toscanini's co-conductor, at the podium),
five in 1927 (again with Toscanini), four in 1928, and two in 1929.

Immediately after the 1929 season, his last as director of La Scala,
Toscanini took *Falstaff* and the entire company to Vienna (18 May 1929)
and Berlin (22 May) – thus duplicating the conclusion of the 1893 La
Scala tour. These performances attracted such figures as Herbert von
Karajan, Paul Stefan, Alfred Einstein, Bruno Walter, Wilhelm Furtwängler,
Fritz Busch, Otto Klemperer, Erich Kleiber, and Paul Bekker (Ibid. pp.
191-4). Karajan later recalled the performance's impact:

From the first bar, it was as if I had been struck a blow. I was completely
disconcerted by the perfection which had been achieved ... To be sure,
Toscanini had employed a stage director; but basically, the essential conception came from him. The agreement between the music and the stage
performance was something totally inconceivable for us.

(Ibid. p. 191)

Toscanini's successes with *Falstaff* continued into the Salzburg Festivals of 1935, 1936, and 1937. His conception of the opera was as unbend-
ing as ever: it was here that he refused to perform it unless Robert
Kautsky's pre-existing Viennese set for III.i, which had Falstaff begin the
act in bed (rather than at a bench outside the inn, as called for in the
score), was totally redone. Of particular documentary value is the live
recording of the performance on 26 July 1937, the earlier of the two
complete Toscanini recordings and the only one with Stabile. Curiously,
this performance (unlike all later recordings, including Toscanini's) was
essentially of the 'Roman' version, not the usual hybrid between the
Roman and Parisian versions (see Chapter 4).

With the Vienna, Berlin, and Salzburg performances, the 'internation-
alization' of *Falstaff* had at last begun. In New York the Metropolitan
Opera performed it in 1938 (under Panizza, with Lawrence Tibbett as

Falstaff), 1943 (Beecham), 1944 (Beecham again – this time it was broadcast), and 1948 (Reiner). On 1 and 8 April 1950 Toscanini conducted *Falstaff* for the radio (half the opera on each date), with the NBC Symphony Orchestra and Giuseppe Valdengo (not Mariano Stabile) in the title role. This broadcast, later released on long-playing records, greatly facilitated the work's dissemination.

*Falstaff* eventually found its way into British favour not so much at Covent Garden but rather at the Edinburgh Festivals of the mid-1950s, in the Glyndebourne production. As early as 1934 Verdi's biographer Francis Toye had been eager to hear this Shakespearean opera 'in such typically English surroundings as those of Glyndebourne' (Hughes 1965: 47). Fritz Busch had hoped to produce *Falstaff* there in the late 1930s – and, indeed, there was talk of inviting Toscanini in 1938 and 1939 as a post-*Anschluss* extension of his Salzburg performances – but these early projects came to nothing. Glyndebourne finally produced *Falstaff* at the Edinburgh Festival of 1955, with Carlo Maria Giulini conducting and Fernando Corena in the leading role. Many reviewers commented on Osbert Lancaster's spare but brightly coloured sets and costumes and Carl Ebert's controversial staging. Ebert demanded, for example, that Fenton slip and fall during one of his duets with Nannetta, and that Alice poke Falstaff in the stomach during their II.ii duet (Shawe-Taylor 1957: 543), and he included among the pranks of III.ii a caricature of Lady Godiva riding a hobby-horse (Hughes 1965: 201). The opera succeeded splendidly and was revived in 1957 (with Vittorio Gui conducting and Geraint Evans as Falstaff), 1958, and 1960 (when the BBC televised and relayed it throughout Europe).

Perhaps the most widely attended productions in recent times have been those designed and staged by Franco Zeffirelli. Zeffirelli's first significant *Falstaff* – for the 1956 Holland Festival, with Giulini and the Glyndebourne cast of the preceding year – pleased through its freshness and originality, which at times contradicted the original instructions of Boito and Verdi. Leo Riemens described the event as

the most perfect *Falstaff* I have ever seen (and I have seen it six times with Stabile!). Scorning all tradition, he placed the period in Shakespeare's own time [almost two centuries later, that is, than the 'proper' period—the reign of Henry IV]. The costumes were so absolutely right that one had the illusion of looking at some very old Dutch masters. The Garter Inn was as perfect as Ford's house, though I was rather disappointed in his two street scenes . . . The action came straight from the music.                                                              (1956: 535)

Five years later Zeffirelli created a new *Falstaff* for Covent Garden.

The production, which was revived in subsequent years, opened on 10 May 1961, and its first audiences 'displayed an enthusiasm for *Falstaff* as never before in London' (Rosenthal 1961: 469). The cast, under Giulini's direction, included Geraint Evans (Falstaff), Mariella Angioletti (Alice), John Shaw (Ford), Regina Resnik (Quickly), Mirella Freni (Nannetta), and Luigi Alva (Fenton). Zeffirelli's spectacular sets and costumes complemented his detailed staging – detailed, once again, beyond the requirements of the score. 'There are too many ideas, too many things happening at once', observed Harold Rosenthal. 'Zeffirelli's production, like his conversation, simply bubbles over with invention' (Ibid. p. 470). Some critics, while admitting the brilliance of the realistic staging, remained sceptical of Zeffirelli's licences: his failure to have Alice show Ford the scene out of the window at the end of II.ii; Sir John's beginning Act III by entering dripping wet, having just pulled himself out of the Thames; Herne's Oak in III.ii being suddenly lifted out of sight into the flies before Falstaff's punishment begins (Jacobs 1961: 744); and the 'Litany' ('Domine fallo casto') staged as a parody of an ecclesiastical procession (Rosenthal 1961: 470).

Zeffirelli pushed his visual reinterpretation further with a sumptuous new production at the Metropolitan Opera on 6 March 1964, conducted by Leonard Bernstein, with Anselmo Colzani (Falstaff), Gabriella Tucci (Alice), Mario Sereni (Ford), Regina Resnik (Quickly), Judith Raskin (Nannetta), and Luigi Alva (Fenton). Zeffirelli's sets again evoked Renaissance England, but were more monumental, realistic, and flamboyantly detailed than at Covent Garden (e.g., the huge wooden beer barrel prominently displayed in the Garter Inn). The general conception, however, took the action far beyond the Renaissance. Zeffirelli explained his intentions shortly before the production opened:

For the Met I'm making a more decorative version, with a nineteenth-century flavor. A rural world, a world of country gentlemen. The women are housewives. In fact, we first see them gossiping in their back yards [in which they hang out the washing] . . . There will be hens pecking outside the tavern, geese in the yards – and for the *féerie* in the last act a white donkey, a pony. The finale should be like a children's picture book. You can't get good animals in Rome. (Weaver 1964: 30)

Clearly, at this point we have gone beyond anything imagined by Verdi, Boito, or Hohenstein. The exuberantly visual extravaganza becomes as much (or more) about Zeffirelli as about the original work of art itself.

With the more general public acceptance of *Falstaff* in the past two decades (particularly as an opera suited to festivals and special productions), producers have felt freer to experiment, to impose their own personalities on the score. The starting point, indeed, may be a sumptuous stage picture with rich, 'historical' furnishings, as in Luchino Visconti's 1966 Vienna *Falstaff* (with Leonard Bernstein and a controversial, *gemütlich* Dietrich Fischer-Dieskau), which included sets and costumes in the style of Vermeer or Hals (Wechsberg 1966: 358). But one also frequently encounters 'extramusical' details and comic effects added to personalize the production as the work of an individual producer. Götz Friedrich's stagings, for example (Holland Festival, 1972; Berlin, 1977), relied heavily on reinterpretation and extraneous activity. Some of the additions had social or political overtones: for instance, portraying Fenton, now an apprentice to Ford, 'making love to Nannetta among the packing cases on her father's wharf' (Sutcliffe 1978: 370). Most, however, were simple visual jokes, sometimes in questionable taste: Sir John peering into Quickly's bodice; a supernumerary deaf widow with an ear-trumpet introduced into the laundry-basket scene; and the entire cast singing 'Tutto nel mondo è burla' while laughing at the audience and dangling their feet into the orchestra pit (Ibid. p. 370).

Sarah Caldwell's busy 1975 production in Boston (sung in Andrew Porter's translation, with Donald Gramm as Falstaff) similarly stressed the visual. Elaborating on Zeffirelli's opening gimmick in the third act, Caldwell inaugurated the action by floating two swans and an empty laundry basket across the set, after which the drenched Falstaff, tangled in river reeds, climbed up from beneath the stage (Baxter 1975: 383). Jean-Pierre Ponnelle's *Falstaff* at Glyndebourne the following year (also with Gramm), which Arthur Jacobs reviewed as 'the most Shakespearean production of Verdi's opera I have ever seen' (1976: 36), varied the Zeffirelli–Caldwell joke: Falstaff entered the third act by climbing out of the orchestra pit.

Notwithstanding its relatively recent entrance into the standard repertory, *Falstaff* will probably always present difficulties for its stage director. Unlike some of the earlier Verdi operas, its rapidity of action, its fleeting musical motives, its closeness of dramatic detail, and, above all, the extreme subtlety of Boito's text with its consciously intellectual content render rapid comprehension virtually impossible. Thus, the danger any producer faces is that a significant portion of the audience will be excluded from the ritual of participation. In our century *Falstaff* productions have dealt with this problem in two ways, the 'solutions' appearing sometimes separately and sometimes intermixed in various proportions. The first solution – Toscanini's – pins its hopes on repetitions and rehearings: in short, on the gradual education of the audience. Much of this education can now be accomplished through recordings:

indeed, recorded performances may have been the strongest factor in launching *Falstaff* into the current repertory. The second solution, particularly favoured where the opera is performed before uninitiated audiences in a language not their own, is to rely on brilliant sets, underscoring the text with explicit gestures, and adding comic or slapstick details (or animals) to cajole the audience into attention. The wise comedy of Verdi's old age lends itself easily (perhaps too easily) to clownish misinterpretation and self-indulgent spectacle. Ultimately, if Verdi's opera is genuinely to succeed, the first solution – the more honest – must prevail.

# 8 *A guide to critical assessments and interpretations*

### The place of *Falstaff* in the Verdian *oeuvre*: the Wagner problem

Most commentators have considered the central problem of *Falstaff* to be that of reconciling it with the rest of Verdi's career. For many, his last opera seems an anomalous work. Besides being his only major comedy and most overtly motivic or symphonic opera, it shows his nearly total dissolution of *ottocento* operatic forms and his surprising elevation of the text to a plane equal to that of the music. How could Verdi have produced such an opera? Does it consciously disavow his past work or grow directly from it? In a genre that had for so long boiled over with music of immediate impact, is the subtlety of *Falstaff* an advance or a retreat?

In the 1890s these questions were conceived under the sway of the prevailing paradigms of musical change: Wagnerianism and symphonic opera. Ever since the Bolognese première of *Lohengrin* in 1871 – of whose impact Gino Monaldi later remarked 'The triumphant entrance of the northern swan struck our national art, personified in G. Verdi, squarely in the breast' (in Jung 1974: 429) – Wagner's music dramas had gradually invaded Italy and fired the minds of young musicians as the most progressive music in Europe. By 1895, two years after *Falstaff*, Italy had heard some 861 performances of *Lohengrin*, 152 of *Tannhäuser*, sixty-two of *Der fliegende Holländer*, fifty to sixty of *Die Walküre*, twenty-five of *Die Meistersinger*, and seven of *Tristan und Isolde* (Ibid. pp. 183-4). And it was widely perceived that the younger generation of Italian composers – especially Puccini and the *veristi* – were experimenting with the techniques of symphonic opera.

The most ardent controversies raged in Milan. By 1895 Monaldi described the Wagnerian issue as having produced sides 'comparable to political factions, with the customary slogans. Thus, the proponents of Wagner brand those faithful to the [traditional] Italian programme as "cabalettisti", "pedanti", "codini" [pigtailed or old-fashioned]. For their part, these opponents use names like "germanisti", "scapigliati" [dishevelled or uncurbed], "avveniristi" [futurists]' (Ibid. p. 429). Small wonder, then, that both inside and out of Italy many critics saw in *Falstaff* Verdi's adoption of Wagnerian methods. It was not a matter of myths and philosophy, leitmotivic construction, or prevailing chromaticism. Rather, *Falstaff* seemed to veer in the direction of orchestral complexity, constant development, attenuation of the melodic line, and subordination of music to text.

Non-Italian critics wrote more comfortably about these matters. Henry Krehbiel's review of the Metropolitan Opera première in 1895 summarizes the perspective well:

The production of 'Otello' and 'Falstaff' created as great an excitement in Italy as the first performance of 'Parsifal' did in Germany; and it must have seemed like the irony of fate to many that Wagner should have to be filtered through Verdi in order to bear fruit in the original home of the art form . . . [In *Falstaff*] the orchestra is the bearer of everything, just as completely as it is in the latter-day dramas of Richard Wagner; it supplies phrases for the singers, supports their voices, comments on their utterances, and gives dramatic color to even the most fleeting idea . . . The flood upon which the vocal melody floats is not like that of Wagner; it is not a development of fixed phrases, though Verdi, too, knows the use of leading motives in a sense, but a current which is ever receiving new waters. The declamation is managed with extraordinary skill, and though it frequently grows out of the instrumental part, it has yet independent melodic value as the vocal parts of Wagner's 'Die Meistersinger' have . . . The finales of 'Falstaff' have been built up with all of Verdi's oldtime skill, and sometimes sound like Mozart rubbed through the Wagnerian sieve.                    (Krehbiel 1909: 248-50)

'This sense of *Falstaff*'s departure from the Italian norm was widely remarked upon, as might be expected, in Germany and Austria. The translator of *Falstaff* into German, Max Kalbeck, blissfully unaware that Verdi and Boito had been confident that they had restored Shakespeare's comedy 'back again to its clear Tuscan source' (see p. 34 above), reviewed La Scala's 1893 Vienna production enthusiastically, and insisted that:

the figure of the wine-drenched, phlegmatic Epicurean with his thick self-satisfaction and merry self-deception, his systematic vulgarity and surpassingly delightful irony, is an old-Germanic device and may count on general understanding only in the north. Just as the content and the ingenious Shakespearean libretto point back from the south over the Alps, so too the music surely employs northern solidity and structure. An Italian comic opera that appeals to German seriousness: that is certainly a remarkable phenomenon and an important sign of the times.

Nicolai's *Lustige Weiber* is without a doubt more Italian than Verdi's *Falstaff*.                    (Kalbeck 1898: II, 35-6)

Such sentiments — undoubtedly widespread — must have been profoundly disheartening in Italy, particularly to those who most closely identified Verdi with the cause of Italian nationalism. Far from 'Mediterraneanizing' music, as Boito had wished, *Falstaff* could easily be misconstrued as a denial of the Italian tradition, a capitulation to the north.

By the end of the century Verdi's presumed assimilation of Wagner had become axiomatic, and writers of textbooks elevated it into the central element of the composer's late style. In Germany, Hugo Riemann wrote in his *Geschichte der Musik seit Beethoven* (1901, pp. 346-7):

A significant change of style separates 'late' Verdi from the works of his middle period. This, quite frankly, is to be traced to the influence of Richard Wagner, who in the meantime had grown into a giant. It is true that Verdi by no means converted to Wagner's musico-dramatic theories. Yet he may have renounced closed melody-structures in favour of declamation, and it seems likely that he adopted Wagner's refined treatment of the orchestra, his harmonic-modulatory technique [!], his animation of inner voices, and the breadth of the execution of certain passages. He assimilated everything that could be accepted to the greatest extent possible without denying his own nature.

In England, the Germanic point of view was carried on in 1905 by Edward Dannreuther in the sixth volume of *The Oxford History of Music* (2nd ed. 1931: 64): '[In *Otello* and *Falstaff*] the master seems to have reversed his artistic direction, and to have adopted a more intellectual speculative "Wagnerian" gait'. Thus, Verdi's late style could be praised and accepted as an advance over (or exorcism of) his earlier, cruder style, which most historians could excuse only by identifying it with a specific historical movement: the *Risorgimento*. The whole 'German' issue was also forcefully introduced into the first major Italian study of Verdi's complete operas: Luigi Torchi's 'Verdi's Works and Their Principal Characteristics' (1901 in Italian). The pro-Wagnerian Torchi, writing immediately after Verdi's death, succinctly described the *maestro*'s emergence out of the purely Italian style of his youth: 'Meyerbeer and Halévy prepared the transformation; Wagner completed it' (p. 294).

To focus one's explanation of Verdi's growth on the influence of Wagner now seems simplistic. As I have suggested in Chapter 5, *Falstaff* (with the exception of its final fugue and — if one concedes its existence — the opening sonata-form) may be largely apprehended within the context of Italian opera traditions, particularly as Verdi had modified them throughout his career. One may argue, probably accurately, that the trends toward motivic construction, orchestral complexity, innovative textual and musical forms, and ongoing continuity originated in the historical pressures of 'progress' and 'originality' as defined by the implicit (and sometimes explicit) aesthetics of nineteenth-century Germanic music. But such 'influences' were general and all-pervasive. Put another way, Verdi might have been aided in his stylistic development by the Wagnerian example, but one need not consider it to have been a precondition of that development. Even in those passages of *Falstaff* most reminiscent of Wagner — Budden rightly notices the resemblance between the polymetrical ensemble near the end of I.ii and the ensemble concluding Act I of *Die Meistersinger* and calls it 'Verdi's most substantial debt to his great contemporary' (1981: 471) — few would dispute the claim that Verdi's personality and integrity remain intact. More to the point, Verdi and Boito almost certainly intended *Falstaff* to reveal how the excesses of Wagnerianism could be avoided. It was to be a counter-example to help stem the Germanic flood (see pp. 33-4 above).

A few early critics detected the impotence of the Wagnerian 'explanation'. Budden (Ibid. pp. 440-1) cites the reviews of Alfred Bruneau and Charles Villiers Stanford, but it was probably George Bernard Shaw who most fervently (and excessively) argued the point:

Of the music of Schumann, Brahms, and Wagner, there is not anywhere in Verdi the faintest trace. In German music the Italian loved what Italy gave. What Germany offered of her own music he entirely ignored . . . But in his defects, as in his efficiencies, his directness, and his practical common sense, Verdi is a thorough unadulterated Italian. Nothing in his work needs tracing to any German source . . . The anxious northern genius is magnificently assimilative: the self-sufficient Italian genius is magnificently impervious . . . Certainly, where you come to a strong Italian like Verdi you may be quite sure that if you cannot explain him without dragging in the great Germans, you cannot explain him at all.

(1901; in Shaw 1956: 137-46)

With the Germanic re-evaluation of Verdi in the 1920s, a 'Verdian Renaissance' due in large measure to the propagandizing efforts of such men as Franz Werfel and Paul Stefan, the Wagnerian explanation fell into disrepute. Now German and Austrian scholars began to stress late Verdi's differences from Wagner and to view *Falstaff* as the logical culmination of his career. 'Italian opera reaches the innermost perfection in Verdi's *Falstaff* (1893), which is simultaneously a point of departure for the musical connecting of antithetical scenes', wrote Guido Adler in his *Handbuch der Musikgeschichte* (1924, rev. 1930: II, 998). Similarly, Ernst Bücken, in his celebrated *Die Musik des 19. Jahrhunderts bis zur Moderne* (1928), could now focus his discussion on the character of Falstaff as a 'typological figure', yet one with idiosyncratic individuality: 'Here the characteristic contrasts with Wagner's art may be clearly observed. Where the German grasps the essence of the purely human in the Idealistic, Verdi understands it within the frame of the Realistic-Typical' (1928: 290-1). By 1937 Alfred Einstein was ingenuously writing of *Falstaff* as a means of legitimizing the composer's other operas:

> *Falstaff* throws a light back over all of Verdi's previous work. It changes the aspect of this work; there must be more to it than we believed; the master who could create such an opera did not write *Trovatore* as mere hand organ music . . . Verdi's secret (I am not now speaking of the so-called secrets of form) lies as deep as Wagner's.
>
> (1937; in Einstein 1956: 87)

In the past fifty years, then, German — along with English and American — historians have felt free to investigate Verdi's development on its own terms. An adequate discussion of those terms, however, has only begun to emerge with the new Verdi research of the past fifteen years.

The whole Wagner issue, however, deeply affected Italy's perception of Verdi. Indeed, some have even argued that it hindered the development of a rigorously intellectual assessment of the *maestro* for many years after his death (e.g., Ronga 1941: 284). Whatever the cause, it is clear that two contradictory views of Verdi's *oeuvre* soon arose in Italy. One group of critics stridently denied that the composer of the last operas was the true Verdi. Considering the essence of *ottocento* opera to be the bold clash of unadorned, elemental emotions, these critics interpreted Verdi's career as rising to a peak in the early 1850s (*Rigoletto, Il trovatore, La traviata*) and declining in inspiration thereafter. In this manner they hoped to render the Wagner problem irrelevant, since it applied only to his latest, weakest, and least characteristic works.

The classic text of this position is Bruno Barilli's argument which first appeared in *Il paese del melodramma* in 1929:

> I am not among those who claim that *Falstaff* is a masterpiece and place it above the other Verdi operas. In this 'great masterpiece', every Kapellmeister's comfort and instructive example, violent contacts and frictions calm down and become reasonable. The lava cools. Nothing remains of the fire but warm ashes . . . The public stays away respectfully, to make room for [the experts'] profitable and loving inventory-work . . . Here Verdi became a Protestant, as far as he could, circumspectly pouring out the last drops of his genius and the melancholy tendernesses of his discrete, senile *verve*.
>
> But his former voice is weak. His attitudes are no longer the marvellous, split-open, superabundant fruits of intuition. His decisions are crossed by a new, troubling element. A sad, brown shadow stretches out page after page in this score. In the sulphurous glow of the footlights the musical comedy of the old misanthrope often seems cold, prudent, indirect, and evasive. He had now . . . met up with a poet who, although imposing, was filled with ideologies and amateurish scribblings. Obliged

to underline a tightly packed, complicated dialogue, sprung entirely from fanciful witticisms and literary devices, the old Verdi (who before had built in the simple, scornful manner of the greats) might have sensed the discord, but he lacked the force to dominate, destroy, and reconstruct the material of the libretto along broad, summary, and powerful lines . . .

In my opinion he actually reached the highest peak of beauty, with a completely southern immediacy, in *Il trovatore* . . . That is where Verdi's art, which is entirely an art of revolt, deformation, and sublime caricature, sets the four corners of the world on fire.      (Barilli 1963: 103-5)

Barilli's assessment has been echoed as recently as 1978, in Giuseppe Tarozzi's *Il gran vecchio*:

The fact is that *Falstaff*, even with all of its stylistic preciosity and technical innovations, is the opera of an *old* artist and not (as is the case with *Otello*) one of an old *artist* . . . Lacking force, mystery, and pain, *Falstaff* is the opera of a now tired genius; of a genius who, although corroded by senility, wants to show himself and the world one more time – for the last time – that he can still sing and make his fantasy work . . . I believe that with *Falstaff* one may say that Verdi remembers having been a genius. But he is one no longer. His blood is lukewarm, almost cold.                                                   (1978: 257-8)

A second, opposing, group of Italian critics rejected the rise-and-fall theory of Verdi's career. This group asserted that his works reveal a 'creative ascent' (*ascensione creatrice*), as Gino Roncaglia called it: a steady climb to perfection. Once again, *Falstaff* was considered the summit of his career, but the Wagner problem was kept at bay by stressing the internal creative development of Verdi's mind. The general shape of ascent, or gradual mastery of material, resembled that found in most German, English, and American discussions of Verdi in the past half-century, but the Italian critics – including Roncaglia, Alfredo Parente, and Massimo Mila – were concerned less with cataloguing analytical detail than with charting Verdi's aesthetic, or spiritual, development. The best discussions here have involved procedures of philosophical and aesthetic classification, often influenced by the thought of Benedetto Croce.

Parente's commentary (1933) on Mila's view of *Falstaff* exemplifies this. Both see the work as a spiritual completion, or the final transcending of emotion that is merely sympathetic – and hence both radically oppose the conclusion of the group represented by Barilli:

Massimo Mila writes [*Il melodramma di Verdi*, Bari, 1933]: 'A world is not complete so long as it has no laughter. And this is certainly the definitive element that an artist can bring to the perfection of his creation – a view of his heroes that is the ultimate and the most difficult for him to take'. In Verdi's case this indicates 'that superior faculty and artistic maturity towards which *Otello* and *Falstaff* tend, as if to a natural conclusion'. A laugh or a smile, which here does not have the value of a particular state of soul, of a feeling among feelings, but instead of a sur-passing of feeling. Verdi probably attained this at the time when he was able to experience [emotion] 'not exclusively *in* his characters, but also outside of them, above them – observing them'.

In this way the somewhat curious research . . . into the comic or joy-ful motives in the pre-*Falstaff* operas acquires a new, richer significance. It readdresses the central problem: that of explaining Verdi's ever-grow-ing artistic potency, his Olympian grandeur in the process of formation.

(Parente 1933: 217-18)

Most recently, Gabriele Baldini (1970) has attempted to forge a synthesis between the two antithetical interpretations of Verdi's career. Baldini agrees with the first group that the true Verdi is to be found in the operas of the 1850s. But he sees the high point as *Un ballo in maschera* (1859), after which a decline sets in until – surprisingly – *Falstaff*, in which 'all hesitations, uncertainties and evasions were swept aside' (trans. 1980: 258). In its brilliance and consistent invention, Baldini argues, *Falstaff* regains the path lost after *Ballo*. The Italian reconciliation to Verdi's late works, one may conclude, is still in the process of formation.

### Falstaff as 'Typological Figure': three recent interpretations

While composing *Falstaff* Verdi realized that, far from being unique, Sir John crystallized in himself an essential aspect of mankind – the pure strain of a character trait generally found mixed in the 'real' world. Thus Verdi wrote on 3 December 1890: 'Falstaff is a sad man who commits all sorts of knaveries, but in an amusing way. He's a *type*! These types are so varied! The opera is completely comic!' (Cesari and Luzio 1913: 712). And in his famous 'Farewell to Falstaff' of 23 May 1893, Verdi hailed Shakespeare's creation as an 'amusing sort of scoundrel' who is 'eternally true, under different masks, in every time, in every place' (see p. 76 above). Verdi conceived of Falstaff as a standard or typological figure – a character-type. Such figures abound in literature: the pedant, the clever servant, the *miles gloriosus*, the heroine, the villain, and so on. Recognizing the presence of such figures can direct one to a work's metaphorical (or symbolic) content. What, then, is Falstaff's character-type? In what sense is he 'eternally true'?

Most literary critics have dealt with Falstaff as he appears in the two *Henry IV* plays, not in *The Merry Wives*. Still, Boito incorporated much of the *Henry IV* Falstaff into the libretto, and most of the traditional discussions of Sir John seem relevant to our understanding of this opera.

A. C. Bradley, for instance, wrote a famous description of the character in 1909:

The main reason why he makes us so happy and puts us so entirely at our ease is that he himself is happy and entirely at his ease. 'Happy' is too weak a word: he is in bliss, and we share his glory . . . A rich deep-toned chuckling enjoyment circulates continually through all his being . . . What we count the graver interests of life are nothing to him. But then, while we are under his spell, it is impossible to consider these graver interests; gravity is to us, as to him, inferior to gravy . . . The bliss of freedom gained in humour is the essence of Falstaff. His humour is not directed only or chiefly against obvious absurdities; he is the enemy of everything that would interfere with his ease, and therefore of anything serious, and especially of everything respectable and moral.

(1909: 261-2)

William Empson's view in 1953 was more psychological and sociological:

Falstaff is in part simply a 'Vice', that is, an energetic symbol of impulses which most people have to repress, who gives pleasure by at once releasing and externalizing them . . . Also (as a minor version of this type) he is in part the 'cowardly swashbuckler', of the Latin play rather than the Miracle Play, whose absurdity and eventual exposure are to comfort the audience for their frequent anxiety and humiliation from 'swashbucklers' . . . Also I think there is a more timeless element about him . . . He is the scandalous upper-class man whose behavior embarrasses his class and thereby pleases the lower class in the audience, as an 'exposure'.

(1953: 244-5)

Within the past decade three provocative discussions of *Falstaff* (and *The Merry Wives*) have emerged to challenge the more traditional inter-pretations of the opera. Each of the three attempts to peer through the flux of surface action to discover a more stable, typological, or meta-phorical content below. The analysis of Peter Conrad finds this in music's ability to become Falstaff's ideal world; Daniel Sabbeth relies on Freud-ian psychological analysis; and J. A. Bryant, Jr, evokes archetypes of myth and sacred ritual. The three perspectives, although radically differ-ent from each other, need not be mutually contradictory. At this level of consideration, as Northrop Frye has pointed out in the introduction to the second essay of *The Anatomy of Criticism* (1957), a great work of art admits investigation according to the principle of multiple or 'polysemous' meaning.

Peter Conrad's starting point in *Romantic Opera and Literary Form* (1977) is the inadequacy of Falstaff's characterization in *The Merry Wives* — a commonplace among literary critics. The ever-resourceful, defiant Sir John of the *Henry IV* plays here loses his quasi-heroic status to be subjected to the most elementary duping and ignominy. 'The comedy is shaming and sullying, marking down Falstaff as a beast' (p. 61). The limitation of any play, argues Conrad, is that it must be restricted to the verbal mode: Falstaff, a habitual liar, can only tell us of his former glories, but the whole demeaning spectacle contradicts his words. The very character of Falstaff is anti-dramatic: he aspires not to act, but to escape the responsibility of acting. In this respect he is analogous to Hamlet, but while the latter escapes into the life of the mind, Falstaff's realm is the body and its fleshly gratification. Both Hamlet and Falstaff 'wish to luxuriate in their sense of themselves, to enjoy the pleasures of stupor – and music, being as Kierkegaard calls it the medium of sensuous immediacy, allows them to do precisely this' (pp. 59-60).

The musical element in Verdi's opera, therefore, succeeds in 'rescuing Falstaff from Shakespeare' (p. 65). Music richly provides those attributes to which the knight aspires – a full, ennobling expression of essence – and which the play, restricted to words, cannot supply.

Music is Falstaff's defense, turning his lies into blameless acts of imagination. Music supplies him with vocal qualities of vitality, juvenility, and inventiveness which belie his ponderous bulk ... While Falstaff merely talks, his versions of himself may seem spurious, his business affairs and political ambitions shabby or preposterous, since he needs constantly to prop up his fictions and intimidate rational objection. Once he begins to sing, he is changed: buoyed up by Verdi's melodic generosity, he becomes the spirit of revelry and jovial disorder which, in speech, he can only pretend to be. (pp. 175-6)

In this manner Conrad amplifies a comment of W. H. Auden, who wrote without sufficient elaboration that Falstaff's 'true home is the world of music' (1959: 21). But Conrad takes the argument a step further. Since Falstaff's goal is to withdraw from responsible society in order to feed his appetites, to seek a static, ever-present voluptuous gratification, he resembles a nineteenth-century decadent – a fairly recent typological figure, but a well-defined one, particularly in the 1890s. The function of the music is to embody the physically sensual, the 'inarticulate' kingdom into which Falstaff wishes to flee (p. 176). According to Conrad, Verdi's music aurally precipitates the knight's essence and translates him out of his proper period into *fin-de-siècle* Europe. This analysis has profound implications for the interpretation of Verdi's *oeuvre*. More than any prior commentator, Conrad stresses how much Verdi (perhaps influenced in this regard by Boito) had renounced the opera of social and political action in favour of the opera of aesthetic and sensual contemplation: *Falstaff*'s swirl of activity masks a more fundamental stasis.

Daniel Sabbeth's discussion of the 'Principles of Tonal and Dramatic Organization in Verdi's *Falstaff*' (a doctoral dissertation of 1976 elaborating an article published two years earlier, 'Dramatic and Musical Organization in "Falstaff"') considers the opera to be a demonstration of personal psychological growth. Closely following the analysis of Norman Holland in *The Shakespearean Imagination* (1964), Sabbeth argues that Falstaff, after an initial scene of paternal authority, regresses to the psychological state of the infant or child. In certain respects he resembles a child in the oral phase of development: 'His sole concern is that his needs be met and his most overwhelming need is to be fed. Falstaff's exaggerated need for food, his insatiable appetite, is symbolized by his stomach' (1976: 18). His primary goal is to achieve 'oral fusion' with various mother-substitutes – and ultimately, this goal is incompatible with acceptable adult behaviour. (This interpretation, too, has a forerunner in Auden, who asserted that 'once upon a time we were all Falstaffs: then we became social beings with super-egos' (1959: 26); cf. also William Empson's comments on Falstaff's character-type, p. 145 above.)

Moreover, argues Sabbeth, Sir John's longed-for liaison with Alice has oedipal overtones. 'Falstaff does not merely want to seduce Alice; equally important is his desire to replace Ford in the latter's relationship with his wife' (1976: 21). Hence he bluntly informs Alice that he desires her husband's death ('Vorrei che Mastro Ford / Passasse a miglior vita', II.ii). Eventually, of course, Falstaff's adventures in quest of oral fusion are frustrated by the wives' stratagems. The desired fantasy, the 'bond of fusion', dissolves. Falstaff undergoes 'individuation', that is, he accepts the adult world by a three-fold operation of 'recognition [of the unattainability of his desires], renunciation [of the fantasy], and acceptance [of the 'real' situation, now as an adult]'. Typologically, Falstaff becomes a psychological Everyman.

Many of the secondary characters experience a similar process of growth. Ford and Cajus are 'mirrors of Falstaff' with related problems of 'oral-oedipal helplessness' (Ibid. p. 24). Ford's fear of being cuckolded resembles the infant's fear of the loss of the mother, and Ford favours his daughter's marriage to Cajus primarily because the doctor is like himself. In this interpretation, which sees Ford's desire to retain Nannetta as incestuous, Ford and Cajus are double aspects of the same personality, a splitting of one character into two (Ibid. pp. 26-9). Cajus, for his part, likewise strives for oral fusion in his naive pursuit of Nannetta, but his regressive fantasy, like those of the others, is consistently thwarted. All three men – Falstaff, Ford, and Cajus – are treated as children, or dupes, by the women. And all meet obstacles that pummel them out of their fantasies and into recognition, renunciation, and acceptance.

The fantasy of oral fusion, Sabbeth insists, has its positive aspects as well. Fenton and Nannetta's concern with kisses ('oral engulfment') is to be interpreted favourably: it springs from the healthier sources of 'tolerance, acceptance, and growth' (Ibid. p. 41) and leads to 'a new beginning of life together' (Ibid. p. 36). And in a much larger sense, to witness the interior of *Falstaff* — the 'play within a play' in which each character pursues his fantasy under masks and disguises — is to permit ourselves to enjoy the fantasy in a non-threatening way, that is, to re-experience our psychic cores while remaining responsible adults. In the last analysis, the opera is didactic, something like a Freudian morality play:

The childish games have an important, almost religious, purpose — that of education. Once the mazes are trodden, the players have a clearer perception of the world around them. It is like the ancient initiation ritual in which old identities are given up for new ones: brittle, dried-up societies dissolve and new, fertile ones are created. Both individuals and society grow.                                    (1974: 422)

Sabbeth's next step — to associate keys and key-relations closely with these psychological observations — radicalizes his discussion beyond the point many analysts are willing to pass. According to Sabbeth, each principal key reflects a dramatic situation, and these emblematic key-areas interact functionally to illustrate the psychological growth process of individuation. C major acts as a frame, or 'a neutral reality from which conflicts emerge and toward which they resolve' (1976: 166). E major is the key of the oral-fusion fantasy, the key of childlike powerlessness and 'the central contests of control' (Ibid. p. 166). The E-conflicts resolve to C by descending through the circle of fifths (E–A–D–G–C), each member of which illustrates the difficult stages of the individuation process. A♭ is a key of isolation (Nannetta and Fenton) and the key of 'the meaningful lessons of the opera' (Ibid. p. 191), particularly as it resolves (grows) into C and escapes enharmonic entrapment by the problematic E major. D♭ often illustrates Falstaff's power; F postpones action or unfolds 'a conflict conceived in E major' (Ibid. p. 201); E♭ can express a final and explicit loss of power (Ibid. p. 201); and so on. Most of Sabbeth's work consists of linear bass graphs (superficially recalling aspects of Schenkerian analysis) that he explicates theoretically and psychologically.

This radical approach to tonality — one of the most controversial topics in current Verdi studies — has met with considerable scepticism.

Andrew Porter, for instance, dismisses it in the *New Grove* as 'an example of "harmonico-psycho-dramatic" argument carried to extremes' (p. 643). Sabbeth's misfortune is to have demanded adherence not merely to one, but to two systems of rigorous belief: Freudian psychoanalysis (as applied to drama) and an unflagging devotion to emblematic tonality in Verdi as filtered through a peculiar adaptation of Schenker. Few scholars are prepared to declare allegiance to both (or, in some instances, to either), much less to embrace Sabbeth's mapping of one system onto the other.

In many respects the opera seems more penetratingly served by recourse to myth, ritual, and standard literary types. J. A. Bryant, Jr, has studied *The Merry Wives* from these standpoints, and his conclusions in 'Falstaff and the Renewal of Windsor' (1974) apply directly to Verdi's opera as well. Bryant begins by observing that the essential action centres less on Falstaff's adventures than on the Fenton—Anne (Nannetta) plot. In true New Comedy fashion (i.e., following patterns also observed in Menander, Plautus, and Terence), the play does not reach its conclusion until the two young lovers have overcome the obstacles to their love and are joined in marriage. This concluding marriage and others of the same type, however, transcend the personal and, by extension, suggest the renewal of society itself. Northrop Frye, for instance, has described the usual formula that orders such comedies: 'The hero's society rebels against the society of the *senex* and triumphs, but the hero's society is a Saturnalia, a reversal of social standards which recalls a golden age in the past before the main action of the play begins' (1957: 171).

Taking his cue from Frye, Bryant (1974) identifies Fenton and Anne with the new, ultimately triumphing society and the other, older characters with the society to be superseded. The afflictions of the established Windsor society go beyond age:

Economic considerations in Windsor have temporarily replaced genetic ones [p. 300] . . . The objective of [Falstaff's] assault on the wives of Windsor is not the satisfaction of lust but satisfaction of the belly [p. 298] . . . Pretty Anne Page is of marriageable age . . . and the senior members of the community are mightily concerned to see that she is disposed of to their advantage... No one of the older generation [except, in the opera, perhaps, Alice] . . . seems to remember the primary purpose of such pairings or to be aware that matches for money are often of the kind that bring a community to extinction [p. 300].

We have, in short, a displaced *Rite of Spring*. The existing order, 'shivering with the counsels and whispers of winter, old age, and death' (p. 300; cf. Falstaff's 'Va, vecchio John' in II.i and opening monologue in III.i), gives way to its replacement. 'Monetary concerns are defeated, biology wins out' (p. 300): thus is the golden age restored. As Bryant reads it, *The Merry Wives* ritually re-enacts an indispensable human myth; it propounds an essentially sacred idea in secular terms.

According to this view, the Falstaff plot provides the mechanism by which the disorders of the older society may be exposed and exorcised. Sir John, the quintessential representative of an aging, corrupt, and possibly impotent generation, becomes a scapegoat who must be humiliated and in some sense banished before social renewal can occur. (Once again, one recalls the work of Northrop Frye (1957: 165), who has written that 'comedy often includes a scapegoat ritual of expulsion which gets rid of some irreconcilable character'. And to the objection that Falstaff, in the end, joins the final feast, Frye could reply that it was in the nature of comedy 'to include as many people as possible in its final society: the blocking characters are more often reconciled or converted than simply repudiated'.) Working from such premises, Bryant is able to explain the 'ritualistic' quality of the Windsor Forest scene:

> While we laugh at the spectacle of Falstaff in the forest, we may also shudder as we laugh; for this last humiliation, involving as it does the victim disguised as an animal and the people's participation in the punishment of that victim, suggests unmistakably the ancient castigation of the scapegoat, whereby an animal, or a man, or a man dressed as an animal was made to take upon himself and suffer for the sins of a whole community. (1974: 298)

Amplifying his discussion still further, Bryant, following Frye, insists that Falstaff's earlier two trials in the play — the ordeal in the laundry basket and the beating while disguised as an old woman — recall certain folkloristic rituals identified in Frazer's *The Golden Bough* as 'Carrying Out Death' or 'Burying Death'. Much as Falstaff may amuse us along the way, his dramatic function is to be defeated. His moment of defeat, appropriately, coincides with the lovers' moment of triumph: his confession and absolution in Windsor Forest, that is, leads at once to Ford's — unwitting — paternal blessing of Fenton and Anne. For Bryant, the ultimate goal of this formulaic action is that 'it makes us once more see the mysterious terms on which we live, accept those terms, and once more concede that the game shall go on' (p. 300).

Thus interpreted, *The Merry Wives* and *Falstaff*, as complete works, become affirmations of generational renewal, the replacement of the old by the young, the resurgent life-cycle. Bryant's work provides an attractive solution for the central stylistic 'problem' of the opera: its shift from the free-flowing, volatile formal procedures of the early scenes to the archaic forms of the Windsor Forest scene — its crystallizing of the final scene's static gestures out of the preceding flux. It now seems quite natural that the scene of revelation should occur within a context of tradition and accompanying ceremonial. Moreover, while it is fitting that Fenton and Nannetta begin their own rite in sonnet and strophic song, one should not ignore the peculiar, almost sacred quality that pervades their music throughout the opera. Verdi consistently sets apart their music and preserves it guileless and without irony. Theirs is the single pure element in an opera so generally alloyed with deceit and self-interest. Surely it is not without significance that the refrain that thrice joins their voices — 'Bocca baciata non perde ventura / Anzi rinnova come fa la luna' — is grounded in the concept of cyclical renewal, for they are the embodiment of that renewal, the crescent moon, the opera's promise.

And, given Bryant's interpretation, nothing is more moving than to contemplate the old Verdi, now ending his last opera, wistfully bidding us farewell by marrying this young couple — stepping aside to permit spring to happen once again. The truth of things, after all, lies in their wide-eyed wonder, not yet blighted by the inevitable autumn and winter.

# A Shakespearean perspective:
# Verdi and Boito as translators

## GRAHAM BRADSHAW

In opera the composer is the dramatist. This is not less true of Verdi than of Wagner, but it is less obviously true. Although *Otello* and *Falstaff* are generally agreed to be supreme operatic masterpieces, assessment of the dramatic achievement they represent is complicated twice over – because they are collaborations, and because they are creative adaptations of works by the greatest of all dramatists. In general terms, we may better understand the nature of Verdi's creative collaboration with Boito by asking where, and how, the two late operas are Shakespearean. *Otello* is a very great work, nor is it diminished by being un-Shakespearean in important respects. But the contrast with *Falstaff* is particularly instructive, since it is part of that opera's miraculous achievement that it *is* profoundly Shakespearean – more Shakespearean than *Otello*, and, paradoxically, more truly Shakespearean than its Shakespearean source.

### I

Boito claimed that in *Falstaff* 'The miracle of sounds guides Shakespeare's sparkling farce back again to its clear Tuscan source, Ser Giovanni Fiorentino' – that is, to the world of Italian *novelle*. One way of characterizing what is un-Shakespearean in *Otello* is to see how Shakespeare's tragedy is led back to its source in an Italian *novella* – the story of the Moor in Cinthio Giraldi's *Gli hecatommithi* (1565) – since Boito effectively restores elements which Shakespeare had eliminated or carefully modified in his own reworking of Cinthio's tale. Further differences between *Otello* and *Othello* appear when we reflect on the fact that very few modern critics can accept the Coleridgean, Romantic view that Iago is a Devil of 'motiveless malignity' and Desdemona a pure Angel or Madonna. That view was prolonged in English dramatic criticism by Bradley's influential *Shakespearean Tragedy* (1912), which provoked an over-reaction in T. S. Eliot and F. R. Leavis – to the effect that Iago is a mere dramatic trigger which sets off Othello's internal mechanism, while

Othello himself is a grossly self-deceiving egoist. From the point of view we have now reached in discussion of the play, Verdi's opera seems the glorious apotheosis of nineteenth-century ways of reading and misreading Shakespeare's play.

Some differences are relatively insignificant: for example, Roderigo is clumsily handled in the opera, so that his role is barely intelligible unless one knows the play. But the major differences concern Iago, Desdemona, the elimination of Shakespeare's first act, and the different character of the love-relationship. Boito's Iago looks back to Goethe's Mephistopheles ('Ich bin der Geist der stets verneint') and Boito's own Mefistofele ('Son lo Spirito che nega sempre, tutto'); he also prefigures the diabolic, dualistic pessimism of Boito's *Nerone*. In a prophetic early fable Boito had written 'Re Orso / ti schermi / dal morso / de' vermi' ('King Bear, beware the bite of the worm'); in *Otello* Iago becomes the Eternal Worm and (after Boito's inspired afterthought) even sings its 'Credo'. This is a very powerful working out of a private creative preoccupation, and is also consistent with the romantic demonization of Iago's 'motiveless malignity'; but it is not Shakespeare, and melodramatizes the fundamental Shakespearean contrast between Iago's habitually reductive prose and Othello's strenuously aspiring poetry.

Nor is Boito's Desdemona closer to Shakespeare's green girl, who is most human and engaging in the girlish impetuosity and 'downright violence' of her passionate, youthfully inexperienced idealism. Seeing Othello 'in his mind', she has disregarded those more obvious differences of age, colour, and race which so appalled her father in Act I; since Boito disregards them too the shock of seeing these lovers together virtually disappears, and the dramatically challenging nature of this idealistic union is defused. Shakespeare's Desdemona badly misjudges her father, who dies of a broken heart, and she misjudges her husband too – most obviously when she disregards Emilia's reassuring report in III.i (one of Shakespeare's significant departures from Cinthio), presses Cassio's case unnecessarily, and even invites Cassio to stay and hear her speak! These complicating critical elements in Shakespeare's characterization are ignored by Boito, whose heroine is sanctified and Marified. This shows how potent the *opera seria* conventions still were: although there is no trace of Rossini's ludicrous Otello in the Boito–Verdi conception, there is more than a trace of Rossini's Desdemona, especially (and worryingly) in the final act. We might even detect the more general influence of Mediterranean idealizations of the woman as donna-Madonna. Whatever the cause, the complexity of the Shakespearean presentation is replaced by a more conventional pathos, dangerously close to melodrama.

This simplifying, sentimentalizing tendency inevitably modifies Boito's treatment of the love-relationship, so that his lovers are in important respects more like Cinthio's than Shakespeare's. In Cinthio's tale the lovers have been married for a long time, and know each other in the biblical as in the other sense. When confronted with the Moor's unaccountable behaviour, 'Disdemona' even wonders whether her husband has grown tired of her after 'using' her so much. By drastically compressing his play's time-span Shakespeare ensures that his lovers have seen little of each other before their elopement, and even after the marriage they are denied the continuing intimacies that time and their circumstances would ordinarily afford: since their moments together in Cyprus are brief and interrupted, it is not even clear that the marriage is consummated – save by the murder on the relaid wedding sheets. Shakespeare's lovers love each other passionately, but scarcely know each other or their passions. They are ingenuous in the good and dangerous senses of that word, and, despite Iago's foul-minded assumptions, sexual appetite has played little part in bringing them together except at a very idealized level (which allows Iago to play on Othello's sexual inexperience of 'subtle' Venetians). Cinthio's Moor is physically passionate in straightforward ways, and is tortured by the thought of travelling without his wife; Shakespeare's Moor repudiates the 'light-wing'd toys' of 'feather'd Cupid' in an ostentatious, awkward way, and is perfectly prepared to leave his bride behind, until she takes the initiative and shows her lovable impetuosity by begging to accompany him. Cinthio's presentation is very much less complex in psychological terms: Shakespeare's changes suggest that the dangers his lovers face will not be merely external.

We might be reminded of the ways Shakespeare modified another story which originally appeared in Cinthio's collection of tales: in *Measure for Measure*, which was written not long before *Othello*, Angelo and Isabella are turned into youthful, inexperienced idealists, who are as ignorant and terrified of sex as they are convinced that their respective secular and Christian ideologies resolve the problems of an alarmingly complex world. Idealists and sceptics figure largely in Shakespeare's plays of this period, which repeatedly return to the radically sceptical question posed in *Troilus and Cressida*: 'What's aught, but as 'tis valued?'; Hamlet's 'There is nothing either good or bad, but thinking makes it so' is a variant. The idealistic Othello has given his life meaning through various acts of self-commitment – to Desdemona and marriage, to the Venetian state which 'makes ambition virtue', and to the Christian religion he adopts. His need to endow life with significance is explored and opposed to Iago's reductive nihilism, and it would be more accurate to describe *Othello* as a tragedy of idealism than as a tragedy of love. But these larger tragic issues are either contracted in Boito's libretto or appear, like Iago's over-explicit nihilism, in the simplified terms of Italian *melodramma*. In this sense Boito offers a powerful concentration of the nineteenth-century view: the Romantic critics (and Bradley later) could not eliminate the first act as Boito did, but neither could they see why the 'real' play about Love and Evil takes so long to get started, or why Desdemona is hardly more prominent than Cassio. And Boito, who knew Cinthio's story but never seems to have asked why Shakespeare made such drastic changes, provided Verdi with an Act I love-duet which makes a curious impression in Shakespearean terms. The text for the duet very cleverly stitches Shakespearean fragments, yet its effect is un-Shakespearean since the psychological complexities and tension have not been 'translated'.

Yet the case becomes more complicated, and *Otello* more Shakespearean, when Verdi takes over as dramatist. The objection that Iago is inflated in a brilliant yet typically Romantic and melodramatic fashion is less damaging, as soon as one attends to Iago's *musical* characterization and to the ways in which this is integrated within the larger musical-dramatic structure. The cataclysmic violence unleashed in the opening bars presents terrifying elemental forces, which are apparently alien to the human world; but then the remarkably fluid musical development (as heard, for example, in the persistent broken arpeggio figures) links the storm-music to the fire-music and to those elemental *human* passions which are released in and by the *brindisi*. The music reveals that the rending forces of Chaos are inside, as well as external to, man. As for Iago, his characteristic chromatic slides, trills, broken rhythms, and spikily unpredictable phrase-endings both set him apart from the other characters and establish his relation with the destructive energies. The musical contrast between Otello's strenuous 'Esultate!' and the disintegrative chromaticism of Iago's 'Beva, beva' is absolute, and parallels the Shakespearean contrast between Othello's aspiring poetry and Iago's reductive prose in tonal, melodic and rhythmic terms. And, in Verdi as in Shakespeare, the hero who triumphantly asserts that the forces of Chaos can be governed feels his own blood beginning to rule, as he quells the riot. In the love-duet Otello's passionate outbursts also register an inner urgency and instability which is alien to Desdemona: the music conveys Otello's vulnerability while placing the lovers' affirmative lyricism within a disturbing musical-dramatic world.

Similarly, the dramatic definition is essentially musical when Iago's poison begins to work. Here we might contrast 'Dio! mi potevi' with a much discussed orchestral passage in Act IV. In 'Dio! mi potevi' Boito and Verdi are both faithful to Othello's great speech ('Had it pleas'd heaven'), and indeed understand better than F. R. Leavis in his famous essay on *Othello* (reprinted in *The Common Pursuit*, 1952) what that speech is doing in Shakespeare's play. Othello searches out the ultimate source of his agony; when it is eventually located – 'There, where I have garner'd up my heart' – there is a swell of horror and revulsion, and everything (including the strenuously controlled syntax) breaks down as Othello's mind is flooded with obscenely bestial Iago-images of Nature as a filthy, meaningless process. Verdi keeps close to Shakespeare's dramatic structuring of this determined, agonized introspection, so that the music also moves in carefully distinguished stages towards the imaginative grasping of the worst agony before the violent collapse. At first the heroic, characteristically aspiring lyricism of Otello's melodic line is entirely smothered: his *voce soffocata* is heard against obsessive repetitions of a triplet figure which pointedly recalls Iago's 'Credo'. He broods on the sufferings he could bear, and the vocal line only begins to climb away from the A♭ when (with the piercing modulation at 'ciel') he thinks directly of Desdemona. In the beautiful *cantabile* section that follows Otello recovers and, as it were, concentrates his imaginative sense of all that Desdemona means or has meant to him; but this also concentrates his sense of the ultimate agony which cannot be endured, so that there is, in the music as in Shakespeare's poetry, a swell of violent emotion before the horrible collapse into incoherence.

In the final act the first reappearance of 'un bacio' presents a similar conflict and collapse in purely orchestral terms. The initial effect of the recalling of past felicity in present anguish is extraordinarily lyrical, as the dismal minor sixth gives way to the major sixth that launches the 'bacio' melody. But the movement from minor to major is at once undermined, as well as enriched in harmonic terms, by a chromatic descent in the bass, by semitones at first and then by larger intervals. In contrast with this downward tug the romantically ardent melodic line arches up to G♯, then B, then finally C♯, before its own slithering collapse down to C♮. Those who are blessed with absolute pitch and an absolute belief in Verdi's command of long-distance tonal relationships may recall earlier associations of C with chaos and ruin, but the immediate effect of this astonishing shift into F minor is in itself sufficiently shocking: if the healing growth from A minor into A major sounded a positive note of hope, this plunge into a remote minor key drops us into a horribly quiet vestibule of Hell. And, as in 'Dio! mi potevi', there is a terrible inevitability in the way that the climax of recalling all that has been lost brings about the helpless collapse. The psychological dynamics of Otello's tortured consciousness are presented in purely musical terms.

Purely musical? It might indeed be objected that without the libretto we would not have the conceptual references we need — even if it is also true that Boito's way of conceptualizing Iago's nihilism and Otello's vulnerability is less subtle than Verdi's musical characterization. But my immediate concern is to establish a point which A. W. von Schlegel had grasped when he realized that prose translations of Shakespeare could not suffice, but which is less familiar in discussions of opera translations. The Shakespearean character of an operatic adaptation is determined not merely, nor even primarily, by fidelity to the Shakespearean plot and big set speeches, but rather by the ability to recreate in musical-dramatic terms the reciprocal relationships of poetic drama. These relationships appear not only in the propositional content of dramatic poetry, but also in its rhythms, its images, its different stylistic registers. So, for example, these elements all contribute to the horrible coup in Shakespeare's *Othello* (IV.i), when Othello collapses into Iago's prose and the bestialities of Iago's reductive imagination. Schlegel recognized that a literary translation which used prose throughout could not reproduce such shifts of register. An operatic adaptation of Shakespeare is also a translation, and a creative critique: for the composer-dramatist, the fact that music can enrich and deepen a libretto's conceptual references is in itself not enough — he must also create an independently articulated, imaginatively coherent musical world which allows for comparable reciprocal relationships. *Falstaff* illuminates and resolves this creative problem in a complex and fascinating way, since its music articulates a drama which is more thoroughly Shakespearean in its reciprocal relationships than its primary Shakespearean source. It should become clear that in advancing this claim I am not using the term 'Shakespearean' in a loose, impressionistic sense; since I shall first need to say more about the reciprocal relationships of Shakespearean poetic drama, I should also crave the indulgence of the reader whose interests are primarily musical, and plead that it will soon become clear how the Shakespearean *excursus* helps us to characterize Verdi's and Boito's achievement.

## II

Tolstoy's difficulties with Shakespeare resulted from his inability to cope with the alien conventions of English poetic drama; people do not speak in blank verse. But, precisely because these conventions are not 'realistic' transcriptions of human speech and behaviour, they may permit nuances and discriminations not otherwise available – helping us to 'see' as well as feel an emotion. I have mentioned the devastating effect of Othello's collapse into Iago-like prose; in Shakespeare any shift from a poetic to a prosaic register invariably matters. In a highly artificial comedy like *A Midsummer Night's Dream* each group of characters has its distinctive poetic or prosaic register, like orbiting stars in a constellation. The stylistic register is itself a constituent of meaning.

The meaning of Falstaff's Catechism on Honour – and my reason for choosing this as a 'test case' will be obvious enough – actually depends on its context within the reciprocal relationships of *Henry IV*. It matters that it is in prose, and indeed that (with one insignificant exception) Falstaff always speaks prose: like Iago, he represents a denial of the human potentialities and aspirations which are treated in poetic registers. If Shakespeare himself had transplanted the Honour Catechism from *Henry IV* to *The Merry Wives*, like Boito three centuries later, the same words would have meant far less. Dramatic meaning depends on dramatic context, and the meaning of the Catechism is affected not only by its being in prose but also by its contributive place within an intricate series of contrasts involving Falstaff, King Henry, Prince Hal, and Hotspur – and indeed the fate of England. Falstaff's body is his commonwealth and flourishing empire, but as *Henry IV* begins we first hear of the bleeding body of the commonweal – of the England Henry would heal and reunite by a politic, and possibly pious, crusade. Henry's conspicuously high poetic register asserts his kingship, as if to dispel the charge that he is an usurper and 'vile politician', but the poetic register drops, revealingly, when he leaves his dream for more pressing realities: 'bootless 'tis to tell you we will go'. The king and politician is also a father, and the theme of Honour is introduced when he sadly contrasts his Harry (Prince Hal) with Harry Percy – Hotspur, 'the theme of honour's tongue'. In the next scenes this contrast is developed, as different stylistic registers reveal an ethic or its absence, an aspiration or a limitation. The prince enters speaking prose, albeit a courtly, beautifully cadenced prose, and only moves into verse in his soliloquy – as though this is his natural register although he chooses to address Falstaff in prose. Falstaff never speaks anything else, and in the next scene we hear the very different, huffing register of Hotspur's intemperately vigorous, emotionally impetuous verse: Hotspur is entirely incapable of Hal's guarded reserve and limber command of different registers, or modes of feeling and being.

As it explores the concept of Honour the play also investigates Englishness, adapting any historical facts which obstruct the mythopoeic exploration of national identity. Which Harry is the more honourable — and the more truly English? The questions interlock, and the answers the play throws out condition any impulsive identification of Falstaff with Merrie England. Falstaff's only allegiance is to self: this is wonderfully liberating in a world where declared aspirations and principles like Honour coincide disquietingly with undeclared self-interest, but we also see why the comedy of the second part of *Henry IV* is so much darker. The humour of the later scenes admits Doll Tearsheet; the scenes with Shallow ache with a remarkably Chekhovian pathos. Not only is Falstaff's souring Carnival opposed to the Lord Chief Justice's Lent, his body's empire is ravaged from within by age and sordid diseases which parallel those afflicting the body of an ungoverned England. The Honour Catechism offers a truth, which the play 'places'; it is much more than a striking and detachable set piece.

Just how subtly this play's reciprocal relationships interact may be illustrated by the scene in Bangor. To Hotspur, Glendower represents an alien culture, alien values and a total disregard for truth. The Welsh bard's vatic posturing is intolerable to the bluff, ultra-English Northerner; so is the poetry Glendower learned when 'train'd up' in an effete, dreamily dishonest English court. When Glendower boasts of the 'helpful ornament' he gave the 'tongue' Hotspur erupts, opposing Glendower's affected courtly 'virtue' and 'mincing poetry' with the discordant images, sounds, and activities of a real world in which cats mew and dry wheels grate on axle-trees. Once again, reality is opposed to a dream or fantasy, sport to work; and in metrical terms there is an unexpected confrontation between the poetics — that of the mid-sixteenth-century miscellanies, and that of the aggressively 'masculine', 'strong-lined', and anti-courtly satirists of the 1590s. In making Hotspur sound like a contemporary Angry Young Poet, Shakespeare finds a pointedly un-medieval way of dramatizing a generation gap and cultural gap, while also furthering his investigation of Englishness and developing the contrast with Falstaff's kind of realism and Hal's complex courtliness. Even as Hotspur opposes the outmoded music of courtly, vapid Mastersingers with the Music of the Future, it is evident that neither truth nor beauty nor true Honour are represented by his own unbridled impulses and blinkered chauvinism. His vehement but limited truths may explode a Welsh windbag, but they remain as inadequate as Falstaff's and as 'altogether govern'd by humours'. The relevant contrasts and correspondences are established through the different stylistic registers and imagery: although Hotspur seems like Falstaff's antithesis — and nowhere more so than in his attitude to Honour – they are also alike. The Hotspur who would push a kingdom topsy-turvy down and who thinks it an easy leap to 'pluck bright honour from the pale-faced moon' is as remote from daylight realities as Diana's fattest forester – the Falstaff who declares himself to be 'governed as the sea is, by our noble and chaste mistress the moon'. They are both 'moon-men', priding themselves on their realism but governed by fantasies and humours. The one will be killed, and the other firmly 'governed' by the future *roi soleil* – the sun-prince who calculatingly plans his 'reformation' but offers the mangled Hotspur 'fair rites of tenderness' when nobody is looking or listening, and who shows his indifference to conventional notions of Honour by allowing Falstaff the credit for killing Hotspur.

That pregnantly private gesture follows soon after Falstaff's Catechism, and brings the play's first part to its conclusion; but the debate on Honour continues. So, for example, Prince John provides another perspective, no less 'realistic' than Falstaff's, when he breaks faith with the rebels and has them executed after their surrender. Why let loyal Englishmen die, if the necessary end can be secured by other means? Why, indeed – but if we still do not like the smell of this, we must go on asking what Falstaff's Catechism left out. As so often in Shakespeare, the dramatic method is perspectival and radically sceptical: there are no objective values (we are not shown what Honour incontrovertibly *is*), but the human need for values is an objective fact about human nature, however incomprehensible or derisory this seems to Shakespeare's cynics and 'realists' like Iago and Falstaff. Verdi makes that connection, as we shall see, and Boito was perhaps departing from his immediate text, but in a wholly Shakespearean way, when his Falstaff describes Honour as a 'bel costrutto'.

These extended remarks should help to make clear why *The Merry Wives* is not only very inferior but also uncharacteristic – un-Shakespearean in a precise sense. Its reciprocal relationships are sketchy and show nothing like the (arguably unsurpassed) richness of those in *Henry IV*. Instead of a complex and beautiful interplay of stylistic registers, through which Shakespeare investigates Englishness, we have a confined, prosaic citizens' comedy in which different characters murder English. Falstaff is inevitably a pitiful shadow of his *Henry IV* self, not so much because his own speeches are inferior (although they are) as because the busy farce provides no larger imaginative space within which a Falstaff could meaningfully exist as something more than the Fat Boy butt of a series of Italianate *lazzi* or tricks. This point needs to be made carefully, since it is so easy to slip into misleading ways of discussing a character's existence — like those old-fashioned critics who discussed the marvellous 'gallery of characters' in Dickens or Tolstoy as though it hardly mattered where and when the characters appeared. Tradition has it that Shakespeare wrote *The Merry Wives* when Queen Elizabeth I expressed a wish to see Sir John in love; the queen's fancy was less regally imperceptive than earlier critics supposed, since modern scholars have established that *The Merry Wives* was written *before* the second part of *Henry IV* had been staged, and the queen could know nothing of Falstaff's liaison with Doll Tearsheet in *Henry IV: Part Two*. Nonetheless, a dramatic character is not as transposable or disposable as a dutiful subject or playwright. Falstaff 'exists' as a part of the *Henry IV* complex of meanings; that he is so reduced in the respectably prosaic world of middle-class Windsor is not the cause but a consequence of that play's slack and diminished reciprocal relationships.

Like Hal and his father, Falstaff could exist in another play, but only by being recreated within another independent, integrated design. Shakespeare faced another difficulty, once he had chosen (time was pressing) to write a farce. For now the intricately Italianate plotting required that Falstaff should become more passive and, as Neil Rhodes puts it (1980: 125), 'merely material'. As Boito quickly saw, *The Merry Wives* recalled the world of the Tuscan *novelle* and the Italian *commedia*, just as its vivid flights of abuse recalled writers like Aretino and stimulated Boito to produce a glorious pastiche of scurrilous Renaissance Italian. But the essence of such plotting is that it is situational. If a character really suffers — like Shylock in *The Merchant of Venice* or Malvolio in *Twelfth Night* — the psychological inwardness is disruptive, complicating, much harder to contain and control. Any dynamic apprehension of character and feeling could only disturb the *élan* and neatness of the carefully, quickly contrived situations of *The Merry Wives*. These were perfectly suited to a Rossinian or Cimarosan *opera buffa*, and indeed Nicolai's delightful work thrives on the limitations of Shakespeare's farce. But Verdi and Boito wanted to translate Shakespeare's Falstaff, to achieve a deeper fidelity to the spirit of Shakespeare's *oeuvre*, not that of the uncharacteristic farce.

So, in our 'test case', the *Henry IV* Catechism was transposed — detached from the dramatic context which originally gave it dramatic significance, and then spliced together with two different fragments from *The Merry Wives*. The result is indeed 'skilfully stitched', as Julian Budden and others have claimed — but then, as Professor Hepokoski brings out, the stitching also shows. Bardolfo's unexpected invocation of 'L'onore' is an obviously contrived cue: as Professor Hepokoski puts it, 'the inconceivable occurs'! And Pistola's reference to 'Messer Pandarus' and pimping reminds us, like Falstaff's surviving references to battlefield injuries, that the Catechism originally had a richer, less restrictingly sexual and suburban, context. The local difficulty parallels the larger dramatic problem, of how to graft the 'real' Falstaff of the histories onto the very slender Windsor stem. Boito is invariably praised for his stitchings and transpositions, and rightly so: they are cleverly managed, and an indispensable part of the attempt to present the Shakespearean Falstaff. But they were also risky, and potentially disastrous: only Verdi could integrate the disparate elements.

### III

The literary felicities of Boito's libretto are innumerable and often untranslatable. English can only hint at the deftness of Falstaff's pun on the art of stealing and the art of *rubato* in 'Rubar con garbo e a tempo'. Ford's great aria culminates in a desperate attempt to see his jealousy as a fortifying source of strength: he even tries to beatify – but how could that register fully on a non-Catholic, non-Italian audience, unused to hearing the phrase 'Laudate sempre sia' followed by 'in nomine Maria'? In Act III, 'Cool his hot lust' will not really do for 'Gli svampi l'uzzolo', but what would? The negating 's-' in 'svampi' could only be rendered awkwardly in English by some word like 'de-sizzle'; and 'svampi' gives 'l'uzzolo' a concretely physical (tumescent) reference. A libretto may be an independent literary masterpiece (and here Boito is rivalled only by da Ponte and Hofmannsthal): no disparagement is intended in the remark that a libretto's efficacy as a dramatic scenario is ultimately more important. It has been suggested that Boito's supreme literary achievement was the first version of the *Nerone* libretto, but this was certainly not effective as a scenario, and Boito the composer-dramatist recognized that it had to be revised and savagely cut. In preparing the libretto for *Falstaff*, Boito's decisive contribution was to present Verdi with six tautly related scenes, in contrast to the twenty-three in *The Merry Wives*, which few Shakespeareans could reconstruct from memory. The local literary miracles are a glorious bonus, to which Verdi was no less gloriously responsive; but in compressing and stream-lining *The Merry Wives* Boito was not so much pointing the way for Verdi as brilliantly clearing it.

Dispensable characters like Nym disappear or are welded into a composite creation, as Professor Hepokoski shows happened with Dr Cajus.

Collecting the Shakespearean Ford's scattered squibbish outbursts into one explosive 'jealousy aria' showed the same genius for *brevità*; in eliminating Mr Page and making Ford Nannetta's domineering father as well as Alice's jealous husband Boito made a crucial change, as we shall see. The ensembles remind us that some of these striking condensations were dictated by the practical need to secure appropriate vocal groupings: it is better to oppose Falstaff with one baritone, not two, just as it is essential that the women's characters and vocal registers should be sharply distinguished – this matters far more to the opera's reciprocal relationships than making Mistress Quickly like her *Merry Wives* counterpart (who is not like her *Henry IV* namesake). Whereas Nicolai cheerfully stops everything for a serenade, Boito's bipartite act-structure is exceptionally taut and purposeful: it concentrates the contrasts between Falstaff's world and the wives', between the *ladri* of the Garter Inn and the folk of middle-class Windsor, as each world calculatingly invades the other. Having eliminated the tautologous episode with the Fat Woman and postponed the Thames dunking to the concertato finale of Act II, Boito could also subtly differentiate the effects of Falstaff's two exposures: at the beginning of Act III Falstaff is wholly isolated and most nearly suppressed; at the end of the act, after his second humiliation, there is a finely disconcerting assimilation, when the Windsor folk are content to follow Falstaff in the fugue. Another structural subtlety allows a strikingly Shakespearean effect: the first two acts move between two very different interiors, but Act III takes us outside the inn and then into the ancient wood. Here, as in the 'green world' of Shakespearean comedy (which *The Merry Wives* dimly echoes), social constraints and elaborate *costrutti* are magically dissolved: the two worlds which have hitherto been sharply opposed, within the inn and Ford's house, now mingle in a moonlit setting which is alien to both, though not to the lovers' enchanted world-within-a-world. *È sogno, o realtà*? Which world is real?

While moving towards these wholly Shakespearean perspectival ironies, the 'scenario' also ensures that everything centres on Falstaff: as in *Hamlet*, the equivocal hero dominates the stage when he is on it and everybody else's discussions and intrigues when he is not (again excepting the lovers). This does not happen in *The Merry Wives*, or in Nicolai's opera; for quite different reasons Shakespeare's Falstaff does not dominate *Henry IV* either. The Hamlet analogy is worth pressing in a different direction, since it also suggests why Falstaff had to dominate the opera. Hamlet was and probably still is the most complex character

ever to have stepped onto a stage; in terms of complexity and rich in-
exhaustibility his nearest Shakespearean rival was Falstaff. Arguments
ʻbout whether Falstaff emerged from the Gads Hill grilling in disgrace
or triumph still continue, like arguments about Hamlet. The fat butt of
*The Merry Wives* is never so complex; but then in *Henry IV* — a play
which no character dominates — Falstaff's complexity depends on his
place within the complex relationships of the play he inhabits. A translated, transplanted Falstaff could not be suppressed by the requirements
of farce but would inevitably dominate, and convert a Herne's Oak
*débâcle* into an equivocal Gads Hill triumph. To recreate the richness
and complexity of the Shakespearean Falstaff, Verdi and Boito had to
recreate the formidable virtuoso and the darker aspects of Falstaff's
archetypal, self-serving energy. Boito transposed these elements but this,
as we have seen in considering the Catechism, posed new problems. In
the case of the Catechism, Verdi resolves the problem very much as he
had resolved the teasingly parallel problem posed by Iago's implanted
'Credo'. Overall integration, rather than the musical equivalent of stitching, was required; how Verdi achieved this becomes clearer once we see
how Falstaff is indeed the consummate virtuoso who adapts himself to
each new situation.

Like Thomas Mann's Felix Krull, Verdi's Falstaff is the amoral con-
noisseur of his own prodigious powers of creative self-transformation;
he is his own work of art, and even relishes the distance separating his
virtuoso performances from their occasion and audience. In the opera's
first episode, the cause of all the furious commotion rises above it as
the very principle of self-regarding calm; the orchestra registers this sublime effrontery in an imperturbably measured ascending figure, which
rises from the low strings to the absurd heights of the ubiquitous piccolo.
Having despatched the first threat to the well-being of his thousand-
tongued belly's kingdom, a suddenly different Falstaff silences his minions, then favours their dirty uncomprehending ears with a brief hymn
to his own supreme art: 'Rubar con garbo' presents the Confidence Man
as Artist. Through the rest of the first part of Act I, and much of Act II,
Falstaff's music offers proof upon proof of his Protean, dizzyingly
opportunistic self-transformations. The self-pitying, self-delighting tirade
on what his clumsy craftsmen cost him leads to a *maestoso* celebration
of his belly's *regno*, and then to new, staggering transformations as
Falstaff *amoroso* plans his progress through two wives' skirts to their
husbands' cashboxes. Here too Falstaff relishes, even as he demonstrates,
his own seductive registers: sex will be an acceptable spin-off — a means
to self-aggrandizement, something he will cheerfully take but does not

need – and it is characteristic that Falstaff thinks not of the women's bodies but of his own massive person being 'gilded' and transfigured by *their* desire.

When his minions refuse to take the letters, anger launches Falstaff into the tirade on Honour; the anger abates in the *meno mosso* as he settles into another self-relishing display of virtuosity, and revives when the needs of 'la pancia' are opposed by the 'bel costrutto'. Here, as in the Act III monologue, or in the casual savagery with which he gleefully imagines the anguish of a cuckolded Ford, the darker aspects are in evidence. Yet a shift of mood or situation will release the small, lovely miracle of 'Quand'ero paggio' – in which the energy and tension released by the grotesque contrast between what we see and hear is deliberately exploited, as the bolstered knight is transformed by his unexpectedly fleet melody. Shakespeare's Falstaff recalls his days as a page, and is also given a diminutive page by Hal as a good visual joke. Verdi's joke is wittier, more devious, and Krull-like. Opera repeatedly provides contrasts between the physical spectacle of an amphora tenor, or a huge tub of female flesh that is somehow Senta, and the emanation of spirit in music. Such contrasts may seem grotesque, or insensibly humbling. Here, the effortless, defiantly casual dissociation of the Inner Me from its bodily case reminds us, in a teasingly reflexive way, that the ease and versatility of Falstaff's self-transformations depend on Verdi's art. We see too how, in restoring and recreating the Shakespearean Falstaff's virtuosity, Verdi's musical-dramatic conception gives complexity and depth to the farce: for this sublimely assured, amoral professional the worst humiliation will be that of being duped by amateurs, *rozzi artisti* and *ogni sorta di gente dozzinale*.

Just as Verdi's musical characterization subtilized and integrated Iago's too demonic 'Credo', Verdi's musical and dramatic development of Falstaff's outburst on Honour conveys a remarkable insight into the darker implications of Falstaff's values, and into the Shakespearean *oeuvre*. The parallel with Iago's 'Credo' is no local accident. It is established, in the libretto's conceptual terms, in the parallel between Iago's 'Credo . . . che tutto è in lui bugiardo' and Falstaff's assault on the 'bel costrutto'; in musical terms, it registers through the reappearance of Iago's jagged phrase-endings, declamatory leaps, slides, and broken rhythms – and the resemblance cuts deep, as is seen if we ask where Falstaff's antithesis, or opposing principle, is located in the music. There is of course no sun-king or Lord Chief Justice; the musical relationship between Alice's sparkling, tripping devilry and Falstaff's grosser, un-domesticated energies is one of distant kinship, not opposition; Ford is

Falstaff's most dangerous enemy, but, as we shall see, he complements Falstaff in musical and dramatic terms (and is of course also a baritone). Musically and dramatically Falstaff's antithesis is provided by the lovers and their ineffably tender, youthful *bel costrutto*. Falstaff's morality, his principle of being, is that of the biological cell – predatorially assertive, voracious, endlessly adaptable, recognizing no commitment or responsibility to anything other than itself. 'In this abdomen there are a thousand tongues that announce my name. This is my kingdom; I shall enlarge it.' The lovers' ardent lyricism opposes love to self-aggrandizement; the *bel costrutto*, or ideal aspiration, to a reductive and cynical 'realism'; a kinder, fostering Nature to the elemental, amoral energies of the Nature that drives a Falstaff – or an Iago.

This also suggests why Ford is so important, within *Falstaff*'s remarkably Shakespearean complex of relationships. If Alice is the pivot of the farce – she stirs the porridge, as Verdi put it – Ford is the pivot of the drama. He is not only Falstaff's most formidable and dangerous antagonist. He is also – after Boito's crucial decision to make Ford Nannetta's father – the obstacle to the lovers' happiness, and the man who will be exposed, with Falstaff, at the end of Acts II and III. And it is important, if we are to see how Verdi's dramatic values are human values, to attend to the complementary relationship between the two baritones. Falstaff neither has nor acknowledges any need for significant human relations; but Ford's sexual and family relations touch the twin nerves of Verdian drama. He is not only a jealous husband in the line including Stiffelio, Renato, King Philip, and Otello; he is also the last in a (revealingly) long line of domineering fathers which includes Montfort, Stankar, Rigoletto, Fiesco, Count Walter, Germont, King Philip, and Amonasro – and almost included Lear. But, far from guaranteeing Ford some kind of automatic reflex of Verdian sympathy, these two lines should remind us of Verdi's concern with profoundly important distinctions. These could be represented by conflating both lines and then redividing them on a very different, but essentially Verdian principle: ranging, on the one side, those who assert their own needs even at the expense of their children or lovers, and are protected from the worst agonies of spirit by the hard carapace of ego; on the other side, those whose capacity for a self-transcending love makes them terribly vulnerable. The depth and strength of Verdi's creative preoccupation with different kinds and perversions of love appeared early on, in his courageous determination to challenge Italian audiences with *Stiffelio*; the preoccupation is not in itself Shakespearean – we find it in Shakespeare too, but also in artists as unlike as Henry James and Janáček – but in *Falstaff* it takes a Shakespearean form, with a pertinent Shakespearean parallel. Ford's jealousy is essentially unlike Otello's, since Ford is incapable of loving, and therefore of suffering, like Otello. The same point may be made in a Shakespearean context, in distinguishing the jealousy of Othello from that of Leontes in the second scene of *The Winter's Tale*. Verdi's Ford and Shakespeare's Leontes come from the same marital bestiary. Both are dangerous egotists who, even as they erupt at the presumed infidelity, show how they regard their wives as 'property' in a way that is degrading and degraded. In their obsessive, driving fury both are clinical 'cases'; they hurt horribly, but without beginning to suffer the spiritual agony of an Othello, or Otello, or even Stiffelio.

In Leontes' 'Go play, boy, play' Shakespeare works with the resources of poetic drama: we notice Leontes' foul images, the deranged violence of the metrical enjambments, the inability to keep his thought to any trajectory, the obsessive preoccupation with horns and with what others may think. A possessed man is raging at the loss of a possession. Yet we do also feel how the fool hurts: diagnostic understanding and imaginative empathy are brought into a complex relation, to which traditional distinctions between tragedy and comedy are inappropriate. The tragi-comic mode corresponds with a particularly comprehensive kind of moral and imaginative understanding that is distinctively Shakespearean. In contrast, Shakespeare's Ford is an uncomplicated and unalarming dolt, seen from the outside in a way that rather recalls Jonsonian comedy. Boito's Ford is more alarming and is vigorously characterized, as Professor Hepokoski shows (Chapter 5); but he too is seen from the outside, like one of Ben Jonson's monsters. But Verdi uses the resources of music drama to achieve something very like the Shakespearean tragi-comic intensity, so that Ford's aria cannot be fitted into the compartmentalized categories of *buffo* comedy or tragic *melodramma*.

Ford's aria begins with a telling musical-dramatic coup. As he asks 'È sogno?', an augmented chord conveys his stunned disorientation in tonal terms; when he puts the alternative, 'o realtà?', the augmented chord resolves into a major triad — but the dramatic effect of this is clear-eyed and drily ironic, since the 'dream' has been mistaken for 'reality' and Ford's question has been *wrongly* resolved. Ford is trapped in a cage of his own making, and although the music shows that he feels decidedly tragic it never allows his swells of self-pity and rage to pass themselves off as tragedy. In 'E poi diranno' the music appears to open out as though it might become expansively lyrical and heartrending, like the great aria of King Philip which the passage for horns has fleetingly recalled; but an incomplete cadence leads to a return of the original, quicker tempo as the obsessional throb of the 'cornifico' triplets is heard again. Throughout the aria each reappearance of this 'horn-mad' figure (which has grown so tellingly from the 'dalle due alle tre' triplets) reminds us that this man is indeed a painfully but comically obsessed 'insensato' — just as he fears, but for quite different reasons, which his wife very well understands. It is surely no accident that the music to which Alice sings 'Quella mania feroce' in Act III recalls Ford's 'Quella crudel beltà': she has not heard this, but knows her man.

I am suggesting that the protracted 'either—or' debate on whether Ford's aria is tragic or comic fails to see how the music itself frames that problem and thereby resolves it in a remarkably Shakespearean way — by helping us to see (in the objectively astringent, diagnostic sense) and feel (empathetically) Ford's state of mind as a grotesquely funny, horribly painful perversion. Ford's compromised intensities actually heighten the comedy, while also giving it a depth that is quite alien to *opera buffa*. It is a wonderfully rich irony when Ford's attempt at role-playing back-fires, and leads to his having an insupportable role thrust upon him; and it is an incomparably comic moment when his would-be-tragic intensities are interrupted by the reappearance of spruce Jack. But the comedy cuts deep. Those who believe that if Ford's aria were transposed up two tones it could be sung by Otello should listen again to the furiously blustering *buffo* crescendo on 'Prima li accoppio'. This man is no Otello — but he really is capable of murder (like Leontes). Indeed, Ford's intensity is disturbing for the same reason that it is *not* tragic: it reveals an ugly, perverted nature.

Indeed, the complementary relationship between Ford and Falstaff may be restated in terms of the Shakespearean contrast between 'nature' and 'nurture' in *The Winter's Tale* and *The Tempest*; this in itself suggests how Verdi's drama left *The Merry Wives* far behind, in becoming not less but more Shakespearean. Falstaff's subversive, entirely amoral nature recognizes no social or human bonds and is, in the Shakespearean sense, unnurtured. For Falstaff, as for the Caliban whose *natural* instinct is to paunch Prospero with a stake and to rape Miranda, the constraining values and sanctions of society are *unnatural*, artificial *costrutti*. That corresponds with a truth about Nature, which the lovers in *Falstaff*, or in *The Tempest*, unconsciously (or instinctively) oppose in assuming that Nature itself fosters the values and aspirations of human nature. In contrast with Falstaff, Ford is a warped social product, a father, husband, and man of property who has perverted the natural human bonds; and he is a more dangerous, nasty piece of work than Falstaff for the same reason that the civilized perversions of Antonio or Sebastian in *The*

*Tempest* are worse than Caliban's unnurtured Nature. Verdi's shrewd diagnosis and the complicating inwardness both issue from a deep concern with normative human relations that is as essentially Verdian as it is Shakespearean, but finds no parallel expression in Boito.

## IV

Those who find these remarks too 'serious' to be appropriate to *Falstaff* should consider whether they are not assuming that Verdi and Boito failed, after all, in their attempt at creative translation. For the joyous, complex life of the Shakespearean Falstaff has its darker aspects and thrives in a serious play — just as it is smothered in a mere farce. To argue that a searchingly perceptive, critically human intelligence plays through *Falstaff* is not to moralize the comedy.

A few remarks may here be appended to Professor Hepokoski's discussion in Chapter 8 of Daniel Sabbeth's curious, critically ambitious, and influential account of *Falstaff* — in the first place, because Sabbeth's account shows the inappropriateness of a moralistic approach. For Sabbeth, *Falstaff* presents a 'ritual drama of growth' in which characters 'try to enact their fantasies', 'undergo trials, uncertainty and suffering', and eventually 'grow to an acceptance of their own limitations and a new awareness of life'. I doubt whether we should generalize about 'Falstaff and the others' as though they form a homogeneous group; more seriously, I doubt whether any character 'progresses' in Sabbeth's radical, moralistic sense. True, Ford admits his errors (like Falstaff, he has no choice), and Nannetta and Fenton are united; but this hardly warrants references to 'initiation rituals' through which 'brittle, dried-up societies dissolve and new, fertile ones are created'. Nor is it easy to see how Falstaff becomes 'an adult member of society now acceptable to all', since the striking thing about the fugue is that Falstaff leads it and that the Windsor folk are willing to be led: exuberant, festive release is the keynote, rather than some strenuous progress towards Adult Integration. Sabbeth's Spock-like preoccupation with the contrast between child and adult leaves little room for Nannetta and Fenton, who are neither adults nor children and will doubtless, as they grow older, become more like their parents. In general terms Sabbeth's preoccupation with 'progress' is too schematic and too optimistic: recognizing that you cannot have something is, alas, not the same as understanding that you should not want it, and renouncing an unattainable desire may bring disillusion and atrophy, not Acceptance and Growth. Seeing the world as a joke may be anything but mature; conversely, seeing that 'tutto nel mondo è burla' might allow a damagingly ironic view of the moral and psychological categories Sabbeth takes so earnestly.

But there is a second, more positive reason for mentioning Sabbeth: he is right to want some account of the dramatic and human implications of the ways in which Ford's jealousy or Falstaff's self-aggrandizement are 'placed' within the drama. What is the effect of the contrast between the gross and subdued appearances of 'Va, vecchio John'? *Henry IV* ends with the somewhat overcast triumph of the sun-king's 'government', *The Merry Wives* ends with a routine triumph of middle-class values, and *Falstaff* ends with the fugal vision of life as a joke: how have we got there, why are we left there? If Verdi's dramatic values are human values, it will not do to evade such questions by resorting to Vaughan Williams's irritable remark: 'It never seems to occur to people that a man might just want to write a piece of music.'

I have suggested that Falstaff's amoral, archetypal vitality is not that of Sabbeth's 'child' but that of unnurtured Nature. The forces of society are ranged against the predatorial, self-aggrandizing Falstaff – he must be taught a lesson. But he has the whole of non-human Nature behind him, and when he is at his lowest ebb he revives with the vision of existence as a vast alcoholic trill – an incessant process of blind becoming, wholly indifferent to the autonomous human world of concepts, values, and *bei costrutti*. The disturbing power of this vision of life as anarchic, amoral process should neither be overstated nor underestimated. To be sure, it is not as explicitly Schopenhauerean and morally alarming as Hans Sachs's burdened reflections on 'Wahn' in *Die Meistersinger*, when his monologues recognize, and recoil from, a vision of life as an incessant, casually destructive, and ethically meaningless process. Nonetheless, the seething, anarchic energies unleashed at the beginning of *Falstaff* are as elemental and subversive as those unleashed at the beginning of *Otello*. These energies are rapidly identified with Falstaff in the one work, with Iago in the other, so that the relationship between *Falstaff* and *Otello* parallels that between Falstaff and Iago. Those with an interest in mythology and anthropology will identify Falstaff's archetypal vitality with that of the Trickster, but that is merely another route to a similar conclusion. This does not vindicate Iago's 'Not I for love and duty', or Falstaff's corresponding view of the *bel costrutto* as a chimera: the human needs, the morally and imaginatively constructive aspirations which Iago and Falstaff deny do not have to be seen as unreal fabrications. Shakespeare – the directing, disposing intelligence at work within the plays – is more sceptical than his idealists, more tentatively affirmative than his cynics and nihilists; the idealistic and nihilistic perspectives correspond with different, opposed views of Nature and human nature. Similarly, in *Otello* and *Falstaff* Verdi opposes the *costrutti* of Otello, Fenton, and indeed all human society with elemental energies which are cataclysmically destructive or profoundly subversive. Verdi was not the only late nineteenth-century artist to feel the conflict between Nature as anarchic process and the Nature that fosters human life; but seeing how that conflict runs through the Shakespearean *oeuvre* was perhaps his most essential insight as a Shakespeare translator.

Do we hear too much of *Falstaff*'s 'mellow humanity'? It may be unwise to ask, since nebulous generalizations about the effect of complex masterpieces are pointless, unless they send us back to the work with fresh questions. But the effect of *Falstaff* seems less mellow than astringent, like Verdi's favourite maxim: 'To trust is good, not to trust is better.' Its 'humanity' and 'wisdom' appear in its bracing readiness to see what life is like and accept the odds against its being what it should be like. This defeats tragedy not by seeing through it but by looking round it. Nothing, it seems, is ever as good or as bad as it appears to be; our situation is desperate but not serious; *tutto nel mondo è burla*, life is a joke, a dream, a trill, a fugue, a *costrutto*. As Boito's former mistress, Eleonora Duse, remarked to him: 'Com' è triste la tua commedia' ('How sad your comedy is').

# Bibliography

Abbiati, Franco. *Giuseppe Verdi*. 4 vols. Milan, 1959

Adler, Guido. 'Die Moderne: Allgemeines', *Handbuch der Musikgeschichte*. Ed. G. Adler. 2nd ed. Berlin-Wilmersdorf, 1930, II, 997-1002

Auden, W. H. 'The Fallen City: Some Reflections on Shakespeare's "Henry IV"', *Encounter*, 13 (Nov 1959), no. 74, pp. 21-31

Aycock, Roy E. 'Shakespeare, Boito, and Verdi', *The Musical Quarterly*, 58 (1972), 588-604

Baldini, Gabriele. *The Story of Giuseppe Verdi*, trans. [of *Abitare la battaglia*, Milan, 1970] by Roger Parker. Cambridge, 1980

Barbiera, Raffaello. 'Alla vigilia del "Falstaff"', *L'illustrazione italiana* (5 Feb 1893), 87

Barblan, Guglielmo. 'Incontentabilità di Verdi', *La Scala* (March 1957), 13-19

*Un prezioso spartito del 'Falstaff'*. Milan, [1957]

'Spunti rivelatori nella genesi del "Falstaff"', *Atti del I° congresso internazionale di studi verdiani*. Parma, 1969, pp. 16-21

Barilli, Bruno. *Il paese del melodramma e altri scritti musicali*. Florence, 1963

Baxter, Robert. 'Boston', *Opera*, 26 (1975), 382-4

Boito, Arrigo. *Lettere di Arrigo Boito*. Ed. Raffaello de Rensis. Rome, 1932

Bradley, A. C. 'The Rejection of Falstaff', *Oxford Lectures on Poetry*. London, 1909, pp. 247-73

Bryant, J. A., Jr. 'Falstaff and the Renewal of Windsor', *Proceedings of the Modern Language Association*, 89 (1974), 296-300

Bücken, Ernst. *Die Musik des 19. Jahrhunderts bis zur Moderne*. Wildpark-Potsdam, 1928

Budden, Julian. *The Operas of Verdi: From Oberto to Rigoletto*. London, 1973

*The Operas of Verdi 2: From Il trovatore to La forza del destino*. London, 1978

*The Operas of Verdi 3: From Don Carlos to Falstaff*. London, 1981

Busch, Hans. 'Apropos of a Revision in Verdi's *Falstaff*', *Music East and West: Essays in Honor of Walter Kaufmann*. Ed. Thomas Noblitt. New York, 1981, pp. 339-50

*Carteggio Verdi–Boito*. Ed. Mario Medici and Marcello Conati. 2 vols. Parma, 1978

Cesari, Gaetano, and Luzio, Alessandro. *I copialettere di Giuseppe Verdi*. Milan, 1913

Chusid, Martin. 'Verdi's Own Words: His Thoughts on Performance, with Special Reference to *Don Carlos, Otello,* and *Falstaff*', *The Verdi Companion*. Ed. William Weaver and Martin Chusid. New York, 1979, pp. 144-92

Cone, Edward T. 'The Old Man's Toys: Verdi's Last Operas', *Perspectives USA*, 6 (1954), 114-33
    'The Stature of *Falstaff*: Technique and Content in Verdi's Last Opera', *Center*, 1 (1954), 17-20

Conrad, Peter. *Romantic Opera and Literary Form*. Berkeley, 1977

Craft, Robert. 'Verdi, Shakespeare, and *Falstaff*', *Current Convictions: Views and Reviews*. New York, 1977, pp. 114-24

Dallapiccola, Luigi. 'Su un passo del "Falstaff"', *Appunti incontri meditazioni*. Milan, 1970, pp. 29-32

Damerini, Adelmo, and Roncaglia, Gino, Eds. *Volti musicali di Falstaff*. Siena, 1961

Dannreuther, Edward. *The Romantic Period, Oxford History of Music* VI [1905]. 2nd ed. Oxford, 1931

Einstein, Alfred. 'Opus Ultimum' [1937], *Essays on Music*. Ed. Paul Henry Lang. New York, 1956, pp. 64-89

Empson, William. 'Falstaff and Mr Dover Wilson', *The Kenyon Review*, 15 (1953), 213-62

Frye, Northrop. *The Anatomy of Criticism: Four Essays*. Princeton, 1957

Gál, Hans. 'A Deleted Episode in Verdi's "Falstaff"', *The Music Review*, 2 (1941), 266-72

Gatti, Carlo. *Verdi nelle immagini*. Milan, 1941
    *Verdi*. 2nd ed. Verona, 1950
    *Il teatro alla Scala nella storia e nell'arte: 1778-1963*. 2 vols. Milan, 1964

Gossett, Philip. 'Verdi, Ghislanzoni, and *Aida*: The Uses of Convention', *Critical Inquiry*, 1 (1974), 291-334

Hepokoski, James A. 'The Compositional History of Verdi's *Falstaff*: A Study of the Autograph Score and Early Editions'. Diss., Harvard Univ., 1979
    'Verdi, Giuseppina Pasqua, and the Composition of *Falstaff*', *19th-Century Music*, 3 (1980), 239-50

Hughes, Spike. *Glyndebourne: A History of the Festival Opera*. London, 1965

Jacobs, Arthur. '*Falstaff*. Covent Garden, October 7', *Opera*, 12 (1961), 743-5
    '*Falstaff*. [Glyndebourne,] June 11', *Opera*, 27 (1976), Autumn, Festival Issue, 36-8

Jung, Ute. *Die Rezeption der Kunst Richard Wagners in Italien*, Studien zur Musikgeschichte des 19. Jahrhunderts XXXV. Regensburg, 1974

Kalbeck, Max. *Opern-Abende: Beiträge zur Geschichte und Kritik der Oper* II. Berlin, 1898

Kovács, Janos. 'Zum Spaetstil Verdis', *Atti del I° congresso internazionale di studi verdiani*. Parma, 1969, pp. 132-44

Krehbiel, Henry Edward. *Chapters of Opera*. New York, 1909

Linthicum, David. 'Verdi's *Falstaff* and Classical Sonata Form', *The Music Review*, 39 (1978), 39-53

Loewenberg, Alfred. *Annals of Opera: 1597-1940*. 3rd ed. Cambridge, 1978

Luzio, Alessandro. *Carteggi verdiani*. 4 vols. Rome, 1935-47

Monaldi, Gino. *Verdi: 1839-1898*. Turin, 1899

Osthoff, Wolfgang. 'Il sonetto nel *Falstaff* di Verdi', *Il melodramma italiano dell'ottocento: studi e ricerche per Massimo Mila*. Turin, 1977, pp. 157-83

Parente, Alfredo. 'Il problema della critica verdiana', *La rassegna musicale*, 6 (1933), 197-218

Porter, Andrew. 'Edinburgh', *Opera*, 6 (1955), 654-7
    'Introduction' to trans. of *Falstaff* by Giuseppe Verdi and Arrigo Boito. New York, 1979
    'Verdi, Giuseppe (Fortunino Francesco)', *The New Grove Dictionary of Music and Musicians*. Ed. Stanley Sadie. London, 1980, XIX, pp. 635-65

Rhodes, Neil. *Elizabethan Grotesque*. London, 1980

Ricordi, Giulio. 'Come scrive e come prova Giuseppe Verdi', *Verdi e il Falstaff* (Numero speciale della *Illustrazione italiana*, Feb 1893), 23

Riemann, Hugo. *Geschichte der Musik seit Beethoven: (1800-1900)*. Berlin, 1901

Riemens, Leo. 'Gebouw v. K. & W., Den Haag: *Falstaff* (June 29)', *Opera*, 7 (1956), 535-6

Ronga, Luigi. 'Difficoltà della critica verdiana', *Verdi: studi e memorie*. Ed. Sindicato nazionale fascista musicale. Rome, 1941

Rosenthal, Harold D. *Two Centuries of Opera at Covent Garden*. London, 1958
    '*Falstaff*. Covent Garden, May 10, 20, and 27', *Opera*, 12 (1961), 469-74

Sabbeth, Daniel. 'Dramatic and Musical Organization in "Falstaff"', *Atti del III° congresso internazionale di studi verdiani*. Parma, 1974, pp. 415-42
    'Principles of Tonal and Dramatic Organization in Verdi's *Falstaff*'. Diss., City Univ. of New York, 1976

Sachs, Harvey. *Toscanini*. Philadelphia, 1978

Seltsam, William H. *Metropolitan Opera Annals: A Chronicle of Artists and Performances*. New York, 1947

Shaw, George Bernard. 'A Word More about Verdi' [from *The Anglo-Saxon Review*, March 1901], *Shaw on Music*. Ed. Eric Bentley. New York, 1956

Shawe-Taylor, Desmond. 'Glyndebourne', *Opera*, 8 (1957), 543-4

Sutcliffe, James Helme. 'Germany: Friedrich's "Falstaff"', *Opera*, 29 (1978), 369-71

Tarozzi, Giuseppe. *Il gran vecchio*. Milan, 1978

Torchi, Luigi. 'L'opera di Giuseppe Verdi e i suoi caratteri principali', *Rivista musicale italiana*, 8 (1901), 279-325

Vaughan, Denis. 'Discordanze tra gli autografi verdiani e la loro stampa', *La Scala* (July 1958), 11-15

Walker, Frank. *The Man Verdi*. New York, 1962

Weaver, William. 'Franco Zeffirelli: The Patience for Infinite Detail That Makes Dramatic Miracles', *High Fidelity* (March 1964), 30-4

Wechsberg, Joseph. 'Bernstein as Saviour?', *Opera*, 17 (1966), 358-9

# Discography

## MALCOLM WALKER

| | |
|---|---|
| *F* | Falstaff |
| *A* | Alice |
| *N* | Nannetta | all recordings are in stereo unless otherwise stated |
| *M* | Meg | ⓜ mono recording |
| *Q* | Quickly | ④ cassette version |
| *Fen* | Fenton | ⓔ electronically reprocessed stereo |
| *For* | Ford |

1930    Rimini *F*; Tassinari *A*; Alfani-Tellini *N*; Monticone *M*; Buades *Q*; D'Alessio *Fen*; Ghirardini *For*/La Scala Chorus and Orch/Molajoli
EMI ⓜ 3C 153 00695-6
CBS (US) ⓜ EL8

1937    (live performance – Salzburg Festival) Stabile *F*; Somigli *A*; Oltrabella *N*; Vasari *M*; Cravenco *Q*; D. Borgioli *Fen*; Biasini *For*/Vienna State Opera Chorus, VPO/Toscanini
Cetra ⓜ LO46/2

1939    (in German – broadcast performance) Hotter *F*; Neumann-Knapp *A*; Wulf *N*; Tegetthoff *M*; Fichtmuller *Q*; Rasp *Fen*; Schellenberg *For*/Leipzig Radio Chorus and Orch/Weisbach
Preiser ⓜ 012 046-7

1950    (broadcast performance – Carnegie Hall, New York) Valdengo *F*; Nelli *A*; Stich-Randall *N*; Merriman *M*; Elmo *Q*; Madasi *Fen*; Guarrera *For*/Shaw Chorale, NBC SO/Toscanini
RCA ⓜ AT301
RCA (US) ⓜ LM6111

1951    (broadcast performance) Taddei *F*; Carteri *A*; Pagliughi *N*; Canali *M*; Pini *Q*; Renzi *Fen*; Meletti *For*/Turin Radio Chorus and Orch/Rossi
Cetra ⓜ LPO2019 ⓜ MPO2019
Everest-Cetra ⓔ S-416/3

1951    (live performance – La Scala, Milan) Stabile *F*; Tebaldi *A*; Noni *N*; Anon. *M*; Elmo *Q*; Valletti *Fen*; Silveri *For*/La Scala Chorus and Orch/De Sabata
Cetra ⓜ LO14/3
Turnabout ⓜ THS65114-5

1956    Gobbi *F*; Schwarzkopf *A*; Moffo *N*; Merriman *M*; Barbieri *Q*; Alva *Fen*; Panerai *For*/Philharmonia Chorus and Orch/Karajan
HMV SLS5211 ④ TC-SLS5211
Angel SCL3552

1957 (live performance – Opera House, Glyndebourne) Evans *F*;
Pastori *A*; Moscucci *N*; Cadoni *M*; Dominguez *Q*; Oncina *Fen*;
Boyer *For*/Glyndebourne Festival Chorus, RPO/Gui
Replica ⓜ RPL2454-6

1963 Evans *F*; Ligabue *A*; Freni *N*; Elias *M*; Simionato *Q*; Kraus *Fen*;
Merrill *For*/RCA Italiana Chorus and Orch/Solti
Decca 2BB104-6 ④ K110K3
London OSA1395

1965 Fischer-Dieskau *F*; Ligabue *A*; Sciutti *N*; Rossl-Majdan *M*; Resnik
*Q*; Oncina *Fen*; Panerai *For*/Vienna State Opera Chorus, VPO/
Bernstein                               CBS (UK) 77392
(US) D3S-750

1967 (in Russian) Nechipailo *F*; Vishnevskaya *A*; Zvezdina *N*; Arkipova
*M*; Levko *Q*; Raikov *Fen*; Valaitis *For*/Bolshoi Theatre Chorus
and Orch/Melik-Pashaev         Melodiya C0961-6

1980 Taddei *F*; Kabaivanska *A*; Perry *N*; Schmidt *M*; Ludwig *Q*; Araiza
*Fen*; Panerai *For*/Vienna State Opera Chorus, VPO/Karajan
Philips 6769 060 ④ 7654 060

1982 Bruson *F*; Ricciarelli *A*; Hendricks *N*; Boozer *M*; Valentini-
Terrani *Q*; Gonzalez *Fen*; Nucci *For*/Los Angeles Master Chorale,
Los Angeles PO/Giulini
DG 2741 020 ④ 3382 020

1962 (excerpts) Corena *F*; Ligabue *A*; Marimpietri *N*; Cadoni *M*;
Resnik *Q*; Alva *Fen*; Capecchi *For*/New SO/Downes
Decca SDD429
London OSA1164

## Creators' recordings

'Quand'ero paggio'
    Antonio Pini-Corsi (rec. 1904)      Columbia (US) 10247
    Victor Maurel (rec. 1907)         Fonotipia 62016

# Index